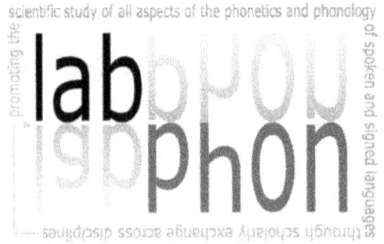

Studies in Laboratory Phonology

Chief Editor: Martine Grice
Editors: Doris Mücke, Taehong Cho

In this series:

1. Cangemi, Francesco. Prosodic detail in Neapolitan Italian.

2. Drager, Katie. Linguistic variation, identity construction, and cognition.

3. Roettger, Timo B. Tonal placement in Tashlhiyt: How an intonation system accommodates to adverse phonological environments.

ISSN: 2363-5576

Tonal placement in Tashlhiyt

How an intonation system accommodates to adverse phonological environments

Timo B. Roettger

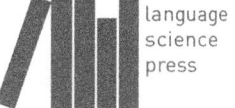
language
science
press

Timo B. Roettger. 2017. *Tonal placement in Tashlhiyt: How an intonation system accommodates to adverse phonological environments* (Studies in Laboratory Phonology 3). Berlin: Language Science Press.

This title can be downloaded at:
http://langsci-press.org/catalog/book/137
© 2017, Timo B. Roettger
Published under the Creative Commons Attribution 4.0 Licence (CC BY 4.0):
http://creativecommons.org/licenses/by/4.0/
ISBN: 978-3-944675-99-2 (Digital)
      978-3-96110-008-8 (Hardcover)
      978-3-96110-009-5 (Softcover)
ISSN: 2363-5576
DOI:10.5281/zenodo.814472

Cover and concept of design: Ulrike Harbort
Typesetting: Sebastian Nordhoff, Timo B. Roettger
Illustration: Sebastian Nordhoff
Proofreading: Alexis Michaud, Amr Zawawy, Andreas Hölzl, Eitan Grossman, Eran Asoulin, Ikmi Nur Oktavianti, Jason Mattausch, Klara Kim, Maria Isabel Maldonado, Myke Brinkerhoff, Teresa Proto
Fonts: Linux Libertine, Arimo, DejaVu Sans Mono
Typesetting software: X∃LATEX

Language Science Press
Unter den Linden 6
10099 Berlin, Germany
langsci-press.org

Storage and cataloguing done by FU Berlin

Language Science Press has no responsibility for the persistence or accuracy of URLs for external or third-party Internet websites referred to in this publication, and does not guarantee that any content on such websites is, or will remain, accurate or appropriate.

Contents

Acknowledgements vii

List of abbreviations xi

1 Hic sunt dracones 1

2 Theoretical background 5
   2.1 Phonetics and phonology 5
   2.2 Suprasegmental phonology 8
      2.2.1 Prosodic structure 10
      2.2.2 Intonation 13
   2.3 Tonal events 15
      2.3.1 Edge tones 16
      2.3.2 Pitch accents 17
   2.4 Tune-text-association 17
      2.4.1 Tune-text-adjustments 19
      2.4.2 The representation of tune-text-adjustments 23
   2.5 Summary 27

3 Tashlhiyt, a Berber language 31
   3.1 The Imazighen 31
   3.2 Historical overview 33
   3.3 Berber in Agadir 35
   3.4 Tashlhiyt 36
      3.4.1 Orthography 36
      3.4.2 Phonology 37
      3.4.3 Morphology 39
      3.4.4 Syntax 39

4 Word stress in Tashlhiyt 43
   4.1 Word stress: a working definition 43

Contents

	4.2	Evidence for word stress in Tashlhiyt	45
		4.2.1 Early observations	45
		4.2.2 Gordon and Nafi (2012)	46
	4.3	Production study: Word stress in Tashlhiyt revisited	48
		4.3.1 Method	48
		4.3.2 Results	52
	4.4	Summary	59

5 The intonation of questions and contrastive focus in Tashlhiyt — 61
  5.1 Introduction — 61
  5.2 Theoretical background: questions and focus — 62
    5.2.1 Questions: a working definition — 62
    5.2.2 Focus: a working definition — 63
  5.3 The intonation of questions and focus — 64
    5.3.1 The intonation of questions — 64
    5.3.2 The intonation of focus — 66
    5.3.3 Intonational differences between marking questions and marking focus — 67
  5.4 Questions and contrastive focus in Tashlhiyt: qualitative observations — 68
    5.4.1 Questions in Tashlhiyt — 69
    5.4.2 Contrastive focus in Tashlhiyt — 70
    5.4.3 Intonational differences between flagging questions and marking contrastive focus in Tashlhiyt — 72
  5.5 Production study — 72
    5.5.1 Method — 72
    5.5.2 Results: pitch scaling — 76
    5.5.3 Results: pitch peak timing — 80
    5.5.4 Discussion — 83
  5.6 Perception study — 89
    5.6.1 Method — 90
    5.6.2 Results and discussion — 92
  5.7 Summary — 95

6 Tonal placement in adverse phonological environments — 97
  6.1 Introduction — 97
  6.2 Tonal placement in absence of sonorants — 98
  6.3 The status of schwa in Tashlhiyt: a review — 101
    6.3.1 The epenthetic vowel account — 101

		6.3.2	The transitional vocoid account	102
	6.4	Production study		108
		6.4.1	Method	108
		6.4.2	Results and discussion	110
	6.5	The status of schwa revisited		118
		6.5.1	Schwa as a sociolinguistic marker	118
		6.5.2	Schwa as reflecting gestural reorganisation	119
		6.5.3	Schwa as a prosodic marker	125
	6.6	Summary		129

7 Towards an intonational analysis — 131
  7.1 Introduction . . . 131
  7.2 Recapitulation of observations . . . 131
  7.3 Analysis of the rise-falls . . . 133
    7.3.1 Rise-falls in Tashlhiyt: primary association to prosodic constituents . . . 134
    7.3.2 The internal structure of the rise-fall . . . 138
    7.3.3 Secondary association to tone bearing units . . . 141
  7.4 Formalising variability . . . 145
    7.4.1 Discrete variability in intonation . . . 145
    7.4.2 Gradient variability in intonation . . . 148
  7.5 Summary . . . 151

8 Concluding remarks and future directions — 153
  8.1 Tonal placement without word stress . . . 153
  8.2 Phonotactic restrictions on tonal placement . . . 154
  8.3 Future directions . . . 158

Appendix — 161
  A.1 Media Access . . . 161
  A.2 Participant Information . . . 161

References — 163

Index — 183
  Name index . . . 183
  Language index . . . 189
  Subject index . . . 191

Acknowledgements

The person I would like to express my deepest gratitude to is my supervisor Martine Grice. She was my most important advisor through my academic life and she constantly advanced my development with her unique and charming way of giving me feedback. From her, I learned how to ask the right questions and how to communicate these questions in a precise and diplomatic way. Martine always provided the right amount of support and pressure I needed, while leaving me great freedom in finding my way through the jungle of academia. She always had an ear for any kind of problem, be it overly dramatic doubts about the scientific method itself or be it being lost in the process of writing. She always believed in me and my development as a scientist and cheered me up on cloudy days. I truly believe she did not only make me a good linguist but will always be a personal role model. Thank you, Martine.

I would like to express my gratitude to Rachid Ridouane. He constantly advanced my understanding of Tashlhiyt and generously introduced me to his home in Morocco, to his culture, and to his heritage. He led me through the depths of the Agadir Souk, taught me the art of pouring Moroccan tea, and warmly welcomed me in the midst of his family and friends. I am very grateful to these memories. Thank you, Rachid.

I also thank all members of the faculty of Amazigh studies at the Ibn Zohr University in Agadir. Without the help of the faculty, none of the data could have been collected. In this context, one man deserves particular credit: Abderrahmane Charki helped us find consultants, organise our recordings, and conduct our experiments. Even though he constantly ate all the chocolate that was supposed to be for our consultants, he did a terrific job and made my life in the field much easier. I am very happy to have met him. Generally, I am grateful to all consultants that patiently participated in my tiresome experiments. It was a beautiful experience full of positivity and support. Tenemmirt, Agadir.

Bodo Winter has played a major role in my scientific and personal development. He was always two steps ahead of me and that way sparked my interest with his enthusiastic and positive way of looking at things. Over the many years, he has become my teacher and a dear friend.

Acknowledgements

The first person to incubate my early interest in language was Kay González-Vilbazo. He taught the introduction to linguistics at the department of German language and literature in Cologne. He told us the most interesting narratives about the mesmerising nature of Universal Grammar, genetically endowed language acquisition devices, and sign language development in Nicaragua. I was instantly hooked due to his convincing and inspiring way. While I have started questioning his view onto language, cognition, and evolution shortly after, I am eternally grateful to have had him as one of my first university teachers. He sparked the flame and made me want to become a linguist.

Jan Menge has been an inspiring character in my development as a linguist. Unfortunately, Jan has long left the field of linguistics. I don't think he is aware of the major impact he has had on my professional career. During my days as an undergraduate, he used to always put my know-it-all allures into perspective, challenged me, and showed me alternative views. I am very grateful to him.

I would like to thank Frank Domahs to put his faith in an overly-motivated undergraduate. I met Frank in 2007 during a research internship at the neurological department of Aachen. He believed in my abilities to conduct my first full-fledged psycholinguistics experiment. Despite me being terrified of writing in English, he persuaded me to write up the results. The write-up turned out to be my first journal publication and gave me important insights into the scientific machinery.

Alongside these amazing scholars, I had many great teachers that I encountered during my academic journey. Many thanks go to Beatrice Primus, who saw potential in a presumptuous undergraduate and hired me as a student assistant. I would like to thank Walter Huber and Richard Wiese to give me the opportunity to have a first peak into neurolinguistic methods in Aachen and in Marburg. I am grateful to Nikolaus Himmelmann who fortunately was my teacher for a couple of years. He taught me a lot about the linguistic craftsmanship and scientific integrity. Many thanks go to James Kirby who was my most important advisor during my year in Edinburgh. Patiently, he spent hours on discussing data with me and always gave me great advice. He continued to be a colleague and has become a friend. Besides the exchange with James, I cannot value my student experience in Edinburgh high enough. The School of Philosophy, Psychology and Language Science is a beautiful and inspiring place and hosts remarkable teachers. I did not only learn a lot about a multitude of different topics, but learned how communicating knowledge is done right. Thank you Alice Turk, Bob Ladd, Simon Kirby, Graeme Trousdale, Antonella Sorace, and James Hurford.

Many other people in the Institute of Phonetics in Cologne have helped to make my work not only easier but, most notably, enjoyable. The exchanges with past and present colleagues and students over the now seven years were always inspiring, exciting and, most of all, fun. I have learned important lessons from many of you and I am grateful for your support: Anna Bruggeman, Anne Hermes, Aviad Albert, Bastian Auris, Christian Weitz, Christine Riek, Christine Röhr, Doris Mücke, Francesco Cangemi, Henrik Niemann, Janina Kalbertodt, Jessica Di Napoli, Martina Krüger, Mathias Stoeber, Simon Ritter, Simon Wehrle, Stefan Baumann, and Theo Klinker.

I would like to thank the a.r.t.e.s. graduate school of humanities in Cologne to award me with a scholarship that made this endeavour financially possible.[1] I am particularly thankful to Andreas Speer, the hard working motor behind a.r.t.e.s., who has enabled dozens of academic careers and will hopefully continue to do so.

Besides these people that walked next to me in my academic life, gratitude is long overdue to the people that were there for me in my personal life and without whom none of my professional achievements would have been possible. I would like to thank my mother, Andrea, and her husband Andreas as well as my father, Frank, and his partner Anna to keep believing in me. Even though unfamiliar with the world I entered, they always trusted my judgments and rewarded me with their support.

I am lucky enough to have great friends, but I would like to thank two amazing men in particular. Dennis Köhler always challenged my view on this world and has had a huge impact on my desire to learn new things and look beyond my limited experiences. He was always an authority to me and a valuable advisor during my personal development.

Christopher Arnold - nothing less of an authority in my life - showed me that faith in yourself and your goals can indeed move mountains. Despite being struck by fate again and again, despite forces that tried to break him down, he always remained unbroken. He is a constant inspiration for me. In times of discouragements, it was always his voice that had told me to get up and move on.

Cologne, May 2017

---

[1] The work presented in this book is based on my doctoral dissertation which was accepted by the Faculty of Arts and Humanities of the University of Cologne in 2016.

List of abbreviations

Throughout this thesis, phonetic and phonemic transcriptions are stated according to the IPA (1999). Phonetic acoustic transcriptions are enclosed in square brackets []. Phonological representations according to a particular analysis are indicated by slashes //. In addition to a phonemic transcription, these representations can also entail information about syllabicity and syllable boundaries (see below). In line with common practice in academic publications on Berber languages, geminate consonants are transcribed as a double consonant (e.g. /tt/).

-	word-internal morpheme boundary or small phrase edge tone
*	(asterisk) precedes an ungrammatical form or indicates a starred tone
.	(period) syllable boundary
+	(plus) indicates the juncture of two tonal targets belonging to the same tonal complex
%	(percent) indicates an intonation phrase edge tone
ṣ ġ	(subscript/superscript vertical line) marks the syllable nucleus according to a particular analysis
AD	/ad/ complementiser
AM	Autosegmental-Metrical model
BS	bound state
C	consonant or segment that does not occupy the syllable nucleus
CS	contrastive statement
dB	decibel
EQ	echo question
EEQT	Eastern European question tune

List of abbreviations

F	feminine or final syllable
F0	fundamental frequency
H	high tonal target
Hz	hertz = frequency of cycles per second
INT	/is/ interrogative preverb
IPO	Institute for Perception Research in Eindhoven
L	liquid or low tonal target
LRT	Likelihood Ratio Test
M	masculine
N	nasal
OT	Optimality Theory
PL	plural
PTEV	postlexically triggered epenthetic vowel
PU	penultimate syllable
S	sonorant consonant
SE	standard error
SG	singular
ST	semitones
TBU	tone bearing unit
V	vowel or segment that occupies syllable nucleus
VOT	voice onset time
Y/N	yes-no question
β	estimated coefficient

1 Hic sunt dracones

"Stress and intonation in Tashlhiyt are still terrae incognitae."
François Dell and Mohamed Elmedlaoui (2002)

Urban legends claim that English cartographers placed the phrase "here be dragons" (Latin: hic sunt dracones) at the edges of their known world.[1] Ancient maps are often found to depict fable creatures, sea serpents, and exotic animals in unknown areas. The present book explores the unknown territories referred to in the quote by François Dell and Mohamed Elmedlaoui. Tashlhiyt, a Berber language spoken in South Morocco, can indeed be considered an exotic case on the linguistic-typological map. The language is characterised by exceptional phonotactic patterns, allowing for whole utterances without a single phonological vowel. These structures make an analysis of prosodic aspects in Tashlhiyt, notably those involving pitch, both interesting and challenging. We take on this challenge and shed light on the as of yet under-explored areas of stress and intonation in Tashlhiyt. With the presented analyses, we aim to make three contributions to the literature.

First, this book presents a quantitative exploration of stress and intonation in Tashlhiyt. The results will contribute to a currently small body of instrumental studies on sound patterns in Tashlhiyt in particular and in Berber languages in general. Apart from impressionistic observations, stress and intonation are mostly neglected in available descriptions of Berber languages. For instance, Kossmann & Stroomer (1997) do not even mention the terms "stress" or "intonation" in their concise overview of Berber phonology.

Second, the findings presented here contribute to intonational typology by supplementing our knowledge of intonation systems with data from a Berber language. Intonation has long been neglected in the study of languages in general. While there has been a noticeable increase in interest within the last three decades, intonation is still under-represented in linguistic descriptions leaving

---

[1] However, there is only one known map that actually carries this phrase (the Lenox Globe, da Costa, 1879).

1 Hic sunt dracones

the majority of documented languages under-documented with regard to intonation. While there are a great number of intonational descriptions for most European languages, systematic instrumental investigations of less documented languages are still rare. To understand how intonation systems differ from each other and what generalisations can or cannot be made across languages, thorough descriptions of typologically diverse languages are necessary. The linguistic system of Tashlhiyt exhibits two structural properties that make it an important case study for suprasegmental description and analysis. On the one hand, Tashlhiyt has been described as lacking word stress and, on the other hand, it allows for phonotactic patterns that are adverse to the production and perception of pitch.

In well-investigated languages, for instance West Germanic languages, certain tonal events often co-occur with lexically stressed syllables. Investigations of languages that do not exhibit word stress are very rare. The question arises as to how well the generalisations about intonation based on languages with word stress hold for languages without such word-prosodic patterns. Since early description, Tashlhiyt has been argued to lack lexically determined word stress by numerous authors. We will evaluate this claim and investigates the placement of intonational events, contributing to a small body of literature on intonation in languages without word stress.

In addition to the important role of word prosody, intonation cannot be understood in isolation, disregarding its segmental structure. Intonational pitch movements – the pragmatically relevant variation of the rate of vocal fold vibration - is superimposed onto segments. For the realisation of intonational pitch movements, certain articulatory and perceptual requirements need to be met. Most importantly, the segments on which the pitch movements are realised need to be voiced to enable pitch modulation in the first place. This is not a trivial requirement. Most languages are characterised by a systematic occurrence of vowels within words. Each word (or syllable) has at least one element of high intensity and rich harmonic structure enabling the realisation of pitch movements and the perceptual retrieval of pitch. As opposed to that Tashlhiyt exhibits exceptionally rare phonotactic patterns. There are whole utterances without a phonological vowel and words can be comprised of voiceless segments only. In these cases, the phonetic opportunity for the execution of intonational pitch movements is exceptionally limited. The present book explores how these typologically rare phonotactic patterns interact with intonational aspects of linguistic structure. Tashlhiyt turns out to be an intriguing case study of how an intonation system can accommodate to adverse phonological environments.

Third, in addition to descriptive and typological contributions, the intonational patterns in Tashlhiyt turn out to be of great importance for evaluating existing intonation models in particular and phonological theories in general. The observed patterns in Tashlhiyt exhibit an unusual high degree of variability. This variability is probabilistic in nature. Discretely definable tonal events occur in different locations with a certain likelihood, but are never fully predictable in a deterministic way. Current models of intonation do not offer concrete formalisation mechanisms for these probabilistic distributions. We will argue that this variability reflects different ways to resolve functional conflicts between the necessity to express tonal movements in privileged positions and the lack of phonetic material to realise these tonal movements. The discussion of tonal placement patterns in Tashlhiyt will contribute to our understanding of the interaction between intonation and segmental phenomena and will shed new light on the applicability of current intonation models.

The present book is organised as follows: chapter 2 will introduce relevant concepts and terminology of intonation and prosodic theory within the conceptual framework of the 'Autosegmental-Metrical' model, the currently most commonly used formal apparatus to describe intonation.

Chapter 3 will introduce Tashlhiyt Berber. First, we will discuss the historical roots of the Berber people in North Africa and Morocco. Then, we will introduce the speaker community on which the results of this book rest upon: Tashlhiyt speakers living in Agadir. Subsequently, we will sketch the linguistic system of Tashlhiyt including basic word order, morphological categories and, particularly relevant, phonological structures. During the discussion of the latter, we will introduce relevant findings on phonotactic patterns and syllable structure.

Following these introductory chapters, three empirical studies will be presented: chapter 4 will explore the possibility of Tashlhiyt having word stress. We will show that, as opposed to recent claims, there is no empirical evidence for the existence of lexically determined metrical structures within the word.

Chapter 5 explores the intonational marking of two communicative functions: flagging questions and marking contrastive constituents. We will show that the intonational expression of these functions resemble each other to a certain degree but differ systematically. Both functions are expressed by specific tonal events that differ with respect to pitch scaling and their temporal alignment with the phrase. Moreover, these differences in production are evaluated in a perception experiment. We will show that both scaling and alignment are relevant perceptual cues to distinguish ambiguous syntactic constructions. Aside from systematic interactions between tonal placement and communicative function,

1 Hic sunt dracones

the placement of tonal events exhibits an unusual degree of variability. While there are several competing factors affecting tonal placement in a systematic way, there remains a significant amount of unexplained variability. Crucially, the placement of tonal events is sensitive to segmental characteristics such as sonority and syllable weight.

Chapter 6 will expand on these findings and explore the realisation of tonal events in light of Tashlhiyt's exceptional phonotactic flexibility. The investigation will focus on tonal placement in words that are comprised of only voiceless obstruents. In these cases, tonal placement exhibits a high degree of variability and interacts with the segmental level in intricate ways. We will argue that patterns of tonal placement may be informative for an evaluation of the linguistic status of particular segmental structures.

Chapter 7 will summarise the aforementioned instrumental observations and will attempt to account for the results with a phonological analysis within the Autosegmental-Metrical model of intonation. This analysis will allow a parsimonious formalisation of the majority of observations. However, we will show that intonational patterns in Tashlhiyt present certain challenges to the current Autosegmental-Metrical model.

Finally, Chapter 8 will recapitulate the main contributions of this book, situating these in the context of cross-linguistic observations, and will discuss possible theoretical implications. We will conclude by pointing out potential avenues for future research.

2 Theoretical background

2.1 Phonetics and phonology

When speakers produce speech, they modify their larynx and vocal organs in a particular way, shaping the cavities through which air passes. This results in specific patterns of disturbance to the air-molecules that spread outwards and eventually reach the ear of the listener where they are processed by the auditory system. For example, bilabial stops are common sounds in human languages. They are characterised by a complete closure of the lips, during which air cannot escape through the oral tract and intra-oral pressure builds up. When the closure is released, the compressed air escapes in a characteristic burst. Both the closure interval and the release phase create a certain disturbance to the air molecules. The resulting subtle differences in air pressure variation can then be detected by the human ear.

For a complete scientific assessment of human speech, these physical and biological mechanisms must be investigated. At the same time, humans use these mechanisms in a very particular way. Speakers classify objectively different instances of articulatory / acoustic / auditory events. The resulting categories can further be described to have a certain functional value for the communicative system. This allows the listener to perceive two observations differing in a particular physical dimension as two instances of the same category. At the same time, another two observations exhibiting the same difference in a different context may be perceived as two different categories. Take for example voice onset time (VOT). VOT is defined as the interval between the release of an oral stop consonant and the onset of voicing. It is a parameter that can vary continuously. However, many languages exhibit systematic clusters of VOT values corresponding to different sets of words. For example, in English, syllable-initial stops in words like *bear* have been reported to exhibit VOT values around 0 ms, i.e. the voicing starts with the release of the stop. Syllable-initial stops in words like *pear* have been reported to exhibit positive VOT values around 60 ms (e.g. Lisker & Abramson 1964). Within a particular part of the continuum, VOT values differing within a certain range are interpreted as belonging to the same category. However, the same absolute difference in VOT values elsewhere on the continuum may reflect instances of two different categories (e.g. Liberman et al. 1957).

Thus, understanding speech not only involves comprehensive models of the physical and biological prerequisites of speech, but also involves understanding of how speakers categorise speech phenomena, form functional categories, and how these categories interact with each other within a system. These two sides of the coin are traditionally attributed to the linguistic subfields of 'phonetics' and 'phonology', respectively. Phonetics can be conceived of as the assessment of speech sounds from an objective perspective based on physical and biological observations. Phonology can be conceived of as the assessment of speech sounds from an internal perspective, analysing the functional relevance of them in relation to other elements within the same system.

For the latter, phonology, we can distinguish between two traditions. These traditions differ with respect to the methodologies applied as well as the assumed scope of phonological analysis. Note that, for exposition purposes, the following discussion simplifies the diversity of phonological schools. The scientific landscape is, of course, more complex.

On the one hand, there is a tradition that we will refer to as 'theoretical phonology', which is based on linguistic structuralism (Sapir 1925; Bloomfield 1933; Trubetzkoy 1939; De Saussure 1989). In this tradition, phonological units are considered as functional elements that have to be defined by their functions within the language system (e.g. Trubetzkoy 1939). Functional elements are represented as symbols, i.e. they are represented as symbolic abstractions of their actual physical manifestation. This systemic approach later led to the development of phonological analyses that are theoretical in nature. Similar to theoretical physics, structures and principles are proposed that account for the observations, regardless of whether they are observable themselves (Gussenhoven 2015). An example is the concept of allophony. Two phonetically distinct speech segments can be considered contextual variants of an underlying phoneme (if these variants are in complementary distribution and sufficiently similar). Take for example voiceless oral stops in syllable-initial sibilant clusters in English, like in the word *sport*. These stops are characterised by VOT values around 0 ms. As discussed above, corresponding voiceless bilabial stops in absolute syllable-initial position (e.g. *pear*) are usually characterised by VOT values around 60 ms. Despite these two sounds being physically distinct, they are commonly analysed as allophones of one underlying phoneme (/p/). Thus, the phoneme /p/ is assumed to have contextual variants, one with aspiration (long VOT, [pʰ]) and one without aspiration (zero VOT, [p]). While the phoneme itself cannot be observed or measured directly, since it is an abstract notion, it can be considered a relevant concept to describe distributional observations of the English sound system in a parsimonious way. The tradition of theoretical phonology focuses on contrasting features of a sound system. This allows for a description of a sound system by proposing a small inventory of symbols and a finite set of interactions between these symbols. This type of phonological analysis is an important prerequisite for the academic communication of critical properties of a sound system, enables language teaching, and allows a straightforward cross-linguistic comparison of sound systems.

Alternatively, phonology can also be conceived of as the scientific study of the cognitive underpinnings of sound patterns. Such a cognitive understanding of speech was most prominently formulated by Chomsky & Halle (1968) who stated their primary interest in the "competence" of a speaker. Competence refers to the knowledge of "the grammar that determines an intrinsic connection of sound and meaning for each sentence" (Chomsky & Halle 1968: 3). Although many phonologists have moved past the ideas of generative phonology, a focus on cognitive aspects of speech has since then dominated phonological analysis. It is most prominently defined by the 'Laboratory Phonology' movement (e.g. Pierrehumbert, Beckman & Ladd 2000), according to which language is conceived of as a phenomenon of nature. In that vein, language has to be explained in terms of general facts about the physical world, biological and cognitive capabilities of humans, and their interaction with the environment. Rapid technological advancements have led to a multitude of methods enabling the investigations of cognitive representations that underlie speech communication. The physical aspects of speech are studied in the context of memory formation, categorisation, as well as the cognitive development of categories during language acquisition.

While a descriptive formalisation of a sound system in the tradition of theoretical linguistics may be taken as a departure point for hypotheses about linguistic knowledge, the former should not be confused with the latter. It is necessary to distinguish between these two definitions of the scientific object explicitly. Traditional phonological descriptions are formalisations of phonetic observations within an abstract symbol system, mainly disregarding non-contrastive phonetic information. As opposed to that, a large body of research has argued that the cognitive representation of speakers is less abstract, but rather contains a large amount of non-contrastive information (among many others Goldinger 1998; Hawkins 2003; and see Hawkins 2012 and Pierrehumbert 2012 for overviews).

This book will explore certain phonetic aspects of stress and intonation in Tashlhiyt that convey contrastive meaning. Based on quantitative observations, we will propose an abstract description of the phonetic facts in the tradition of structuralism and theoretical phonology. These abstract formalisms serve descriptive purposes and allow for cross-linguistic comparison, but their use should not be interpreted as capturing how the actual knowledge of a speaker is represented. For the purpose of formalisation,[1] we choose the Autosegmental-Metrical model. This model is introduced in subsequent sections alongside relevant concepts and terminology of intonation theory that will be used to describe stress and the placement of intonational tones in Tashlhiyt.

First, the two broadly used notions 'intonation' and 'prosodic structure' will be introduced and distinguished (§2.2). Subsequently, the mapping between tonal events and prosodic structure will be discussed with regard to two descriptive categories: 'edge tones' and 'pitch accents' (§2.3). Edge Tones are tonal events that are associated to the edges of prosodic constituents. Pitch accents are tonal events that are associated to specific prosodic units, so-called 'tone bearing units' (TBU). In some cases, the available TBUs are insufficient to carry pitch movements, i.e. there is not enough segmental material available to realise the pitch movement, or the segmental material is phonetically not suited to bear a pitch movement. Intonation systems allow for different adjustments of the segmental tier or the tonal tier in order to accommodate such conflicts. The nature of these adjustments is controversial. They can either be considered to be adjustments of the phonetic realisation of tonal contours or reflexes of phonological differences. The different adjustments as well as their theoretical treatment is discussed to prepare the investigation of tonal placement patterns in Tashlhiyt in later chapters (§2.4).

2.2 Suprasegmental phonology

Phenomena that refer to domains larger than segments (phones/phonemes), such as the syllable, the word or entire phrases, are referred to as 'suprasegmental'. Postlexical suprasegmental properties of speech encode phenomena that are not lexically determined but dependent on the postlexical structure of the discourse. These aspects of speech not only encode paralinguistic functions, such as emotions, speaker involvement, and attitude; they also play a crucial role in linguistic organisation. Their central role has been tremendously under-represented in linguistic research in the 20th century leaving the majority of documented languages, in fact, under-documented with regard to their suprasegmental phono-

---

[1] Of course, this does not exclude the possibility that proposed phonological formalisms are adequate departure points for further psycholinguistic modelling.

logical system. The language investigated in this book is a good example of this lack of documentation.

Yet, anyone who has tried to communicate a relevant message with a mouth full of food ("can you pass me the gravy, please.") is likely aware of the immense role that suprasegmental properties of speech play when the actual segments are unintelligible. Suprasegmental parameters convey the intended illocutionary act, structure the utterance into smaller meaningful units, and emphasise certain units while de-emphasising less important pieces of information. The entire discourse, including turn-taking between interlocutors, is controlled by suprasegmental aspects of speech. When we talk about suprasegmental properties of linguistic structure, two terms are often used interchangeably: intonation and prosodic structure. In the following, we attempt to arrive at working definitions for these terms within the terminology and conceptual framework of the 'Autosegmental-Metrical' model, henceforth referred to as AM model (Pierrehumbert 1980; see Ladd 2008 for an overview).

The reason for using the AM model are twofold: first, it is the most commonly used model to describe intonation systems. Thus, many languages that have already been documented with regard to prosodic and intonational structure are described within this analytical framework. In this respect, AM has proved to be flexible enough to adapt to the analytical requirements of typologically diverse languages. There is of course a high degree of variability as to how the model is interpreted and applied to the language under investigation by a given analyst. The basic descriptive devices it offers, however, allow one to compare languages reasonably well. Second, the AM model captures common properties of prosodic and intonational systems, which explains the great success this model had after its initial development in the 1980's.

The 'Autosegmental' aspect of AM is based on the assumption that there are separate levels of description for segments on the one hand (i.e. consonants and vowels) and tonal events on the other hand. The 'Metrical' aspect of AM is based on the assumption that elements within the segmental levels of description are incorporated into hierarchically organised sets of constituents. These assumptions are discussed in detail below.

In the AM model, the terms 'prosodic structure' and 'intonation' are defined in a narrow sense (Grice 2006; Ladd 2008). Prosodic structure is the system that groups utterances into smaller units and assigns relative prominence to elements within these units. Intonation is the system that associates tonal events with this prosodic structure.

2 Theoretical background

Prosodic structure and intonation are phonetically manifested in a multitude of different channels including perceived pitch (acoustically approximated by fundamental frequency), loudness (relative intensity), vowel quality (formant bandwidth, spectral tilt, voice source), and length of certain units (relative duration). Consider for example the following English sentences:

(1) Helen LOVES cheese.

(2) Helen loves cheese straws.

For example, the word *loves* in (1) can be made prominent by realising a rise in pitch, accompanied by longer, louder, and more clearly articulated segments, than it would otherwise be. Similarly, the word *cheese* can be marked as phrase final in (1) as opposed to (2) where it is phrase medial. Finality in (1) can be marked by a fall in pitch on *cheese* accompanied by creaky voice, a decrease in loudness, and lengthening of its final segments.

2.2.1 Prosodic structure

The AM model assumes that utterances can be broken down into prosodic units that are hierarchically organised. Although certain prosodic units have been claimed to be found in all languages, their universality has been called into question. Moreover, the validity of such claims is very much dependent on how the units are defined (e.g. Schiering, Bickel & Hildebrandt 2010; Hyman 2011). Crosslinguistically, some prosodic units are found to be more common than others, such as the following: the highest level in the hierarchy is commonly referred to as either the 'utterance' (υ) or the 'intonational phrases' ("ι" or "IP") which itself can contain one or more 'smaller phrases' (here referred to as "SP"). Depending on the analysis, either there are no levels between the intonation phrase and the phonological word, the next level in the hierarchy, or there are one or more levels. These levels have been referred to as phonological phrases ("φ" or "PP", e.g. Gussenhoven 2004, for English), accentual phrases ("α" or "AP", e.g. Pierrehumbert & Beckman 1988, for Japanese) or intermediate phrases ("ip", e.g. Beckman & Pierrehumbert 1986, for English; and Grice, Baumann & Benzmülller 2005, for German). Regardless of how it is labelled, any SP is assumed to contain one or more phonological words ("ω"). Words might be organised into metrical feet ("Σ" or "F") which themselves are organised into one or more syllables ("σ"). Syllables can be further organised into subsyllabic constituents subsuming the segments ('onset' and 'rhyme', the latter of which can be further decomposed into 'nucleus' and 'coda'). Alternatively, some accounts propose the mora ("μ"), which

2.2 Suprasegmental phonology

divides the syllable into rhythmic units. An example hierarchy of prosodic units in English is shown in Figure 2.1.

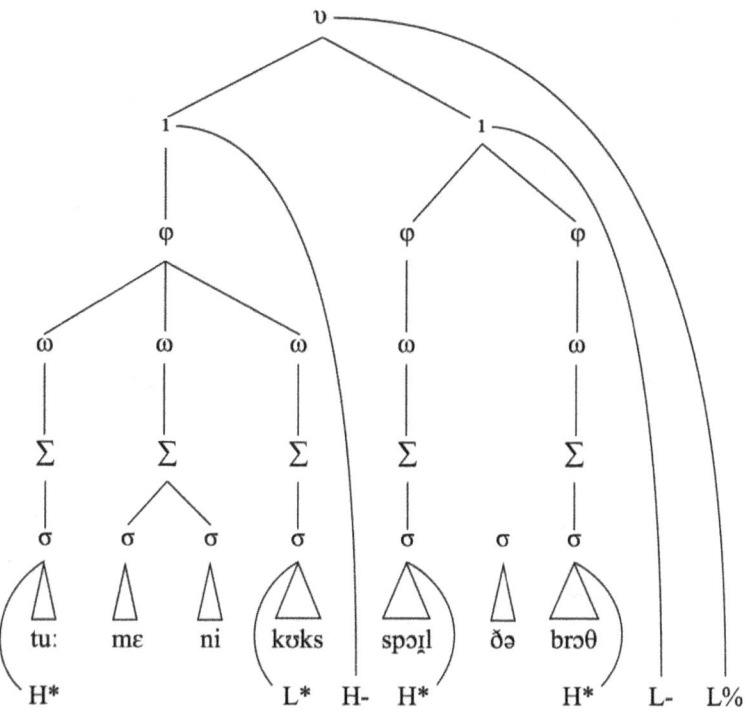

Figure 2.1: Schematised example of a hierarchically organised prosodic structure for the English sentence "Too many cooks spoil the broth". At the bottom, the tonal structure is represented in accordance with Beckman and Pierrehumbert's analysis of English (1986). See Gussenhoven (2002) for an alternative analysis. This example has been presented by ibid. (2002:271).

The proposed level of prosodic structure can be justified by distributional diagnostics. For example, in English, the IP and the ip have been defined intonationally (Beckman & Pierrehumbert 1986), i.e. certain tonal events appear at their edges. For instance, a rise in pitch, may only occur at the right (or left) edge of the proposed prosodic unit. So in Figure 2.1, there is a high edge tone at the right edge of the initial ip (notated with '-', i.e. H-) and a low edge tone at the right edge of the final ip (L- coinciding with the right edge of the IP, notated with '%', i.e. L%). Other phonetic aspects can be taken to back up this descriptive choice. In addition to the presence of the tonal event, there can be a clear pause after the

11

2 Theoretical background

proposed unit. Further evidence is sought in modifications of segmental properties. First, specific segmental processes such as assimilations have been argued to operate only within certain prosodic phrases but not across their edges (Nespor & Vogel 1986). Second, it has been repeatedly shown that fine phonetic detail is used to encode prosodically privileged positions, such as edges of prosodic domains. This segmental marking of prosodic structure is henceforth referred to as 'edge-induced strengthening'. Edge-induced strengthening comprises the modification of temporal and spatial phonetic parameters of prosodic phrases. Many languages have been shown to mark certain prosodic edges by phonetically enhancing segments either before or after the boundary. There are two major phenomena described in the literature that fall under the umbrella of edge-induced strengthening: 'initial strengthening' and 'final lengthening'. The former refers to spatio-temporal adjustments at the left edge. For example, it has been shown that acoustic parameters that are contrastive are enhanced in phrase-initial position. For instance, in languages that have aspirated stops, voice onset time (VOT) is longer in phrase-initial position than in phrase-medial position (Cooper 1991; Pierrehumbert & Talkin 1992; Jun 1993; Cho & Jun 2000; Choi 2003; Cole et al. 2003). The latter, final lengthening, refers to the spatio-temporal adjustment of segments at the right edge of a phrase. For example, it has been shown that the syllable rhyme is longer in phrase-final position than in phrase-medial position in English (e.g. Turk & Shattuck-Hufnagel 2007).

The proposed hierarchically organised prosodic units involve strength relationships. This concept is borrowed from the tradition of 'Metrical Phonology' (Leben 1976; Liberman & Prince 1977). To demonstrate this idea, consider the compound *statistics instructor* (cf. Figure 2.2). The compound consists of two prosodic elements corresponding to the nouns *statistics* and *instructor*. Both words consist of three syllables. One syllable of each word is considered to be the metrically strongest syllable, i.e. the stressed syllable (/stə.ˈtɪs.tɪks/ and /ɪn.ˈstrʌk.tə/). Strength relations are phonetically manifested via parameters such as duration and intensity (see Chapter 4 for a detailed discussion). In addition to the strength relation within each noun, there is a strength relation on the level of the whole compound. The first part of the compound is stronger than the second part.[2]

This hierarchy of strength relations results in one single most prominent syllable of the whole compound. It is the strong syllable of the strong noun (/ˈtɪs/). This is reflected in the perception of that syllable as the most prominent syllable of the compound overall. The strongest element of a unit is called the 'designated terminal element' (Liberman & Prince 1977; Ladd 2008). It is the docking site for

---

[2] For exposition purposes, we ignore the level of the metrical foot here.

2.2 Suprasegmental phonology

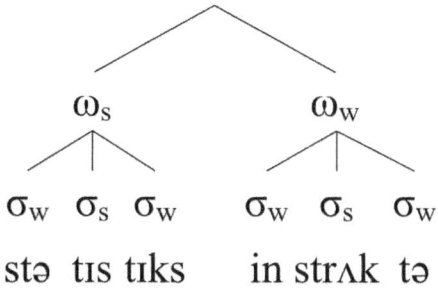

Figure 2.2: Schematised example of strength relationships in the compound *statistics instructor*. The two parts of the compound have at least one strong syllable and the compound itself is characterised by a strong first element and a weak second element

particular tonal movements, linguistically significant parts of the intonation contour.

2.2.2 Intonation

In the AM model, prosodic structure is taken as a grid that determines where significant aspects of the intonation contour may occur. Of the phonetic dimensions described above, pitch has been regarded as the primary channel of intonation as defined here. Acoustically, pitch corresponds roughly to the perception of fundamental frequency (f0). Changes in pitch, such as a pitch glide or jump up or down from the pitch of surrounding segmental material, are perceptually most prominent. These changes in pitch often co-occur systematically with a particular pragmatic or semantic function and are therefore considered to be phonological units formally integrated into the phonological system as abstract entities.

Tonal movements can be conceptualised as configurations, i.e. holistic contours that directly reflect functional aspects of speech (e.g. Bolinger 1951; Crystal 1969; Halliday 1967; O'Connor & Arnold 1973; Kohler 1991; Hirst & Di Cristo 1998; Xu 2005). Alternatively, tonal movements can be considered to consist of sequences of tonal targets. These are compositional in that the function of the whole utterance can be deduced from the functions of its parts. The latter approach assumes that tonal structure consists of a sequence of local tonal targets and that the pitch values between such tonal targets are phonologically underspecified, i.e. they are merely transitions from one target to the next. These tonal targets are formally represented as either H(igh) or L(ow) tones and are assumed

2 Theoretical background

to systematically co-occur with certain structural landmarks. Commonly, tones co-occur with prominent elements of the prosodic structure and / or edges of prosodic constituents.

Configurational approaches have been criticised due to their inability to account for certain characteristics of intonational contours. If intonational contours were holistic undivided forms, one would expect them to stretch or compress according to the length of the utterance (Arvaniti 2011). This is, however, not the case. Figure 2.3 depicts an intonational contour that has been prominently discussed by Hirschberg and Ward (Ward & Hirschberg 1985; Hirschberg & Ward 1992).

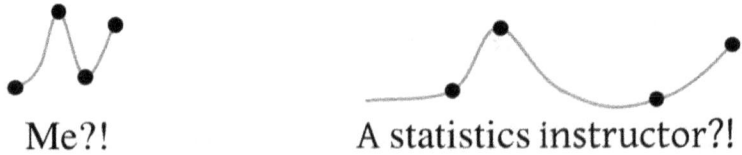

Figure 2.3: Schematic depiction of the 'incredulity contour' (Hirschberg & Ward 1992; Ladd 2008; Arvaniti 2011)

This contour is described as being used to express a "lack of speaker commitment" to the appropriateness of a proposition in general (Hirschberg & Ward 1992: 243). More specifically, it is used to express incredulity. Imagine a scenario in which my supervisor approaches me and suggests that I give a course in statistics next semester. At this particular point in time, I may consider myself still very poorly educated within the depths of statistical thinking and do not feel suited for this assignment. My surprise and incredulity would potentially be expressed by the contour depicted in Figure 2.3 (in the very rare occasion in which I used native English intonation contours appropriately).

This contour can be holistically described as a rise-fall-rise. If this were an appropriate description of the contour expressing the proposed function, we would expect it to be evenly distributed across the segments, when comparing the short utterance *Me?!* with the longer utterance *A statistics instructor?!*. The contour on *Me?!* is, however, not simply stretched to fit the longer utterance. There are at least two separate tonal events: the rise and subsequent fall through the prominent lexically stressed syllable (here: stə.ˈtɪs.tɪks) and the utterance-final rise. These tonal events are matched with certain very specific structural landmarks. Between these tonal events, there is a long stretch of low pitch dependent on the length of the utterance. This is in line with evidence that intonational contours differ in their alignment in utterances of varying length, prosodic structure, and information structure. This was first instrumentally recognised by proponents of the Institute for Perception Research model in Eindhoven (IPO, Cohen & t'Hart 1968; t'Hart & Cohen 1973; t'Hart & Collier 1975). They found that in Dutch a sequence of pitch movements is realised on specific landmarks in the utterance. These landmarks are sometimes realised on one syllable and are sometimes realised on two non-adjacent syllables separated by a longer stretch of segments. Subsequent research on unrelated languages supported the observation that certain aspects of the contour timed with certain landmarks of the prosodic structure are important for listeners, but overall contour shape is not. For instance, Pierrehumbert & Steele (1989) recreated an artificial contour for the expression *only a millionaire* that can be described as a rise-fall followed by a rise utterance finally. They created a continuum consisting of 15 positions for the rise-fall differing by 20 ms. Speakers interpreted the continuum as two different contours: one contour with an early aligned rise-fall and one with a late aligned rise-fall. These two different contours correspond to two different pragmatic interpretations. This demonstrates that certain tonal events systematically co-occur with very specific landmarks of the prosodic structure. Similar observations have been made by Rietveld & Gussenhoven (1995) for Dutch, and D'Imperio & House (1997) for Neapolitan Italian. Contours with the same overall shape are interpreted as different communicative functions dependent on the temporal co-occurrence of certain tonal events with certain structural landmarks.

Configurational approaches cannot capture the systematic co-occurrence of parts of the contour and certain structural landmarks in the utterance. It is necessary to decompose the contour into separate parts, which are located in specified positions of the utterance. This allows the analyst to model the differences between intonation contours associated with different functions successfully, and allows, at the same time, to capture the shared structure of superficially different looking contours expressing the same function. This requires a level of abstraction that is achieved in the AM model by decomposing the intonation contour into separate tonal events that are associated to particular prosodic positions.

2.3 Tonal events

In the AM model, a tonal event can either co-occur with a tone bearing unit of a prosodic constituent (TBU) or co-occur with the periphery of a constituent itself. The co-occurrence of a phonological tone with a certain segmental or prosodic landmark can be expressed in terms of 'phonological association' and 'phonetic alignment'. Henceforth, association is taken to be discrete, referring to the phono-

2 Theoretical background

logical linking of a tone with a phonological entity (a TBU or a boundary), and alignment to be continuous, referring to the exact position of a tone in relation to a landmark in the speech signal (see e.g. Ladd 2008). The former is an abstraction away from the phonetic instantiation captured by the latter. The mapping of a tonal event (tune) onto the segments it co-occurs with (text) is referred to as 'tune-text-association'.

There is a crucial distinction between edge tones, i.e. tones found at the beginning or end of a prosodic constituent, and pitch accents, i.e. tones marking strong elements of prosodic constituents. This distinction is made in the AM model, as well as in some models preceding it. Trubetzkoy (1939) distinguished between tones having a 'culminative' and a 'delimitative' function. Culminative tones lend prominence; delimitative tones mark edges. Trager & Smith (1951) made a distinction between 'pitch phonemes' and 'juncture phonemes'. The IPO model distinguished between 'accent lending' and 'non-accent-lending' pitch movements (Cohen & t′Hart 1968; t′Hart & Cohen 1973; t′Hart & Collier 1975). In the AM model, this distinction is made using the terms 'edge tones' and 'pitch accents'. Generally, these two types of tonal events are widely used descriptive categories that capture tonal events in intonation systems across languages.

2.3.1 Edge tones

Tonal events can co-occur with the beginning or end of a prosodic constituent. These tones are called 'edge tones' or 'boundary tones'. Edge tones mark edges but also express utterance-wide functions such as sentence modality. In the incredulity contour shown in Figure 2.3, the final rise always occurs at the right edge of the phrase. It has been analysed as a H(igh) intonation phrase-final edge tone (Hirschberg & Ward 1992). In Figure 2.1, the right boundary of the first ip is marked by a high edge tone marking non-finality (H-), while the final ip is marked by a low edge tone (L-). Ladd defines edge tones as "any tone that is associated with the periphery of a prosodic domain" (Ladd 2008: 47). This phonological association is often manifested as the tone being aligned close to the edge of the phrase. This is made explicit by Pierrehumbert & Beckman (1988: 127): they claim that "tones are produced at the phonetic boundary of the node with which they are associated [...]." They go on and state that "the initial and final tone [...] are produced at about the same time as the initial and final segments [...]". Thus, the most relevant characteristic of an edge tone is its alignment with the margins of a prosodic phrase.

2.3.2 Pitch accents

After having explored the properties of tones that are located at the periphery of prosodic phrases, we now turn to tones that occur with prominent units inside these phrases. Pitch accents have been described as marking the strongest elements (or the heads) of prosodic constituents.[3]

In English and German for example, a pitch accent is usually associated with the primary stressed syllable of the most prominent word of a phrase. Going back to the short incredulity contour in Figure 2.3, the rise-fall in pitch has been described as a rising pitch accent, associated with the primary stressed syllable of *statistics instructor*. The pitch accent that co-occurs with the stressed syllable of the most prominent unit of a phrase is commonly described as the nuclear pitch accent of that phrase. Commonly the nuclear pitch accent occurs within focused constituents, i.e. communicatively the most relevant elements of the utterance (for a brief discussion of 'focus', see Chapter 5). The concept of marking the head of a constituent is directly linked to the idea of strength relationships within the prosodic structure and is determined, among other things, by lexical strength relationships within the word.

2.4 Tune-text-association

The previous discussion highlighted two descriptive categories of tonal events in the AM model: edge tones and pitch accents. These tones are mainly distinguished by their temporal co-occurrence with certain segmental landmarks. An edge tone is aligned with the edge of a phrase and a pitch accent is aligned with the head of a phrase. Phonetic alignment is taken as direct evidence for any proposed phonological association (Arvaniti, Ladd & Mennen 2000). Proposing the association of a tone to an edge is often justified by the consistent alignment of the tone to that edge. Proposing the association of a tone to a TBU is justified by the consistent alignment of the tone to that TBU.

The last two decades of research investigating phonetic alignment have yielded the insight that certain tonal targets can be aligned in a highly systematic way with respect to reference points in the segmental string. In a number of European languages, specific turning points (local F0 minima and F0 maxima as well as elbows) are predictably realised within a small time frame determined

---

[3] Please note, that the term 'pitch accent' has also been used to refer to lexically determined tonal properties of certain languages, most prominently used in the description of Japanese. The term is used here only to refer to post-lexical pitch accents.

2 Theoretical background

by the segmental make-up of the text (e.g. Arvaniti, Ladd & Mennen 1998; Atterer & Ladd 2004; Arvaniti & Ladd 2009; Mücke et al. 2009, and Ladd 2008 for an overview). Importantly, patterns of phonetic alignment relative to segments, which are consistent within rather than across language varieties, are typically taken as the phonetic manifestation of phonological association to a structural unit like a stressed syllable or a phrase edge (Arvaniti, Ladd & Mennen 2000). This, in turn, goes hand in hand with a classification of the tonal event as belonging to a descriptive category like pitch accent or edge tone.

Similarly, the existence of varying alignment patterns where the same tonal targets are aligned differently relative to a stressed syllable has frequently been used to posit a distinction between pitch accent categories within a language variety (Pierrehumbert & Steele 1989; D'Imperio & House 1997; Face & Prieto 2007), which we will turn to now.

In the AM model, pitch accents are analysed as consisting of minimally one tone which is 'starred' (e.g. H*, L*). The starred tone can optionally be combined with an 'unstarred' tone (e.g. H*+L, L+H*, signalled by '+', but see Gussenhoven 2002, for a critique of this notation). In those bitonal cases, one common argument for choosing which tone is the starred tone and which is the unstarred tone relates to the phonetic alignment of the starred tone with respect to the segmental material. Figure 2.4 depicts two different pitch accent types for English. Both involve a rise in pitch close to the TBU, the stressed syllable (grey box), but they differ in terms of phonetic alignment. The solid line corresponds to a rise starting within the stressed syllable and reaching its pitch maximum in the following syllable. The dashed line corresponds to a rise starting in the syllable preceding the stressed syllable and reaching its pitch maximum within the stressed syllable. This difference in phonetic alignment can be accounted for by means of the notation of the starred tone, which indicates which tonal target is reached in the stressed syllable.[4]

Later work, however, has challenged the assumption that the relationship between phonological association and phonetic alignment is that straightforward. Often, the tonal targets are phonetically instantiated close to, but not within, the TBU the tones are assumed to be associated with. Arvaniti, Ladd & Mennen (2000) demonstrated that the tonal targets of a rising pitch accent in Greek do not co-occur with the accented syllable but shortly before or after it, respectively.

---

[4] The notation of starred tones is not uncontroversial since it often remains empirically unclear which tone of a bitonal event is the starred one (Arvaniti, Ladd & Mennen 2000). Moreover, it often remains a matter of analysis whether the unstarred tone of a bitonal event really 'belongs' to the pitch accent or whether it might be a reflex of a preceding/following pitch accent or an edge tone.

2.4 Tune-text-association

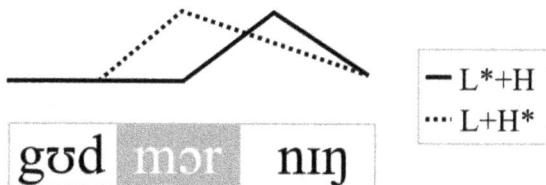

Figure 2.4: Schematised pitch contours for bitonal pitch accents adapted from Grice (2006: 782).

Moreover, alignment patterns are often idiosyncratic in that they are very much dependent on the language or even the variety under investigation (e.g. Mücke et al. 2009).

In addition to language-dependent factors affecting tonal alignment, there are circumstances in which the phonetic realisation of a tonal target is constrained in predictable ways. In some cases, the number of tonal targets in a tune may exceed the number of TBUs with which these tones can associate. This situation is referred to as 'tonal crowding'. In other cases, the segmental material may be phonetically inadequate for bearing a pitch movement.

To resolve a conflict between the need to realise functionally relevant tonal events and both the amount of TBUs available and the phonetic suitability of these TBUs, linguistic systems appear to adjust either the tones or the segments. The nature of this adjustment depends on syntagmatic, paradigmatic, as well as language-specific factors. One prominently discussed pair of notions is the distinction between 'truncation' and 'compression', both of which refer to adjustments of the realisation of tones themselves. Either a tonal target can be phonetically not reached (truncation) or the rate of pitch change between tonal targets is increased (compression). The tones can also adjust by shifting tonal targets towards less restricted segmental material. Alternatively, the tonal realisation might stay the same, while the segmental material adjusts to fulfil the requirements necessary to realise the tones. In these cases, either the segmental material may be lengthened or additional segments may be added to bear the critical tonal targets. These different strategies will be discussed in the following.

2.4.1 Tune-text-adjustments

2.4.1.1 Truncation and compression

If the segmental tier offers too little sonorant material for the realisation of a tonal sequence, the f0 contour can be truncated or compressed. A useful phenomenon

2 Theoretical background

to shed light on truncation and compression is the lexical pitch accent contrast in Swedish: in Swedish, there are minimal pairs that are differentiated only by their lexical pitch accent (accent I and accent II). Both accent types consist of a high followed by a low target differing only in the phonetic alignment of the high tone (Bruce 1977). In their seminal work, Erikson & Alstermark (1972) discuss how the realisation of a lexical pitch accent is adjusted in the face of phonotactic restrictions. On the one hand, they observed that the actual pitch movement is often reduced with decreasing vowel length, i.e. the pitch movement is undershot, with the fall after the high tone simply ending before it reaches its low target. If the syllable contains a short vowel and a voiceless coda consonant, the fall in f0 may disappear entirely. This mechanism has been named 'truncation'. On the other hand, they discuss "rate adjustments", where the pitch movement is realised more rapidly on shorter vowels. This mechanism has later been named 'compression' (Bannert & Bredvad 1975).

Grabe (1998) investigated truncation and compression in Southern Standard British English and Northern Standard German. She investigated rising and falling contours phrase finally by systematically manipulating the voiced material available to realise the tonal movement, ranging from a disyllabic word with a long vowel (/ʃiːfɐ/) to a monosyllabic word with a long vowel (/ʃiːf/) to a monosyllabic word with a short vowel (/ʃɪft, ʃɪf/). Note that the stimuli contained voiceless consonants, in this way reducing the phonetic opportunity to realise tonal movements to the vowel only. Her results indicate that Southern Standard British English compresses both falls and rises. In contrast, Northern Standard German truncates falls and compresses rises. Moreover, for German, Grabe observed a gradual decrease in f0 excursion of the fall between /ʃiːfɐ/ and /ʃiːf/. For /ʃɪf/, the fall was entirely absent. This complete undershoot has also been observed in high fall-rise contours in German and Dutch (Lickley, Schepman & Ladd 2005; Ladd 2008). In case of tonal crowding, the fall is entirely truncated resulting in a high rise. The tonal adjustment depends on the contour and the language under investigation. For example, Grabe (1998) showed that f0 rises are more likely to be compressed in German and English, while the falling contour is truncated in German but compressed in English. As opposed to Grabe's findings, Rathcke (2009) showed that falling contours in German were partially compressed whereas rising–falling contours were truncated. Moreover, truncation and compression appear to be dialect dependent (Bannert & Bredvad 1975; Grabe et al. 2000) as well as speaker specific (Prieto & Ortega-Llebaria 2009).

2.4.1.2 Shift of tonal targets

A different strategy to resolve conflicts in the tune-text-association is a temporal shift of the tonal target. If there is not enough segmental material to realise a sequence of tonal targets, one or multiple tonal target may be realised earlier. A case in point is Neapolitan Italian. Statements marked by a narrow focus on the final word are characterised by a local rise on the accented syllable followed by a fall within the vowel. Similarly, yes-no questions are characterised by a local rise on the accented syllable followed by a low target at the end of the utterance (D'Imperio 2001). Thus, questions and statements with final narrow focus are expressed with similar tonal events, i.e. a rise-fall in pitch phrase finally. Even though these contours appear to be very similar in certain contexts, they have been described as differing in the alignment of the high tone, which reaches its target later in the accented vowel in questions than in statements (D'Imperio & House 1997). Questions, however, can also display an additional final rise making the tonal movement very complex (a rise-fall-rise). The presence vs. absence of this final rise is dependent on dialect and speaking style (Savino 2012). Cangemi & Grice (2016) looked at the alignment of the high target of the pitch accent across instances with and without an utterance-final rise. They found strong evidence for the high target shifting to the left when a phrase-final rise is present. The tonal sequence starts earlier to ensure the realisation of all tonal targets. The tendency of tones to be shifted leftwards has been observed in many other languages in different contexts (Steele 1986; Caspers & Heuven 1993; D'Imperio 2001; Prieto, D'Imperio & Gili Fivela 2005; Schepman, Lickley & Ladd 2006; Mücke et al. 2009).

2.4.1.3 Adjustments of the text

After having explored cases in which the tune adjusts to insufficient text, we now turn to adjustments of the text to the tune. The text can be adjusted in two ways: existing segmental material can be lengthened or segmental material can be added. The former case has been reported for Spanish and Catalan by Prieto & Ortega-Llebaria (2009). They investigated the intonational marking of focus in phrase-final position. In words with final stress, narrow focus is characterised by a rise-fall on the final syllable. They compared these contours to a simpler falling contour and found that syllables are longer when the tune is more complex. This can be considered to be a mechanism to fit the complex rise-fall tonal sequence, which is not necessary for the simpler falling contour. Similar results have been reported for Bari Italian yes-no questions, which are typically realised (in read speech) with an accentual rise followed by a fall-rise. If a phrase-final accented

2 Theoretical background

syllable bears the rise-fall-rise, it has been found to be considerably lengthened as compared to the same syllable in neutral statements, in which there is a simple fall in the lower portion of the speaker's range (Grice, Savino & Refice 1997; Refice, Savino & Grice 1997). Similarly, Frota (2002) reports on lengthening of the nuclear vowel in phrase-final position when a fall-rise is to be realised in Portuguese yes-no questions. Heston (2014) reports on lengthening of utterance-final vowels when they are accompanied by a final rise-fall in Fataluku, a Papuan language.

In addition to lengthening existing segments, some languages insert additional segmental material to enable tonal realisation. In Bari Italian, speakers producing loanwords ending in closed syllables often insert a schwa-like element word finally ([tɪm] vs. [tɪmə], Grice et al. 2015). The presence as well as the acoustic salience of these schwas is modulated by the complexity of the tune with a greater incidence of schwa and a greater duration of schwa in more complex question tunes. Moreover, the metrical structure of the word predicts the presence and duration of schwa as well. There were more and longer schwas in monosyllabic words than in disyllabic trochaic words. This fits with the idea of schwa occurring to aid in the realisation of tones. Since a disyllabic word already contains one unaccented syllable that can carry some of the tonal complex, speakers are less likely to add an additional element. Frota (2002) reports on similar insertions of non-lexical vowels in Portuguese. A high central vowel is inserted in utterances with a complex tonal movement on the final syllable.

2.4.1.4 Summary

To sum up, the literature indicates different mechanisms for conflict resolution in tune-text-association. The tonal target is not reached (truncation) or the rate of pitch change is increased (compression). The tune can also adjust by shifting the tonal target towards less restricted segmental material (shift). Finally, the segmental material may be lengthened or additional segments may be added to bear the critical tonal target. These strategies are schematised in Figure 2.5.

Importantly, these strategies are not mutually exclusive. Contours can be both compressed and truncated to some degree, a shift may occur together with additional compression, and adjustments to the text may interact with adjustments to the tune. Interestingly, previous research has also demonstrated that there may be a trade-off between text-adjustment and tune-adjustments. Prieto & Ortega-Llebaria (2009) report on a negative correlation between increasing syllable duration and truncation of the contour.

2.4 Tune-text-association

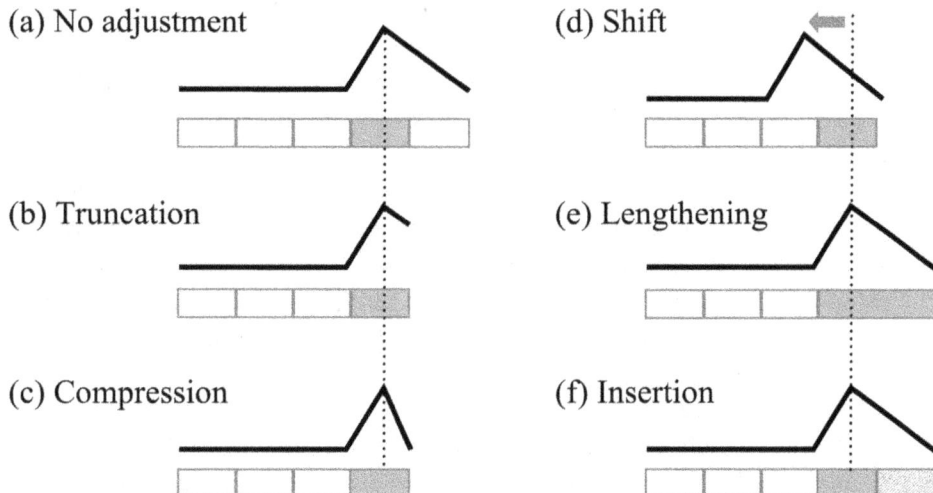

Figure 2.5: Schematic representation of tune-text-adjustments. The grey box indicates the TBU with which the rise up to a high target co-occurs. Panel (a) illustrates a case in which tune and text associate normally. The tune is characterised by a rise towards a high target on the TBU followed by a fall to a low target at the end of the utterance. In (b) the final low target is not fully reached (truncated). In (c) the rate of pitch change is compressed. In (d) the rise-fall shifts to the left. In (e) the accented syllable is lengthened. In (f) an additional segment (light grey) is added.

2.4.2 The representation of tune-text-adjustments

Adjustments to the tune are often considered to be phonetic variants of phonologically identical contours (Grønnum 1989; Grabe 1998; Grabe et al. 2000; Hanssen, Peters & Gussenhoven 2007; Ladd 2008). One strong argument for this claim is the gradual nature of truncation. As discussed above, Grabe (1998) observed a gradual decrease in f0 excursion from /ʃiːfɐ/ to /ʃiːf/ to /ʃɪf/ which resulted in the fall being entirely absent in /ʃɪf/. Furthermore, Grabe notes that speakers hear the target words as having falling pitch regardless of the actual f0 values (Grabe 1998: 140). This is in line with recent findings demonstrating that despite the "missing" parts of the f0 contour, the signal may bear other acoustic correlates that correspond to the intended meanings. Experiments with whispered speech have shown that noise-induced cues can be used to convey meanings that would otherwise be encoded in f0. Speakers of Mandarin compensate for the lack of F0 in whispered speech by using, for example, intensity to maintain the contrast between lexical tones (Whalen & Xu 1992). The use of acoustic substitutes for f0 is

2 Theoretical background

not restricted to whispered speech: recent experiments have shown that in normal speech, speakers consistently make adjustments in voiceless obstruents induced by intonational contexts. In several experiments, Niebuhr and colleagues (Niebuhr 2008; 2009; 2012; Niebuhr, Lill & Neuschulz 2011) showed that frication and aspiration noise of phrase-medial and phrase-final voiceless obstruents corresponds to the expected modulation of f0 (see also Ritter & Roettger 2014). In particular, voiceless parts of the signal corresponding to high/rising tones exhibit higher mean Centre of Gravity and higher mean intensity than counterparts of corresponding low/falling tones. Thus, even in absence of f0, the phonological representation may be phonetically manifested via other channels than f0.

While truncation in Grabe's study appears to be gradual, other phenomena discussed in the literature have rather been regarded as discrete. In these cases, tune-text-adjustments like truncation may be interpreted as contextual variants of the unadjusted tune-text-association similar to allophony in segmental phonology. This sort of phonological account has been proposed within the AM model using the concept of 'secondary association'.

In their influential analysis of the Japanese intonation system, Pierrehumbert & Beckman (1988) proposed secondarily associated edge tones. Consider Figure 2.6. Japanese is analysed as having both lexically specified tonal events (HL on se' and do') and postlexical tonal events (all other tones). Syllables can be mono-moraic or bi-moraic. According to Pierrehumbert and Beckman, both the accentual phrase (α) and the utterance (υ) are delimited by edge tones. The utterance is analysed as having an initial L edge tone and a final H edge tone. The final H is considered an edge tone that is 'primarily associated' with the right edge of the utterance. The initial L tone is –in addition to being primarily associated with the left edge of the utterance– also associated with a tone bearing unit, the first sonorant mora in the utterance.

Similarly, accentual phrases have a left H edge tone and a right L edge tone. Both tones are conceived of as secondarily associated with a sonorant mora. The accentual phrase-initial H tone associates with the second mora, because the higher-level utterance-initial edge tone is associated with the first mora. The accentual phrase-final edge tone, the L, is analysed as secondarily associated with the first mora of the following accentual phrase, pushing the accentual phrase-initial edge tone to the second mora. Note that in this analysis not all edge tones are secondarily associated. For example, the final L edge tone of the second accentual phrase is only primarily associated with the edge and has no secondary association.

2.4 Tune-text-association

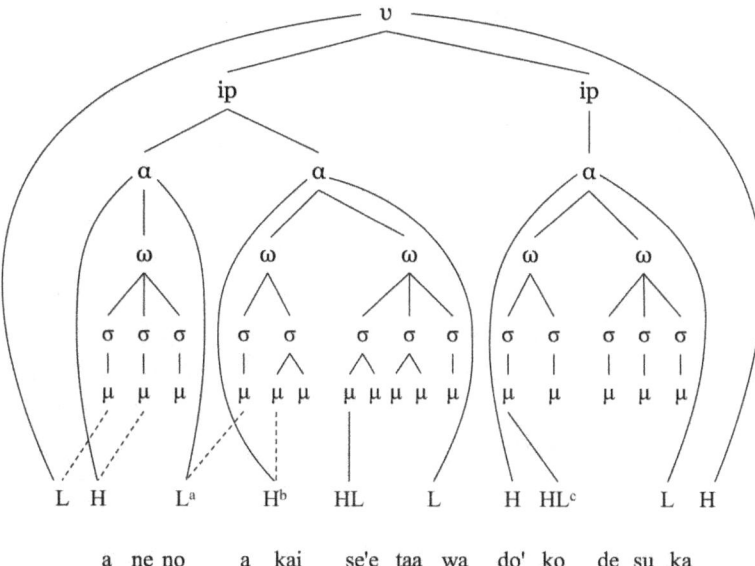

Figure 2.6: Pierrehumbert and Beckman's analysis of prosodic structure and tonal association for following Japanese sentence: Ane-no akai se'etaa-wa do'ko desu ka? ('Where is big sister's red sweater?', adapted from Pierrehumbert & Beckman (1988: 21)). Dashed line indicates secondary association to a TBU.

The accentual phrase-final L tone (indicated by superscripted a) is realised on the first mora of the upcoming accentual phrase if two conditions are met: the first syllable in the phrase must be mono-moraic and unaccented (i.e. here, it does not bear the HL). This results in an association of the accentual phrase-initial H tone (indicated by superscripted b) to the second mora (as in akaise'e taa wa, Figure 2.6).

There are two scenarios in which the first mora of the accentual phrase is not associated with the L tone but instead with a H tone: either the first syllable is bi-moraic in which case phrase-initial H is associated to the first mora (not in Figure 2.6), or the first syllable is accented (bearing the HL, indicated by superscripted c). When the first mora bears a H tone, the L tone realisation is reported to be "phonetically weak", i.e. the pitch is not as low, the rise to the H is shorter and flatter or it is entirely absent. In cases with a short unaccented first mora, the L tone preceding the H is realised as "phonetically strong", i.e. there is a clear rise from low to high pitch.

2 Theoretical background

This analysis attempted to account for the distributional properties of intonational tones in Japanese. The difference in the phonetic realisation of the proposed tones is accounted for by two different phonological association patterns, and in turn, with two different categories of edge tones: an edge tone that has only a primary association and an edge tone that has an additional secondary association to a tone bearing unit.

Grice (1995) has applied this theoretical concept to Palermo Italian question intonation. Yes-no questions in the Palermo variety are produced with a rise-fall in pitch consisting of a rising pitch accent (L+H* in Grice's annotation) and low edge tone (L-). When the final syllable is accented, the subsequent fall does not fully reach a low target. However, if the accented syllable is not final, there is a deep fall towards a full low pitch target. This resembles the truncation phenomena described in §2.4.1. As opposed to Grabe (1998), however, Grice accounts for this difference by means of phonological association patterns. In the case of a final accent, the low edge tone is primarily associated to the edge. In the case of a non-final accent, the edge tone is secondarily associated to the final syllable making it lower in pitch. One argument for this analysis put forward by Grice is the rather discrete nature of this alternation in terms of both distributional observations and auditory impressions.

Gussenhoven applied a similar analysis to tonal phenomena in Venlo Dutch accounting for the alignment properties of low edge tones (Gussenhoven & Vliet 1999; Gussenhoven 2000; 2002). After a high pitch accent marking focus, the low edge tone can be aligned right after the high target, resulting in a sharp fall, or at the edge, resulting in a slow fall towards the phrase edge. If the stressed syllable is bi-moraic, the fall occurs right after the high target of the pitch accent and the high pitch accent is analysed as associating with the first mora of the stressed syllable. Alternatively, if the stressed syllable is mono-moraic, there is a late, imprecise fall towards the end of the phrase. Gussenhoven accounted for this asymmetry by proposing a secondary association of the low edge tone to the second mora of the accented syllable. If not available, the low edge tone remains primarily associated to the boundary with no secondary association.

Whether tune-text-adjustments, as discussed in the previous section, are adjustments of the phonetic realisations, leaving the phonological representation unchanged, or a phonetic reflex of a phonological alternation, remains an empirical question to be answered for each language individually. While the gradual nature of truncation in Grabe's study (1998) indicates a non-phonological nature of tune-text-adjustments in German, Grice's reports on Palermo Italian (1995) suggest a representational difference. Such cases can be seen as context-dependent allophonic alternations paralleling to context-dependent alternations in the segmental domain. Secondary association can be conceived of as a way to formalise such context-dependent allophonic alternations and, in turn, enables an allocation of tune-text-adjustments to the level of phonological representation.

The concept of secondary association was substantially extended and made more explicit in Grice, Arvaniti & Ladd (2000). They used this formal mechanism to account for phonological differences of a particular tune across varieties of Hungarian, Romanian, and Greek: 'the Eastern European question tune' (EEQT). All of these languages express yes-no questions with a similar intonation contour, characterised by a rise-fall. In all investigated languages, the contour can be analysed as having a low nuclear pitch accent on the stressed syllable of the accented word (L*), a rise to a high tone (H), and a fall to a low tone at the right edge of the phrase (L%). However, they differ with regard to the position of the H tone. The H tone occurs either on the stressed syllable in a word occurring after the accented word or on a specific syllable close to the right edge of the phrase (dependent on the position of the accented word and the language under investigation). Take for example Standard Greek. When the nuclear accent (L*) is on a non-final word, the H phrase accent (H-) is secondarily associated with the lexically stressed syllable of the final word (Figure 2.7a). If the nuclear accent is on the final word, the H phrase accent is secondarily associated with the final syllable (Figure 2.7b). Grice et al. account for these contours by proposing a phrase edge tone (H-) that is secondarily associated to a particular syllable (post-nuclear stressed syllable or a syllable close to the phrase edge). Given this analysis, the languages investigated by Grice et al. share the same phonological representation differing only in the unit with which the H tone is secondarily associated. They refer to this tone as a 'phrase accent' and define it as an edge tone with the possibility of a secondary association to a tone bearing unit. These tones, even though clearly not signalling prominence or focus, share some of the properties of pitch accents when they are associated with a TBU such as enhancing the spatio-temporal aspects of the segments with which they co-occur. So phrase accents are argued to be at once edge tones ('phrase-') and prominence lending tones ('-accent').

2.5 Summary

The present chapter has introduced relevant concepts of intonation and prosodic structure. These notions were elaborated on within the Autosegmental-Metrical model (AM). The AM model is characterised by two assumptions. It assumes that

2 Theoretical background

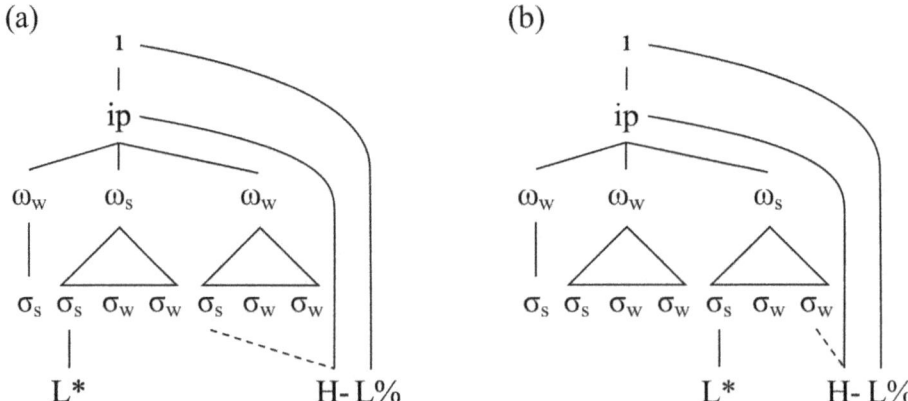

Figure 2.7: The East European Question Tune for Standard Greek analysed as phrase accents that are secondarily associated with the text (according to Grice, Arvaniti & Ladd 2000).

sounds are grouped into hierarchically organised sets of constituents and it proposes separate levels of description for segments and tonal events. These levels are associated with each other. Based on these assumptions, certain key phenomena of intonation were discussed. Tonal events are defined by properties of their phonetic form such as their temporal alignment with the segmental material as well as by the function they express. Edge tones are phonologically associated with the edges of prosodic constituents. Pitch accents are phonologically associated with designated terminal elements of prosodic constituents. These designated terminal elements usually coincide with the stressed syllable of a word. Since the notion of pitch accent presupposes the presence of metrical prominence asymmetries at the word level, it is limited with regard to its applicability. Languages without word stress cannot be described as having a pitch accent in the sense used here, namely a postlexical tone or tonal complex associated with a lexically determined strong syllable.

With regard to functional differences, edge tones are commonly described as marking edges and signalling communicative functions such as sentence modality (questions vs. statement) and (non-)finality. Pitch accents are commonly described as marking prominent elements of the phrase such as new and contrastive information.

In addition to edge tones and pitch accents, certain tones fall in neither category: some of these tonal events can be captured by the concept of the phrase accent. Phrase accents associate to the edge, but do not have to be aligned to it. They can appear on a TBU near the edge, either a stressed syllable or an unstressed syllable that is close to the edge. They do not signal focus, but appear to have prominence-lending qualities. The introduction of the phrase accent constitutes a development in intonation research (and the AM model) that demonstrates the fruitfulness of decomposing typological categories into their distributional and functional characteristics.

It becomes clear that the association of the tune and the text is one crucial criterion for categorising tonal events. This association, however, is not always straightforward. In certain contexts, the phonetic realisation of a tonal event is restricted, either due to crowding of tones or due to the segmental identity of the TBU. Facing such conflicts, linguistic systems adjust either the tones or the segmental material by truncating or compressing the contour, shifting the tonal target, lengthening the available segmental material, or inserting additional segments. Both the choice of strategy as well as its linguistic status depend on the language under investigation and the analysis. Some phenomena exhibit gradual and predictable properties; others appear to be best captured by assigning them (allo-)phonological status.

While most work on tune-text-association has been done on languages in which well-formed syllables usually contain at least a sonorant, work on tune-text-association in languages with more extreme phonotactic possibilities is rare. There are languages that allow whole utterances without phonological vowels and words that are comprised of voiceless segments only. In these cases, the phonetic opportunity for the execution of intonational pitch movements is constrained. The question arises as to how the tune associates with the text in these cases. Here, we will attempt to answer this question by studying intonation in Tashlhiyt, a Berber language.

3 Tashlhiyt, a Berber language

3.1 The Imazighen

The Imazighen (Amazighs, Berbers) are the native inhabitants of wide parts of North Africa extending from the coast of the Atlantic Ocean to the Siwa oasis in Egypt. The language spoken by the Imazighen is henceforth referred to as "Berber" (it is also referred to as "Tamazight").[1] Berber has been classified as belonging to the Afro-Asiatic language family, which also includes Ancient Egyptian, Chadic, Cushitic, Omotic, and Semitic languages (Lewis, Simons & Fennig 2016). For a general overview of the language family see Basset (1952), Applegate (1971) and Galand (1988).

Berber is spoken by a substantial number of people in Algeria, Tunisia, Libya, Egypt, Mauritania, Burkina-Faso, Mali, and Niger with the majority of speakers living in Morocco. Moroccans are often native speakers of one or more Berber languages alongside a Moroccan variety of Arabic. The long-lasting language contact between Moroccan Arabic and Berber is reflected in highly overlapping vocabularies, a result of massive borrowing in Berber (Kossmann 2009).

Morocco is described as having three major Berber languages: "Tarifiyt" spoken in the north, "Tamazight" spoken in the Middle Atlas region and "Tashlhiyt",[2] the variety under investigation here, spoken in the High-Atlas region and south of it (Figure 3.1). While there is a clear geographic separation of Tarifiyt and the southern varieties reflected in a clear-cut linguistic distinction, the distinction between Tamazight and Tashlhiyt is better captured by a continuum. The number of Tashlhiyt speakers is unclear. Estimates range from three million (Chaker

---

[1] In the following, the languages spoken by the Imazighen are referred to as "Berber". This term is used as a neutral term and has no negative connotation in an Anglo-Saxon context. While the term "Tamazight" has become popular among modern Berber intellectuals, we refrain from using the term here because of its ambiguity: Tamazight can be used to refer either to the Berber language as denoting the language family in general or to the specific Berber variety spoken in central Morocco (as opposed to Tashlhiyt in the South).

[2] Alternatively, the language or specific subvarieties of it have been referred to as Shilha and Soussiya (Susiya, Tasoussit). Tashlhiyt has also been spelled Tachilhit, Tashelhaït, Tashelhit or Tashilheet.

3 Tashlhiyt, a Berber language

1992) to 3.9 million speakers in 2004 (Lewis, Simons & Fennig 2016), with Berber in general being currently spoken by about 7.7 million people in Morocco (Lewis, Simons & Fennig 2016). These numbers may diverge so drastically due to the historically loaded multilingual context in Morocco, which will be sketched briefly below.

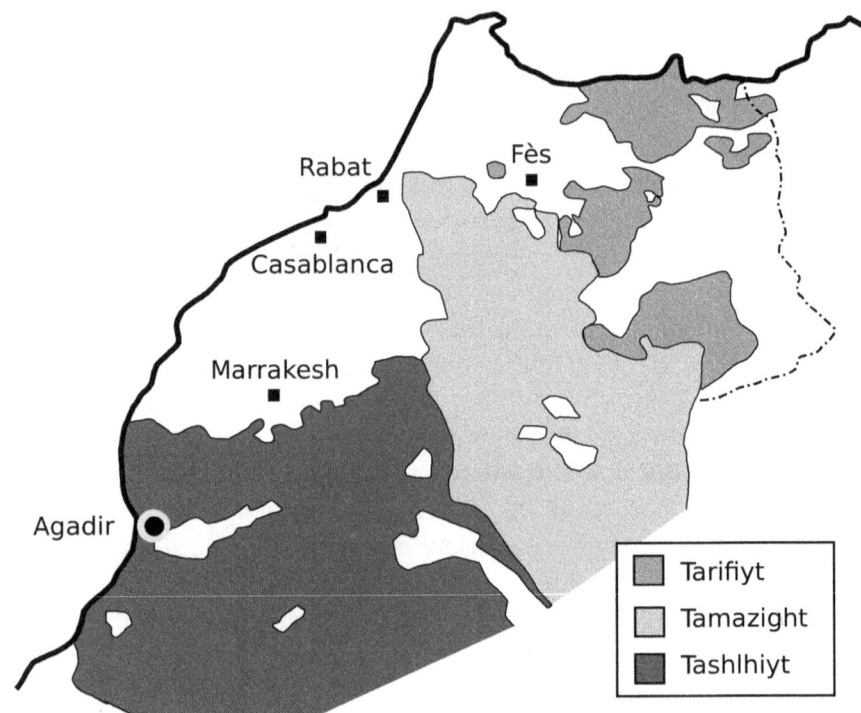

Figure 3.1: Map of the three major Berber languages spoken in Morocco alongside the location of major cities. The large circle indicates the location of Agadir, the city in which the Tashlhiyt variety investigated here is spoken. White spaces indicate non-Berber speech communities. This map is based on the map by Colin (1937: 203).

In addition to at least one Berber variety, Moroccans are often speakers of Moroccan Arabic. In some areas, speakers may additionally have a high degree of proficiency in French, a residual of the French colonisation. It is clear that this intricate multilingual situation in Morocco plays an important role in any evaluation of the linguistic structures of Moroccan languages. Therefore, a brief historical overview of the Imazighen in North Africa and the history of Morocco is given below (§3.2). The linguistic description presented in this book is based on recordings of university students from Agadir. We will briefly discuss relevant facts about Agadir and the speaker sample (§3.3). Subsequently, we will give a succinct overview of the linguistic system of Tashlhiyt (§3.4). This will include an introduction to the orthographic systems used by Tashlhiyt speakers (§3.4.1), a presentation of the phoneme inventory of the language, relevant phonetic properties of phonological contrasts, and relevant aspects of syllable structure (§3.4.2), a presentation of basic morphological patterns (§3.4.3), and a description of basic word order and syntactic constructions (§3.4.4).

3.2 Historical overview

The Imazighen were the first inhabitants of North Africa, as testified by historical, anthropological, archaeological, and linguistic records (e.g. Julien 1966; Laroui 2015). The first Imazighen in Morocco were farmers and merchants trading with people from the Mediterranean early on. Over the centuries, they were heavily influenced by other civilisations such as the Phoenicians, the Carthaginians, the Romans, and the Vandals, all of which left a lasting effect on their religious belief, arts, and language. However, no civilisation had a greater impact on the Imazighen than the Arab civilisation. The Arabs arrived in Morocco in 682 CE. As the Berbers had no significant literary tradition, the Arabic language spread quickly and manifested itself as the language of science, administration, and, of course, the language of the Qur'an.

Another linguistically significant historical event was the French Protectorate. At the beginning of the 20th century, France established a protectorate over Morocco. The French Protectorate lasted from 1912 to 1956 and had, yet again, a huge impact on political, educational, and economic aspects of the country. The French introduced new educational systems, which, crucially, distinguished between a very constrained Islamic system and an Imazighen system that did not contain Islamic studies. Both Arab and Imazighen communities protested. It was perceived as an attack on Moroccans' cultural and religious identity since the education in Classical Arabic was a crucial aspect of religious practice (Zouhir 2013). Later, in 1930, a decree was enacted by the French (and signed by the Moroccan king) that formalised certain practices of Berber tribes by law. The decree entitled areas in which Berber was the dominant language to practice their own tribal law systems. Officially approving the cultural practice of the Berber led to the perception of a straightforward attempt to divide the population. These changes, however, had the opposite effect. A sense of nationalism in Morocco emerged, uniting Imazighen and Arabs under the umbrella of a common language: Arabic (El-Aissati 2005).

3 Tashlhiyt, a Berber language

After the end of the French Protectorate in 1956, Morocco was left with the administrative systems of the French, including their education system. Except for religious studies, all people were still taught in French. During the French Protectorate, knowledge of French was indispensable for obtaining power (Marley 2004) and even after the French left, French remained a language of high prestige. In the now independent Morocco, classical Arabic was aimed to replace the language of the colonisers, and became the official language as part of a general arabisation policy. The incentive here was to unite the country and to reinstate a national language. The whole education system and large parts of the administration system were arabised. This move of the government, however, completely ignored the multilingual reality in Morocco. In the official constitution, which claimed Arabic to be the official language of the country, the Imazighen and their language, Berber, were not even mentioned once (El-Aissati 2005).

This policy made Berbers become increasingly active in promoting their language as an official language in Morocco. In 2000, the Charter of Educational Reform was put into place. Among other things, the reform aimed to reinforce and improve Arabic teaching, diversify languages used for teaching science and technology, and, crucially, open up to Berber languages. The latter aspect is most notable since it constitutes a recognition that the education of Berber speakers, a large part of Morocco's population, could benefit from education in their mother tongue. For many, the Charter was received as a promising development enabling the majority of Moroccans to obtain a high degree of proficiency in the national language and at least some limited proficiency in two foreign languages (Berdouzi 2000). This recognition reached a symbolic high in 2011 when a constitutional reform took place. In the reform, Berber (alongside Arabic) was recognised as an official language, making Morocco the only North African country to give official status to a Berber language.

However, the teaching of Berber has met with mixed reactions. Some advocate that Berber should not be a mandatory subject in school because it is perceived as not particularly useful for professional purposes, which generally require Arabic. Others argue that it will instead encourage students speaking Berber to continue their education and facilitate their socioeconomic integration (Ennaji 2005). These opposing views depend at least partly on the sociolinguistic context in which speakers find themselves. For example, Marley (2004) conducted a survey in a school in Khouribga, a town in central Morocco that is mainly inhabited by native monolingual speakers of Moroccan Arabic (no Berber speakers). Marley found that both teachers and students are convinced of the benefits of learning a European language (French) in addition to Arabic. Learning non-prestigious languages like Berber is generally perceived as less favourable, although speakers generally acknowledge the cultural relevance of the Berber culture.

To summarise, the present linguistic situation in Morocco is characterised by the co-existence of multiple languages, each of which is associated with different degrees of prestige. This diversity is particularly noticeable in large cities that attract people from all parts of the country. Agadir is one of these melting pots.

3.3 Berber in Agadir

Agadir (English: 'wall', 'citadel') is a major city of Morocco and is located close to the Atlas Mountains right at the Atlantic Ocean (cf. Figure 3.1). It is the capital of the Souss-Massa-Drâa region. After its destruction by an earthquake in 1960, the city has been rebuilt. Now, Agadir has a great number of new residents and attracts many tourists. Tourism and fishing are the major economic industries besides agriculture (mainly citrus fruits and vegetables). As one of the biggest cities in the south, Agadir is a melting pot for people from large parts of southern Morocco's countryside who go there seeking education and employment. Linguistically, this results in a speaker population that exhibits different levels of multilingualism, with people coming from communities speaking either only Berber, only Moroccan Arabic, or both to differing degrees (Mountassir 2008). Moreover, speakers come from communities speaking different subvarieties of Tashlhiyt itself. This results in a high degree of tolerance to linguistic variation (for Moroccan Arabic and Berber dialects in other cities, see Maas & Procházka 2012).

The present studies are based on data collected at the Ibn Zohr University of Agadir. The speaker sample consists of students from the Département des Études Amazighes. Speakers are all bilingual speakers of Moroccan Arabic and Tashlhiyt and exhibit comparable proficiencies in these languages, according to their own judgments. These speakers were asked about their attitudes towards languages spoken in Morocco with regard to everyday life, education, professional life, religion, and science. In line with Marley's (2004) findings, speakers indeed consider French to be a relevant language to obtain a job. It is considered the language of business and the most modern and practical language. Speakers explicitly articulate the desire to learn French. However, as opposed to Marley's sample (from a non-Berber village), speakers from Agadir consider Berber to be the language which is most needed for their professional lives alongside French. They believe Berber is the language that should dominate education and should be taught to children. Speakers also attribute great ideological and cultural value

3 Tashlhiyt, a Berber language

to Berber. In line with that, speakers consider Berber to be the language that best embodies Moroccan culture. Speakers are exposed to TV programs, books, and music in Berber on a daily basis. Further, speakers mainly use Berber when engaging with modern communication devices such as cell phone text messages, emails, and social media.

3.4 Tashlhiyt

In the following, we will provide a very brief overview of relevant grammatical aspects of Tashlhiyt. Many grammatical phenomena are well documented (e.g. Stumme 1899; Aspinion 1953; Applegate 1958; Galand 1988; Dell & Elmedlaoui 1988; 2002). A great deal of work has been done on phonotactic patterns, morphophonemic alternations, and prosodic morphology (e.g. Jebbour 1996; Boukous 1987; Lasri 1991; Bensoukas 2001; Lahrouchi 2001; Ridouane 2003). More recently, a number of instrumental studies have looked at phonetic details of certain phonological phenomena (Ouakrim 1994; 1995; Ridouane 2003; 2007; 2008; Ridouane & Fougeron 2011; Gordon & Nafi 2012; Hermes et al. 2011, summarised in Ridouane 2014). Some of these findings are summarised in the following overview.

3.4.1 Orthography

Currently there are three different major orthographic systems in use to write Tashlhiyt: (Neo-)Tifinagh script, Arabic script, and Latin script. Tifinagh is an ancient script that was widely used by Berber speakers from the 3rd century BC to the third century AD. This ancient script has recently been re-established as an official writing system in Morocco. Young speakers are, however, seldom able to read or write in it. Publications exclusively written in Tifinagh are rare, but the script has entered public spaces on town signs and traffic signs. The Arabic script is based on the Arabic alphabet. It has been in use since the 16th century (Boogert 1997). Because the education system in Morocco is still dominated by standard Arabic, speakers are usually fluent readers of the Arabic script.

The most widely used script for Tashlhiyt today is the Latin script. It is the alphabet preferred by researchers and writers across different domains. In most modern printed works, the standard put forward by the Institut National dès Langues et Civilisations Orientales (INALCO) is adopted (Chaker 1996). However, the frequent use of private devices such as cell phones and computers has led to certain idiosyncratic adjustments of the standard in informal contexts. For example, according to INALCO, pharyngealised consonants are written with a subscripted dot (e.g. <iḍgam> /idˤgam/ 'yesterday'), but due to the practical limitations of private devices, it is frequently written with capitalised letters to indicate pharyngealisation (<iDgam>). Even though the speakers that we have worked with were fluent readers and used to communicating with their friends and family using some version of the Latin script, they appeared to be rather insecure when reading out aloud.

3.4.2 Phonology

3.4.2.1 Phoneme inventory

The following will constitute a brief introduction to the phoneme inventory of Tashlhiyt. Additionally, we will discuss some phonetic underpinnings of phonological contrasts following recent descriptions such as Ridouane (2014).

Table 3.1: Consonant inventory of Tashlhiyt Berber, ignoring the singleton/geminate contrast (cf. Ridouane 2014).

	Labial	Dental		Post-alveolar		Velar		Uvular		Ary-epiglottal	Glottal
		plain	pharyngealised	plain	pharyngealised	plain	labialised	plain	labialised		
Plosive	b	t d	tˤ dˤ			k g	kʷ gʷ	q	qʷ		
Nasal	m	n	(nˤ)								
Tap		r	rˤ								
Fricative	f	s z	sˤ zˤ	ʃ ʒ	ʃˤ ʒˤ			χ ʁ	χʷ ʁʷ	ʜ ʕ	h
Approximant				j			w				
Lateral		l	lˤ								

Tashlhiyt has a complex consonant system (see Table 3.1). Each singleton consonantal phoneme has a geminate counterpart. For example, consider the minimal pairs /juf/ 'he was better' vs. /juff/ 'he puffed' and /igwra/ 'frogs' vs. /iggwra/ 'he was the last'. This length contrast is not restricted to word-medial position. It is also found in absolute initial and final positions.

Tashlhiyt contrasts plain and labialised dorsal consonants and plain and pharyngealised coronal consonants. Pharyngealisation, where it occurs, spreads towards adjacent segments. For example, in /tzdˤart/ 'you are able', the pharyngealisation of /dˤ/ spreads throughout the word (cf. Ridouane 2003). The domain on which pharyngealisation operates has been identified as minimally the syllable and maximally the phonological word (Elmedlaoui 1995; Dell & Elmedlaoui 2002).

Tashlhiyt has two approximants, /j/ and /w/, which contrast with the corresponding high vowels /i, u/. Tashlhiyt has a rather simple vowel system with

3 Tashlhiyt, a Berber language

three lexical vowels /i, a, u/. The vowel quality has been reported to be highly dependent on the consonantal environment, especially regarding the presence or absence of adjacent pharyngealised consonants. As opposed to the consonantal system, vowels do not contrast with regard to length, although surface long vowels may occur in case of adjacent identical vowels. Any discussion of the Tashlhiyt vowel system should additionally refer to the existence of a central vowel that is not one of the cardinal vowels. The occurrence and distribution of this central vowel, often referred to as 'schwa', has sparked an as of yet unresolved debate as to whether this element needs to be considered as a phonological entity or a phonetic artefact (e.g. Coleman 1996; 1999; 2001; Dell & Elmedlaoui 2002; Ridouane 2008, see Chapter 6 for a detailed discussion). This element is particularly relevant for the discussion of phonotactics and syllable structure, which we will turn to now.

3.4.2.2 Phonotactics and syllable structure

Tashlhiyt allows for whole utterances without any phonological vowels and has many words that consist of consonants only. Typologically rather rare structures such as (1) are often cited in the literature as extreme phonotactic cases.

(1) /tfttʃtsskkχtkkstʃʃkk/
    'You examined the currency which you checked out'

Throughout this book, Tashlhiyt's syllable structure will be described according to Dell and Elmedlaoui's analyses (Dell & Elmedlaoui 1985; 1988; 1996; 2002) which is mainly based on the Imdlawn variety spoken by Elmedlaoui himself and, therefore, may be argued to have a limited generalisability. Even though we follow their analysis here, controversial aspects will be discussed where relevant.

In addition to typologically common syllables containing vocalic nuclei such as V, CV, VC, and CVC, Tashlhiyt also has consonant-only syllables. According to Dell and Elmedlaoui, all consonant types are allowed in syllable nucleus position, even voiceless stops. This is exemplified in (2–5).

(2) Sonorants: /tl̥.km̥t/ 'You arrived'
(3) Fricatives: /tṣ.χft/ 'You fainted'
(4) Voiced stops: /tḅ.dġt/ 'You are wet'
(5) Voiceless stops: /tf.tk̟t/ 'She sprained it'

3.4.3 Morphology

The following brief sketch of morphological patterns in Tashlhiyt is based on Dell and Elmedlaoui's descriptions (Dell & Elmedlaoui 1988; 2002). Tashlhiyt exhibits two major lexical categories: nouns and verbs. There is also a small group of adjectives, largely derived from verbs. Additionally, there are functional elements like tense and aspect markers, negation markers, complementisers, and conjunctions.

In general, verbs agree with their subjects in person, gender (feminine, masculine), and number (singular, plural) through prefixation, suffixation or both. Adjectives agree with the noun they modify in gender and number. Verb stems alternate according to aspect and mood resulting in four different stems per lexical verb (perfective affirmative, perfective negative, aorist, imperative). Stem alternation involves vowel alternation (vowel quality or alternation with null) or gemination.

Nouns are inflected for gender, number, and 'state' (free, bound). The grammatical category referred to as state (état d'annexion) has certain properties akin to case, e.g. it is dependent on the verbal and prepositional context. A noun is inflected for 'bound state' when it is governed by a preposition, when it follows its verb or a cardinal number. In all other positions, it is in the 'free state'. However, not all nouns inflect for state. A distinction must be made between vowel-initial nouns (such as /agru/ 'frog') and consonant-initial nouns (such as /ssuq/ 'market'). Consonant-initial nouns do not inflect for state, while vowel-initial nouns do. Gender and state are expressed through affixation, while number is expressed through either affixation or stem alternation. While affixation is regular, stem alternation is to some extent lexically determined.

3.4.4 Syntax

The basic word order in Berber has been described as VSO (Basset 1952; Sasse 1984). Tashlhiyt is no exception, as can be seen in thetic utterances and most subordinate clauses (cf. 6–8 taken from Dell & Elmedlaoui 2002: 17). All verbal arguments can be pronominalised. Referential pronouns are cliticised onto the verb (cf. 7):

(6) t-ga   t-fruχ-t   i-fullus-n   ʁ=t-gmmi
    3F.SG-put F-child.BS-F.SG up-chicken-M.PL   in=F-house
    'The girl put the chickens into the house.'

(7) t-ga=tn=gi-s
3F.SG-put=3M.PL=in-3F.SG
'She put them (m) into it (f).'

The verb can carry cliticised pronouns for subject, indirect and direct object, multiple adverbs, and multiple prepositional phrases (in that order). If there is a clitic preponed to the verb, the pronouns cliticise to the preverb. In natural discourse, some verbal arguments are often contextually given and therefore pronominalised, in other contexts they are new information and expressed as full noun phrases. Most commonly, the subject is only expressed via a pronoun cliticised to the verb and the complements of the verb are expressed as full noun phrases (cf. 8).

(8) t-ga   i-fullus-n   ʁ=t-gmmi
3F.SG-put up-chicken-M.PL in=F-house
'She put the chickens into the house.'

In the case of subject and direct object being expressed as proper noun phrases, SVO is also very common. When the subject precedes the verb, it is inflected for free state (cf. 9).

(9) t-afruχ-t   t-ga   i-fullus-n   ʁ=t-gm
F-child-F.SG 3F.SG-put up-chicken-M.PL in=F-house
'The girl put the chickens into the house.'

Both SVO and VSO are commonly used in cases of broad focus, i.e. as an answer to a question like /ma iʒran/ 'what happened (or happens)?'. SVO constructions, however, are considered as carrying more emphasis (Sadiqi 1997; Mettouchi & Fleisch 2010). This is particularly prominent in constructions having free standing pronouns (co-referential with the pronominal subject marker on the verb). These constructions appear to express emphasis if they are in clause-initial position (cf. Mettouchi & Fleisch 2010: 221). Other arguments of the verb can be left dislocated, too. Constructions with the subject or complements in clause-initial position are referred to as 'left-dislocations'. In addition to left-dislocations, there are 'cleft' constructions. In cleft constructions, the subject or a complement of the verb occurs in clause-initial position preceding the verb. It is morphologically marked by a cleft marker (/ad/ cf. 10).

(10) ddisk ad t-sʁa   t-fruχ-t
record ad 3F.SG-bought F-child.BS-F.SG
'It is a record that the girl bought.'

3.4 Tashlhiyt

Left-dislocated and clefted constituents are described as carrying pragmatic emphasis and have been reported to be prosodically separated from the rest of the utterance. Mettouchi & Fleisch (2010) note that in cleft constructions, the clefted constituent is separated from the verb by a "prosodic rupture" (ibid.: 224). On a similar note, Dell and Elmedlaoui speak of an "intonational break" (Dell & Elmedlaoui 2002: 17) between the subject and the rest of the sentence in SVO constructions (see also ; Sadiqi 1997; Boukhris et al. 2008).

Despite these impressionistic observations, higher prosodic aspects like stress and intonation are not yet systematically explored in Tashlhiyt. However, it is of particular relevance for intonation theory for two reasons: first, Tashlhiyt is renowned for cross-linguistically rare phonotactic flexibility, allowing whole utterances to consist of voiceless obstruents. This leads to frequent contexts in which the phonetic opportunity to execute pitch movements is drastically limited. The question arises as to how the language resolves this tune-text-association conflict. Second, impressionistic observations of different scholars throughout the last century have indicated that Tashlhiyt lacks word stress. The absence of lexically determined metrical structure raises the question as to how intonational tones are associated with segments. The question of whether Tashlhiyt exhibits word prosodic metrical structure, will be discussed in the following chapter.

4 Word stress in Tashlhiyt

4.1 Word stress: a working definition

While there are many claims that 'word stress' (or 'lexical stress') is a universal feature of human languages (e.g. Goedemans & Hulst 2009), the universality of this linguistic phenomenon very much depends on how it is defined. Following the main assumptions of the Autosegmental-Metrical (AM) model, word stress shall be defined as an abstract strength relationship between syllables at the level of the phonological word, as reflected in Hyman's definition (Hyman 2014):

(1) Word stress refers to the phonological marking of one most prominent syllable of the phonological word.

This definition crucially presupposes the presence of two linguistic units: the syllable and the phonological word, two units that, although very common cross-linguistically, have been claimed not to be universal. Hyman (2011) analysed Gokana, a Gogoni language spoken in Nigeria, as exhibiting no linguistic evidence for the syllable as a relevant linguistic unit. Schiering, Bickel & Hildebrandt (2010) discuss evidence from Vietnamese and Limbu that suggests that the phonological word is not a universal prosodic domain either. However, since both the syllable and the word have been argued to be relevant linguistic units in Tashlhiyt (e.g. Dell & Elmedlaoui 2002; Ridouane 2008), we proceed by assuming that the proposed definition of word stress is applicable.

Proposing abstract strength relationships within the word needs to be empirically justified. Prototypically, word stress systems are described as exhibiting some of the following phonological properties: the word stress position is phonemic; stressed syllables exhibit greater segmental or tonal contrasts and usually undergo lengthening processes, while unstressed syllables exhibit fewer contrasts and usually undergo shortening processes; stressed syllables are phonetically enhanced; stressed syllables co-occur with postlexical tonal events.

In English, stress has been analysed as phonemic (e.g. Halle & Vergnaud 1987; Hayes 1995). In (2), the noun *import* is distinguished from the corresponding verb by the position of the stressed syllable only. In English, stress is also fre-

4 Word stress in Tashlhiyt

quently associated with a process of vowel reduction. Unstressed syllables are often produced with reduced vowels or syllabic consonants in syllable nucleus position. Example (3) demonstrates the alternation of stressed /ɒ/ in *harmonic* and unstressed /ə/ in *harmony*. The reduction of unstressed vowels results in a smaller vowel inventory in unstressed syllables than in stressed syllables.

(2) import, N /ˈɪm.pɔːt/ vs. import, V /ɪm.ˈpɔːt/

(3) harmonic /hɑː.ˈmɒ.nɪk/ vs. harmony /ˈhɑː.mə.n̩i/

In addition to qualitative differences, stressed syllables are often phonetically enhanced. The phonetic correlates of stress are typically investigated via measurements of duration, intensity, and fundamental frequency (cf. Fry 1955; 1958, for a recent overview see Gordon 2014; Gordon & Roettger in press). Most languages exhibit increased duration, greater intensity, higher fundamental frequency, or some combination of these as acoustic markers of stress. However, although stress is often correlated with phonetic enhancement, some languages exhibit ambiguous phonetic cues as to which syllable is the most prominent. For example, stressed syllables in Modern Welsh have been reported to exhibit shorter vowel durations than vowels in unstressed syllables (Williams 1999).

Moreover, cross-linguistic phonetic studies that have investigated word stress in the past have frequently used methodologies that do not allow word-level phonetic prominence to be distinguished from prominence attributable to higher prosodic constituents. For example, many studies rely on acoustic records of words that are read out from lists making it impossible to disentangle word stress from phrasal phenomena. It is thus crucial for an evaluation of word-level stress in any language to tease apart different levels of prosodic structure (for an overview see Roettger & Gordon in press).

Related to the last point, stressed syllables can interact with postlexical events and can be the designated elements for the association of intonational tones, i.e. pitch accents (or phrase accents, cf. Chapter 2). In English, pitch accents are associated with stressed syllables, i.e. they systematically co-occur with the metrically strong element of prominent words in the phrase. Recall the incredulity example in Chapter 2 (Figure 2.3, *A statistics instructor!?*). Alongside an utterance-final rise, this contour is characterised by a rise and subsequent fall around the metrically strongest syllable in the compound. Although stress is often correlated with the co-occurrence with intonational tones, it does not constitute a sufficient argument in itself for the presence of word stress. Whilst in English, pitch accents go hand in hand with stressed syllables, this is not necessarily the case for other languages (for an overview see Gordon 2014). For example, as discussed in Chapter 2, phrase accents are sometimes associated with specific syllables close to a phrase boundary that are not necessarily lexically stressed (Grice, Arvaniti & Ladd 2000).

In the following, we will discuss possible evidence for the notion of word stress in Tashlhiyt. We will argue that there is no convincing phonological evidence for lexically determined stress in this language. Although a recent study presented phonetic evidence for systematic phonetic prominence asymmetries within the word (Gordon & Nafi 2012), we will argue that these findings are likely the result of post-lexical phenomena (§4.2). Subsequently, we will present a production study that provides evidence for the null, i.e. there are no lexically specified prominence asymmetries within the word (§4.3) leading to the conclusion that there is no word stress in Tashlhiyt. Finally, these results will be discussed in context of comparable languages that have been claimed to lack word stress (§4.4).

4.2 Evidence for word stress in Tashlhiyt

4.2.1 Early observations

Early descriptions of Tashlhiyt have claimed that 'stress' is only found in utterance final position:

> [...] stress patterns referred to here apply only to utterances consisting of a single word. If the utterance contains more than one word, the stress is reduced slightly on all vowels except those in the final word. It can be said, therefore, that primary stress occurs only at the end of an utterance. (Applegate 1958: 9)

It has further been claimed that stress in Tashlhiyt is likely to be a phenomenon of higher prosodic constituents rather than the word:

> Whereas in an English or Italian sentence every polysyllabic word has its own prominence peak, it is highly dubious that the same obtains in Imdlawn Tashlhiyt. If Imdlawn Tashlhiyt has a phenomenon that could be called stress or accent, it is likely that it is a property of units larger than words. (Dell & Elmedlaoui 2002: 14)

These authors acknowledge the presence of certain prominence asymmetries at the phrase level. The authors also make it very clear that there is a distinction to be made between the notion of word stress and the prominence phenomena attributed to higher levels of prosodic organisation.

4 Word stress in Tashlhiyt

In Tashlhiyt, there is no evidence for a phonologically marked prominent syllable in the domain of the phonological word: there are no known phonotactic restrictions on certain syllable positions, i.e. all syllable positions within a word allow the same inventory of phonemic contrasts. To my knowledge, there is no grammatical pattern that takes phonologically prominent syllables into account (in line with observations made by Kossman, p.c. February 2015). Generally, there are few, if any, minimal pairs solely distinguished by phonetic prominence, and speakers report that they confuse these (Ridouane, p.c. October 2013). Stumme (1899) notes that word 'accent' usually falls on the word stem but that it can be shifted by certain word formation processes. Similarly, Sadiqi (1997) notes that stress is not distinctive, however, she proposes that word stress falls on the last vowel of the stem if there is no suffix following. These observations, however, are not supported by experimental evidence.

Moreover, speakers are rather insensitive to phonetic prominence asymmetries within the word. In line with my own experiences, Gordon & Nafi (2012: 708) state explicitly that speakers are not able to consistently identify a syllable as being stressed, neither through direct questioning nor through rhythmic tasks in which speakers had to tap their finger when producing a stressed syllable.

4.2.2 Gordon and Nafi (2012)

Despite the lack of clear phonological evidence and the absence of any indication of native speakers' awareness of stress, Gordon & Nafi (2012) have recently argued that Tashlhiyt does indeed have word-level prominence, namely on the final syllable of the word. They investigated three acoustic correlates of prominence: duration, intensity, and mean fundamental frequency. They recorded six participants that read out di- and trisyllabic target words in two different contexts: (i) in isolation, resulting in the target word forming its own intonation phrase, and (ii) followed by an adverb, resulting in the target word being in phrase-medial position. Target words were selected to cover a wide range of phonotactic patterns with syllables having vowels (e.g. /ba.lak/ 'Get out of the way'), sonorant consonants (e.g. /t.zm̩.zm̩/ 'She squeezed') or obstruents (e.g. /tf.tk̩t/ 'She sprained it') in syllable nucleus position.

The authors found that phrase-final nuclei consistently had higher f0 values than other syllables. However, they interpreted this as a reflex of an intonational tone associated with a lexically strong final syllable in the target word. Irrespective of f0, they found that the syllable nuclei of word-final syllables, especially in phrase-final position, exhibited greater duration and intensity than the nuclei in penultimate syllables. This asymmetry between penult and final syllable has been reported to be robust for vowels (analysis based on two word pairs, n=2) and sonorants (based on n=5). The results were less convincing for obstruents (based on n=6), with no duration differences for voiced obstruents (n=2), and no intensity differences for voiceless obstruents (n=4). Since Gordon and Nafi's study is the only study available that has looked at potential word-level prominence instrumentally, it is necessary to critically evaluate their findings. There are two major methodological concerns:

First, any prominence asymmetries found in their study might ultimately be triggered postlexically, a caveat they acknowledge in their paper. Durational asymmetries in final syllables might be due to postlexical strengthening phenomena such as final lengthening (e.g. Beckman & Edwards 1990; Edwards, Beckman & Fletcher 1991; Gussenhoven & Rietveld 1992; Cho 2005), where lengthening at higher domains (intonation phrase final) is greater than at lower domains (e.g. word final). Although there is no direct instrumental evidence for final lengthening in Tashlhiyt, such asymmetries may explain the results on phrase-final syllables by Gordon & Nafi (2012).

Orthogonal to the possibility of phrase-final lengthening, both longer durations and higher intensity in the final syllable may be postlexically triggered by tonal events. As Gordon and Nafi acknowledge, the final syllable appears to bear a tonal event, which the authors analyse as a "pitch accent". (We will come back to the classification of these tonal events in Chapter 7). The point to be made here is that a postlexically relevant tonal event is located at the right edge of the utterance. This tonal event may be accompanied by phonetic enhancement, in line with numerous studies on pitch accents and phrase accents in other languages (e.g. Harrington, Fletcher & Beckman 2000; Cole et al. 2007; Katsika et al. 2014). This phonetic enhancement of syllables co-occurring with tonal events in Tashlhiyt has been impressionistically described in Grice, Ridouane & Roettger (2015). This applies to syllables at the right edge of the utterance, but also to the final syllable of phrase-medial words (Roettger & Grice 2015). In Gordon and Nafi's study, speakers produced different target words in a constant carrier phrase, thus the target words were implicitly contrasted. Previous findings on Tashlhiyt by Grice et al. (2011) have demonstrated that implicitly contrasted target words in phrase-medial position are realised with a pitch peak on the target word. This tonal event appears to prefer the right edge of the word, which could have been the source of the observed asymmetries in Gordon & Nafi (2012).

Second, there are statistical concerns with Gordon and Nafi's study. The authors analyse their data with analyses of variance (ANOVA) using speakers as the population that is inferred over, i.e. they average over different words. However, any claim that a language behaves in a certain way should be a robust generalisation not only over speakers but also over the lexicon, i.e. over the words of the language. Ignoring one of these levels and generalising, for example, only over speakers of a language, might result in a false positive. This statistical shortcoming has been described as the "language-as-fixed-effect fallacy" (Clark 1973; see Winter 2011, for a discussion related to phonetic research and Roettger & Gordon in press for a discussion related to acoustic studies on word stress). Crucially, when claiming that a language has a fixed word stress position, any statistical generalisation must apply to the population of words. As was criticised by Clark more than forty years ago, statistical inference is often only made over speakers/listeners. Gordon and Nafi used a very limited set of target words. This makes generalising over the Tashlhiyt lexicon conceptually (and mathematically) not feasible.

4.3 Production study: Word stress in Tashlhiyt revisited

This section presents data designed to address the above-mentioned methodological concerns and offers an answer to the question as to whether Tashlhiyt exhibits phonetic prominence asymmetries at the word level or not. To this end, a corpus was designed in which potential word-level prominence is not confounded with any postlexical events. Moreover, statistical methods were used that allow generalisation over both speakers and words of the language.[1]

If we ignore the absence of phonological arguments in favour of word stress and assume that Tashlhiyt indeed has fixed word stress on the final syllable, it is hypothesised that there is a consistent acoustic prominence asymmetry between penultimate and final syllables. Alternatively, word stress may not be fixed in Tashlhiyt, i.e. different words may have different word stress positions.

4.3.1 Method

To test these hypotheses, short mock dialogues produced by ten speakers were analysed. Disyllabic target words appeared in three different sentences in phrase-medial position (cf. 4–6, target words highlighted in bold).

(4) is inna **baba ʁ**akudan?
     'Did he say 'father' then?'

---

[1] Parts of the presented experiment have been published in Roettger, Bruggeman & Grice (2015).

4.3 Production study: Word stress in Tashlhiyt revisited

(5) uhu, inna **dari** ʁakudan.
   'No, he said 'in my house' then.'

(6) inna target **dari** ʁakudan?
   'He said 'in my house' then?'

These sentences were designed to elicit specific intonation patterns: the first context was a yes-no question 4, followed by a negation (/uhu/), and a contrastive statement 5 with the target word in corrective focus. The statement in 5 was followed by a confirmation-seeking echo question 6. As will be further elaborated on in subsequent chapters, the target word in 5 is contrastively focused and is expected to co-occur with a rise in pitch followed by a fall. Echo questions are also expected to co-occur with a rise-fall in pitch but at the right edge of the utterance-final word. Crucially, in 6, the target word is given information and not marked by any apparent tonal movement (cf. Figure 4.1).[2] This enables us to disentangle word-level prominence from postlexically induced prominence.

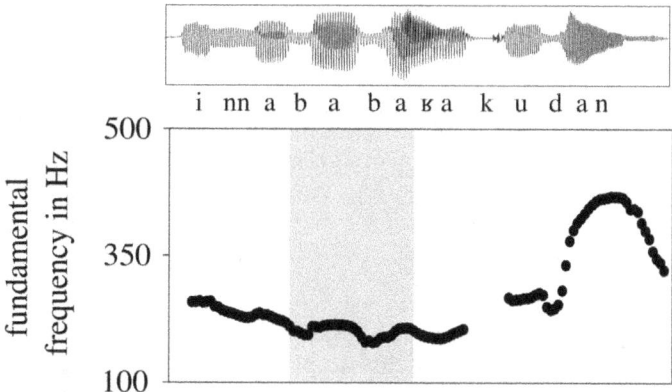

Figure 4.1: Representative waveform and f0 contour for the echo question /inna baba ʁakudan/ 'He said 'father' then?' The target word is highlighted in grey. Note that there is no apparent tonal event on the target word.

4.3.1.1 Participants and procedure

Ten native speakers of Tashlhiyt (6 male, 4 female, mean age = 25, age range: 21-34) were recorded in Agadir in November 2014. One male speaker had to

---

[2] The corresponding sound file of this contour and all following contours that are illustrated in figures throughout the rest of this book can be found at https://doi.org/10.5281/zenodo.815840.

4 Word stress in Tashlhiyt

be excluded from the acoustic analysis due to malfunction of the recording device. All speakers live in Agadir, are fluent in Moroccan Arabic, and have a basic command of French (cf. Appendix A2.1 for participant information). Participants were asked to reenact orthographically presented mock dialogues (in Latin script) presented in cartoon form. Speakers were instructed to produce the dialogues as presented in 4 to 6. Each target word was produced twice in each sentence modality by each speaker.

4.3.1.2 Speech material

A corpus of disyllabic target words was created. All target words were comprised of syllables with a vocalic element in syllable nucleus position. There were some words (n=6) containing two identical syllables (e.g. /baba/ 'father'), such that the target syllable occurs in both penultimate and final position. The other word pairs (n=5) contained non-identical syllables, with the target syllable occurring once in penultimate and once in final position (e.g. compare the target syllable /di/ in /sidi/ 'sir' and /dima/ 'always'). This resulted in 11 comparable target syllables. There were words containing light and heavy syllables, but only syllables with the same syllable weight were compared, i.e. light with light and heavy with heavy (as opposed to Gordon & Nafi 2012). These target words were presented alongside 14 obstruent-only filler words that are not further analysed here. All target words are displayed in Table 4.1.

4.3.1.3 Analysis

Only target words in echo questions were considered in the following analysis. All these target words were predicted to be realised with no pitch peak on the target word, allowing us to analyse prominence asymmetries at the word level, with no influence of the phrase level. This prediction was confirmed by the author via auditory and visual inspection of the f0 contour. Target words in echo questions were segmented and annotated with Praat 5.4 (Boersma & Weenink 2015). All acoustic material was manually annotated employing the following labelling criteria: segment boundaries in the target words were identified in the acoustic waveform by means of an oscillogram and a wide-band spectrogram. All segmental boundaries of vowels and consonants were labelled at abrupt changes in the spectra indicating closure formation or release: this was the case for nasals, laterals (especially in the spectra for the intensity of higher formants), and obstruents (at random noise patterns in the higher frequency regions). To compare the data to Gordon and Nafi's study as closely as possible, duration, average intensity, and

4.3 Production study: Word stress in Tashlhiyt revisited

Table 4.1: Target words (in IPA) and translations. Note: the target word /ʁuni/ is borrowed from Moroccan Arabic (Tashlhiyt: /ʁnni/). The inclusion of this target word in the design was due to a misunderstanding with our consultant. The presented statistical analyses hold even after exclusion of this item.

Target word (1)	Target word (2)	Target syllable
tama 'next to'	ʃita 'brush'	ta
dari 'in my house'	juda 'enough'	da
dima 'always'	sidi 'sir'	di
tili 'ewe'	hati 'here is'	ti
nizi 'of the fly'	ʁuni 'sing'	ni
baba 'father'		ba
bibi 'turkey'		bi
kawkaw 'peanuts'		kaw
kifkif 'it is the same'		kif
tamtam 'drum'		tam
janjan 'one-one'		jan

average fundamental frequency for each target syllable nucleus were extracted. All data were analysed using R (R Core Team 2015) and the "lme4" package (Bates et al. 2015). The continuous variables nucleus duration (ms), mean nucleus intensity (dB), and mean fundamental frequency of the nucleus (Hz) were analysed with linear mixed effects models.

Again, to evaluate our data against Gordon and Nafi's analyses, a subject-based (averaging over all syllables) and a syllable-based analysis (averaging over all speakers) were performed. The predictor was syllable position (penult, henceforth "PU" vs. final syllable, henceforth "F"). Contrasts were deviation coded. In line with Gordon and Nafi's analyses varying intercept-only models were used, i.e. we account for different speakers and different syllables having general higher or lower values for the respective parameter. In other words, this analysis tries to replicate Gordon and Nafi's analysis in the most anti-conservative way. If no effect is found, we can be certain that the analysed acoustic parameters do not vary as a function of syllable position. However, if an effect is found, the results will be subject to further scrutiny. We will employ more conservative analyses by including varying-slopes for subjects and syllables as crossed random effects. These types of models exhibit a lower type I error rate than models with only varying-intercepts (Schielzeth & Forstmeier 2009; Barr et al. 2013). This

4 Word stress in Tashlhiyt

model architecture allows for a generalisation over the speaker population and the word population at the same time.

4.3.2 Results

4.3.2.1 Duration

Looking at the durational patterns displayed in figures 4.2 and 4.3, it becomes apparent that target words exhibit no consistent durational asymmetry. Duration is given as the difference between the duration of the target syllable nucleus in penultimate position and final position. In fact, five of eleven target vowels have negative values indicating that the final syllable is longer, and the other six target vowels have positive values indicating that the penult is longer. Although the final vowel is on average 4 ms longer than the penultimate vowel, this pattern is far from being consistent across the word or speaker sample. These observations are reflected in the absence of any significant influence of syllable position on vowel duration in both the subject-based and the syllable-based analysis ($\beta \leq 0.019$, $SE \geq 0.0035$, $\chi^2(1) \leq 1.68$, $p \geq 0.2$).

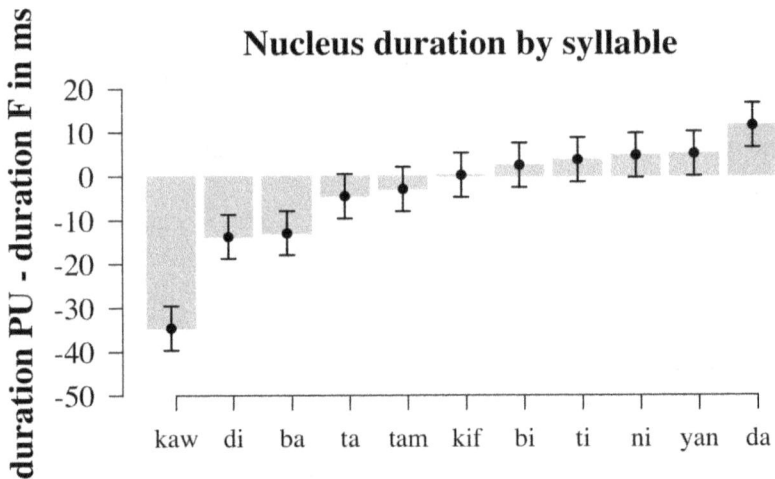

Figure 4.2: Difference scores of vowel duration of penult (PU) minus final syllable (F). Means are arranged according to magnitude for all target syllables. Negative values indicate greater duration for the F; positive values indicate greater duration for the PU. Error bars indicate standard errors taken from the model described above.

4.3 Production study: Word stress in Tashlhiyt revisited

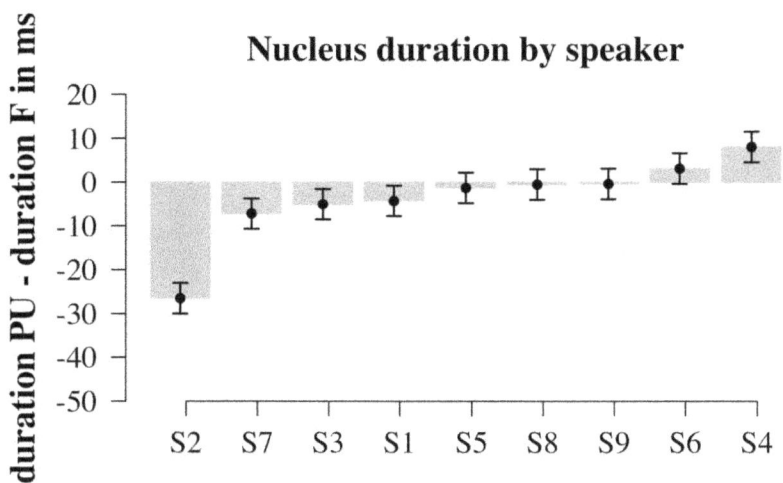

Figure 4.3: Difference scores of vowel duration of penult (PU) minus final syllable (F). Means are arranged according to magnitude for all speakers. Negative values indicate greater duration for the F; positive values indicate greater duration for the PU. Error bars indicate standard errors taken from the model described above.

4.3.2.2 Intensity

Looking at the intensity patterns displayed in Figures 4.4 and 4.5, a slightly different picture emerges. Again, intensity is given as the difference between the mean intensity of the target syllable nucleus in penultimate position and final position. Eight of eleven target syllables and six of nine speakers have positive values indicating higher intensity in the penultimate vowel. This descriptive trend goes in the opposite direction of the trend that Gordon and Nafi reported in their study. While these trends do not hold for the subject-based model inferentially (β=0.36, SE=0.31, $\chi^2(1)$=1.43, p=0.23), there is in fact a significant effect for the syllable-based analysis (β=0.5, SE=0.18, $\chi^2(1)$=6.03, p=0.014).

Despite exhibiting a statistically significant effect, there are three arguments against the assumption that these differences are linguistically relevant. First, the estimation of the effect size is 0.36 dB and 0.5 dB, for the subject-based and syllable-based models, respectively. These values clearly lie below the commonly assumed just noticeable difference of 1 dB for intensity (cf. Lehiste 1970: 119). This average difference, thus, is unlikely to be used by listeners as a perceptual cue to stress.

4 Word stress in Tashlhiyt

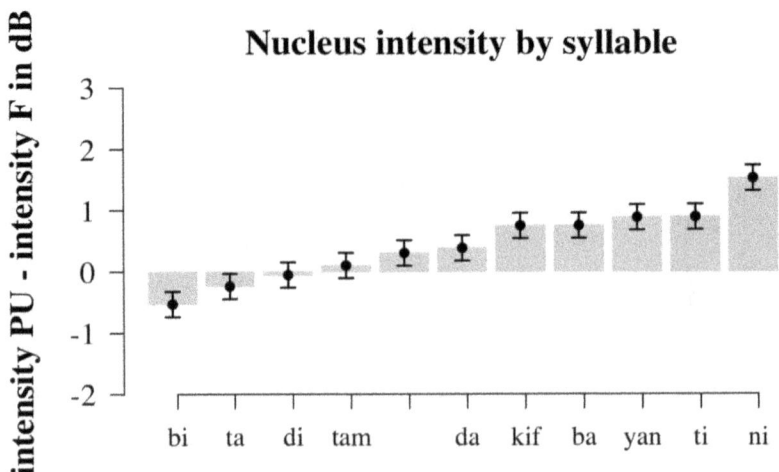

Figure 4.4: Difference scores of vowel intensity of penult (PU) minus final syllable (F). Means are arranged according to magnitude for all target syllables. Negative values indicate greater intensity for the F; positive values indicate greater intensity for the PU. Error bars indicate standard errors taken from the model described above.

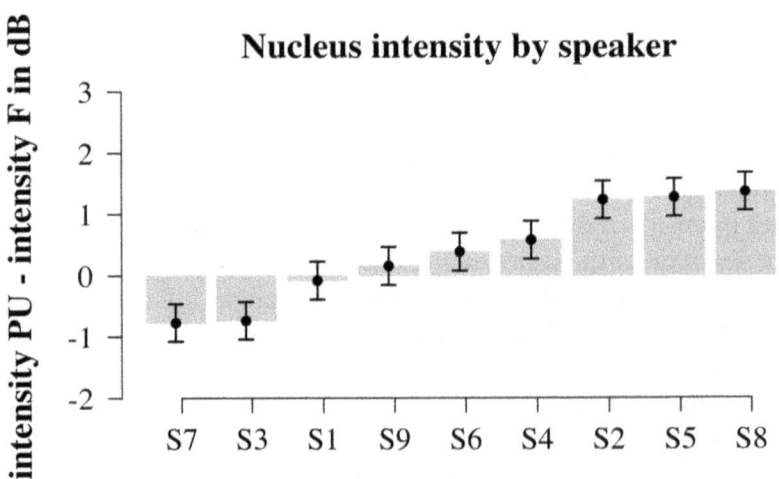

Figure 4.5: Difference scores of vowel intensity of penult (PU) minus final syllable (F). Means are arranged according to magnitude for all speakers. Negative values indicate greater intensity for the F; positive values indicate greater intensity for the PU. Error bars indicate standard errors taken from the model described above.

4.3 Production study: Word stress in Tashlhiyt revisited

Second, the consistent trend for louder syllables in the penult may be an artefact of a general declination of intensity throughout the utterance. This general trend has been observed for other languages (Ladefoged 1972; Lieberman & Blumstein 1988; Vayra & Fowler 1992) and is apparent in other data sets of Tashlhiyt (impressionistic observation by the author). This intensity declination, however, might not be as robust across the speaker population, explaining the lack of a significant effect in the subject-based analysis.

To explore whether the effect of intensity could be due to intensity declination, utterances were divided into ten equally long intervals. For each interval, the intensity mean was extracted. Intensity values were then submitted to statistical analysis. Intensity was modeled as a function of time steps (1-10). Both subject-based (averaging over target words) and item-based (averaging over subjects) analyses were performed. Both the subject-based (β=-0.68, SE=0.11, $\chi^2(1)$=31.2, p<0.00001), and the item-based analysis (β=-0.68, SE=0.07, $\chi^2(1)$=79.1, p<0.00001) showed a significant negative linear trend, i.e. intensity decreases throughout the utterance by an estimated 0.7 dB from one step (1/10 of the utterance) to the next.

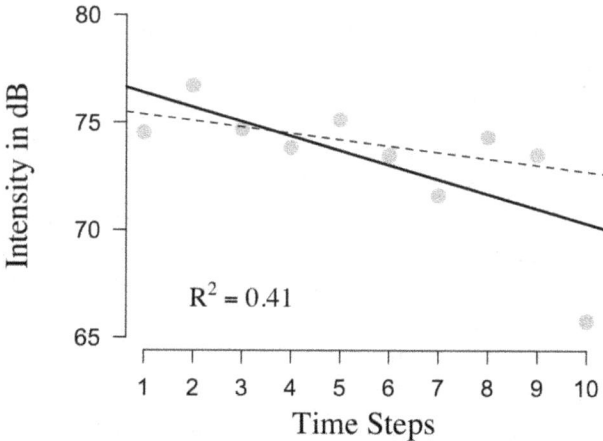

Figure 4.6: Aggregated mean intensity values as a function of time and the corresponding regression line (solid line). The R^2 value corresponds to the adjusted explained variance of the solid line. The dashed line indicates the negative trend excluding the final intensity value.

Figure 4.6 illustrates the negative linear trend throughout the utterance (averaging across both speakers and words). Note that this trend is not an artefact of a sudden drop in intensity at the end of the utterance (although it is certainly in-

4 Word stress in Tashlhiyt

fluenced by it). Even though the estimated negative trend is clearly smaller after excluding time step 10 (β=0.35, corresponding to the dashed line in Figure 4.6), it is still significantly negative indicating a decreasing trend in intensity. The effect size from one time step to the next (0.35 dB) numerically corresponds to the estimated difference between the penult and the final syllable in the analysis performed above (0.36 dB for subjects and 0.5 dB for syllables). Thus, this global downdrift likely accounts for the intensity asymmetries between penult and final syllables. We conclude that the asymmetry found above is unlikely to be the result of lexically specified prominence asymmetries. The effect size is too small to be considered a perceptually relevant cue and better corresponds to a global declination trend across the entire utterance.

Third, applying a more conservative statistical analysis to the intensity patterns across syllable positions including crossed by-subject and by-syllable random slopes, the significant effect vanishes. There remains no statistically generalisable effect of intensity predicted by syllable position (β=0.36, SE=0.27, $\chi^2(1)$=1.9, p=0.17).

4.3.2.3 Fundamental frequency (f0)

Finally, we consider mean fundamental frequency of the vowels in the target syllable. In Figures 4.7 and 4.8, fundamental frequency is given as the difference between the mean fundamental frequency of the target syllable nucleus in penultimate position and final position. The plot clearly indicates a consistent asymmetry across syllables and speakers. The penultimate syllable has on average 9 Hz higher mean f0 values than the final syllable. This asymmetry is significant for both the subject-based and syllable-based analyses (β≤9.55, SE≥1.97, $\chi^2(1)$≤4.6, p≤0.03). Applying a more conservative statistical analysis including crossed by-subject and by-syllable random slopes, the significance of the effect remains robust (β=11.6, SE=3.9, $\chi^2(1)$=6.8, p=0.009).

This consistent but subtle f0 difference may be an artefact of two confounding factors. First, there were strong microprosodic influences of the voiced uvular fricative of /ʁakudan/ following the final target syllable. This leads to a drop in f0 as is illustrated in Figure 4.1. Second, there was a general declination trend of f0 from the beginning of the utterance towards the low pitch target preceding the sharp rise at the end of the phrase. Even though the stimuli were chosen so as not to exhibit phrasal effects, utterance-wide declination trends can be observed that result in consistent, but numerically subtle differences in f0.

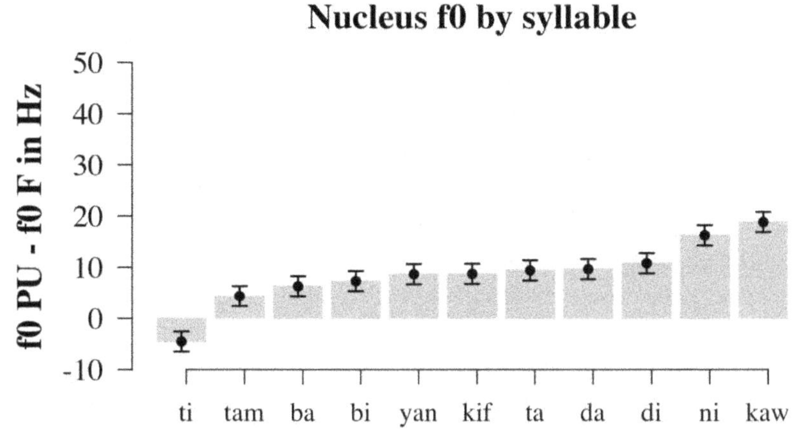

Nucleus f0 by syllable

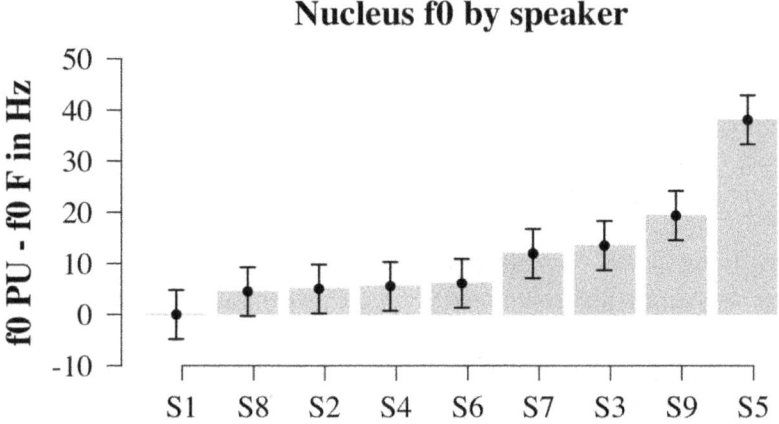

Figure 4.7: Difference scores of fundamental frequency (f0) of penult (PU) minus final syllable (F). Means are arranged according to magnitude for all target syllables. Negative values indicate greater f0 for the F; positive values indicate greater f0 for the PU. Error bars indicate standard errors taken from the model described above.

Nucleus f0 by speaker

Figure 4.8: Difference scores of fundamental frequency (f0) of penult (PU) minus final syllable (F). Means are arranged according to magnitude for all speakers. Negative values indicate greater f0 for the F; positive values indicate greater f0 for the PU. Error bars indicate standard errors taken from the model described above.

4 Word stress in Tashlhiyt

4.3.2.4 Discussion

In sum, the null hypothesis for the assumption of fixed word stress cannot easily be rejected based on descriptive or inferential grounds. There are no acoustic prominence asymmetries between syllables of any given target word in a consistent manner across items or speakers. If anything, descriptive trends and a significant syllable-based analysis point to louder vowels in the penult (as opposed to louder vowels in the final syllable as found in Gordon & Nafi 2012). This intensity effect, however, is below the just noticeable difference threshold, the magnitude of the effect corresponds to a general declination of intensity throughout the utterance, and more conservative statistical analyses do not support the generalisability of this effect. Pitch shows a consistent effect of lower pitch values on the final syllable. This effect is of low magnitude and probably an artefact of independent segmental perturbations. Taken together, the evidence presented here casts reasonable doubt on the claim that Tashlhiyt exhibits word stress as reflected in prominence asymmetries.

While Tashlhiyt often gives the impression that one syllable is more prominent than neighbouring syllables within the word, this impression quickly fades after hearing other instances of the same word produced by the same speaker. The observed patterns in Tashlhiyt resonate well with the following quote on the Salish language Nuxalk, often referred to as Bella Coola.

> [In Bella Coola there are] ... no phonemically significant phenomena of stress or pitch associated with syllables or words... When two or more syllabics occur in a word or a sentence, one can clearly hear different degrees of articulatory force. But these relative stresses in a sequence of acoustic syllables do not remain constant in repetitions of the utterance (Newman 1947: 132, cited after Hyman 2014: 57)

Taken together, these findings lead to a rejection of the very specific claim that Tashlhiyt exhibits acoustic prominence asymmetries at the word level (Gordon & Nafi 2012). The assumption of word stress in Tashlhiyt was only based on Gordon and Nafi's acoustic results. Given that this chapter showed that their results do not replicate and that there are no other phonological arguments for word stress, the general claim that Tashlhiyt exhibits word stress needs to be rejected until further evidence is found to the contrary.

4.4 Summary

Given the present findings, there is no evidence for prominence asymmetries in words containing vowels. Neither duration nor intensity differ across syllable positions. Pitch is generally slightly lower on the final syllable, but this has been argued to be due to microprosody and global declination. Placing these results in a wider context, a number of studies have argued against the presence of word stress in other languages. Three studies that are of particular interest are sketched here: Maskikit-Essed & Gussenhoven (2016) argue that Ambonese Malay lacks word stress (see also Goedemans & Zanten 2007, for evidence on Indonesian). They looked at pitch peak alignment in phrase-final words and were unable to identify a stable landmark that serves as an anchor for the high tone. Moreover, they show that phonetic prominence asymmetries can be attributed to aspects of higher order prosodic organisation, i.e. durational asymmetries are attributed to domain-final lengthening. The latter finding emphasises the methodological relevance of disentangling postlexical aspects of speech from lexical ones (Gordon 2014; Roettger & Gordon in press).

Another language reportedly lacking word stress is Tamil. Tamil has been described as having no distinctive word-level prominence, however, the literature anecdotally reports on the special status of the word-initial syllable. Keane (2006) carried out an acoustic study to address this issue. Her data, based on five speakers, showed no consistent acoustic asymmetry across syllable positions, neither in duration nor in intensity. Interestingly, Keane presents the results for different words descriptively, and, similar to Tashlhiyt, there are large differences across different syllables with some syllables being longer in word-initial position and others being longer in word-medial position. However, initial syllables are consistently produced with a rising tone, which may be interpreted as evidence for fixed word stress. However, as Keane rightly acknowledges, this rising tone may instead be a postlexical tone that is aligned to the left edge of a prosodic constituent smaller than the intonation phrase.

Finally, Brunelle (2017) discusses word stress in Southern Vietnamese. The literature has made contradicting claims about whether Vietnamese can be described as having word stress or not and if so where in the word it is. Brunelle provides acoustic evidence suggesting that there is little evidence for word stress in Southern Vietnamese and that earlier reports of final stress are best interpreted as an artefact of higher prosodic structure, i.e. phrase-final lengthening.

These three case studies highlight the potential confounding of word stress and postlexical structure. As discussed at the beginning of this chapter, many studies

4 Word stress in Tashlhiyt

reporting on word prosodic systems have used a methodology that did not allow for the disentangling of word-level and phrase-level phenomena. Roettger & Gordon (in press) confirm this impressionistic observation based on a corpus of more than 100 studies investigating over 70 languages. Gordon (2014) points to this threat in prosodic research:

> [...] a large portion, if not the majority, of the prosodic typology that is currently understood to refer to stress may actually reflect phrasal prominence associated with tonal events occurring at or near phrasal edges. (Gordon 2014: 111)

The present chapter argued for the absence of acoustic reflexes of phonological word stress in Tashlhiyt by carefully controlling for such confounds. At present, there is no convincing phonetic or phonological evidence for the presence of word stress in Tashlhiyt.

In the following chapters, higher prosodic aspects of the language will be investigated. Findings will show that the placement of intonational events flagging questions and marking contrastive constituents are prone to a vast amount of variation, lending additional support to the conclusion that there is no word stress in Tashlhiyt.

5 The intonation of questions and contrastive focus in Tashlhiyt

5.1 Introduction

Cross-linguistically, the flagging of questions and the marking of contrastive elements represent communicative functions that are prototypically expressed by means of morphosyntactic devices such as word order or morphological marking. In addition to morphosyntax, these functions can be expressed via prosodic structure and/or intonation. The present chapter will investigate the intonational marking of questions and contrastive statements in Tashlhiyt. We will show that under certain circumstances, both functions are expressed by similar phonetic parameters: questions and contrastive statements are characterised by a rise-fall in pitch. However, even though the pitch movements are very similar in some contexts, there are clear distributional properties and acoustic correlates that systematically distinguish the tonal events in questions from the ones in contrastive statements.

The chapter is structured as follows. After a brief introduction to linguistic aspects of flagging questions and marking contrastive elements (§5.2), common cross-linguistic strategies employed to express these functions prosodically and intonationally will be discussed (§5.3). Morphosyntactic constructions and the intonational expression of flagging questions and marking contrastive elements in Tashlhiyt are then described based on qualitative observations (§5.4). Subsequently, a production study will be presented that provides evidence for both global pitch parameters and local tonal events being used to distinguish questions from corresponding contrastive statements. Moreover, evidence will be presented that the location of tonal events is determined by several interacting factors (§5.5). A perception study will be presented that demonstrates the perceptual relevance of the identified cues (§5.6).

5.2 Theoretical background: questions and focus

5.2.1 Questions: a working definition

The distinction between questions and statements is usually defined by a bundle of properties associated with different linguistic levels of description. As a result, the term 'question' is used ambiguously in the literature. First, question can refer to a syntactically defined interrogative structure, irrespective of its pragmatic function. An example is the English yes-no question which is morphosyntactically distinguished from a corresponding statement by auxiliary fronting (cf. 1 and 2 below). Second, the term question can also refer to an utterance that functions as a request for information, regardless of its morphosyntactic form. An example is the declarative question in English, which exhibits a declarative syntactic structure (e.g. (3b) below). Following Bartels (1999) (after Lyons 1977, and Jacobs 1991), the term 'question' shall be used here as a purely functional term referring to utterances that "convey perceived relative lack of information […] regarding a relevant aspect of propositional content" (Bartels 1999: 9). In turn, statements are defined as utterances that lack such speaker uncertainty. The following study is limited to two question types: yes-no questions and declarative questions.

One of the most common and most often discussed question types is the 'yes-no question' (henceforth: y/n question, also known as 'polar question'). It is considered the most basic question type and a near universal across languages (Sadock & Zwicky 1985). Compared to a corresponding statement (cf. 1), y/n questions in English can be marked by auxiliary fronting (cf. 1 and 2).

(1)   Helen ate the chocolate.
(2)   Did Helen eat the chocolate?
(3)   a.   I ate the chocolate.
       b.   You ate the chocolate?

Another closely related type of question is the declarative question. This question type is morphosyntactically identical to corresponding statements and is often reported to be distinguished from statements by intonation only (Haeseryn et al. 1997). Henceforth the term declarative question will be used to refer to requests for information with declarative syntactic structure. This includes both declarative questions and echo questions. The latter are repetitions of either an entire preceding utterance or parts of it, and express either surprise, disbelief or lack of comprehension, indicating that the proposition the question refers to

5.2 Theoretical background: questions and focus

is unexpected or inappropriate. Echo questions often ask for confirmation or clarification, and can be described as having a bias towards a negative response (cf. 3).[1]

5.2.2 Focus: a working definition

A pragmatic notion which is orthogonal to the distinction between questions and statements and which is cross-linguistically frequently expressed by intonation is 'focus'. Krifka (2008) defines focus as the marking of elements to indicate that alternatives to these elements are relevant for the interpretation of the utterance. Consider examples (4) and (5).

(4)   Helen ate [the milk chocolate].

(5)   [Helen] ate the milk chocolate.

The statements are morphosyntactically identical and denote the same proposition but differ with regard to which argument is in focus. In (4) the milk chocolate is in focus, implying that there are alternatives to the milk chocolate that are relevant for the interpretation of the utterance. The part of the utterance that is not in focus is often referred to as 'background' (Lambrecht 1996). In (5) Helen is in focus, implying that there are alternatives to Helen that are relevant for the interpretation of the utterance. Here, the milk chocolate is in the background.

In (4) a friend and I may have been talking about Helen's eating habits and her recent diet, which is mainly based on vegetables and fruits. Yesterday, Helen cheated and, instead of eating a banana, she ate the milk chocolate that I had bought for myself. The milk chocolate and the explicitly or implicitly mentioned alternatives are relevant for interpreting this particular statement here. I contrast the milk chocolate with fruits, for example, by means of focusing the milk chocolate. Alternatively, we may have been talking about the milk chocolate bars in my cupboard. One package disappeared and I ask my friends who took it. The answer in (5) is a compatible response here, since it signals that Helen did it and not someone else. Focus can, moreover, differ with respect to the size or scope of the focus domain. Consider example (5) again, here repeated as (6). It is a compatible answer to all of the following questions in (7):

(6)   Helen ate the milk chocolate.

---

[1] Another common question type is the wh-question, which will be briefly discussed in Chapter 7 (see Bruggeman, Roettger & Grice 2017, for a first exploration of wh-questions in Tashlhiyt).

5 The intonation of questions and contrastive focus in Tashlhiyt

(7) a. What happened? [Helen ate the milk chocolate].
 b. What did Helen do? Helen [ate the milk chocolate].
 c. What did Helen eat? Helen ate [the milk chocolate].
 d. Did Helen eat the banana? Helen ate [the milk chocolate].
 e. Did Helen eat the white chocolate? Helen ate the [milk] chocolate.

Question (a) elicits whole-sentence focus (also referred to as 'broad focus') without pragmatically singling out a specific element in the utterance. Questions (b-e) elicit 'narrow focus' either on the verb phrase (b), the entire compound in object position (c and d), or the modifier of this compound (e). The answers differ with respect to the set of alternatives. An answer to (a) and (b) can either be described as lacking a juxtaposition of alternatives, or as being an alternative to another holistic proposition. In (c) the milk chocolate, on the other hand, contrasts with an open set of alternatives (all possible things Helen could have eaten). In an answer to questions (d) or (e), the focused constituent is explicitly contrasted with the alternative in the question (banana / white chocolate). The examples in (d) and (e) are a specific type of narrow focus, which is referred to as 'corrective focus' or 'contrastive focus'. Focus types such as contrastive focus can be marked by morphosyntactic devices such as word order or focus particles. They can also be marked by intonation or prosodic structure only.

5.3 The intonation of questions and focus

Many languages express both questions and contrastive focus by means of intonation. In some cases, the intonational parameters used to mark these functions look very similar, differing only in subtle ways. Thus, comparing these two functions is a promising departure point from which to gain an understanding of the intonation system of Tashlhiyt. The following section will give an overview of possible intonational devices employed to express these functions in other languages.

5.3.1 The intonation of questions

Languages have been frequently reported to distinguish questions from corresponding statements by means of 'global' or 'local pitch scaling' or certain tonal events. Global scaling, also referred to as 'pitch register' (Ladd 2008), involves the lowering or raising of phrase-length contours. If both the lowest and highest points of a contour are raised, there is an increase in 'pitch level'; if the lowest

5.3 The intonation of questions and focus

point is lowered and the highest point is raised, there is an increase in 'pitch span'. Local scaling involves a specific tonal event, such as a rise or a fall, and typically involves a local increase in pitch span also referred to as 'pitch excursion', i.e. there are lower lows and higher highs for the respective tonal event (Ladd 2008).

Cross-linguistically, both local and global pitch scaling have often been reported to be significantly different for questions and statements with questions generally exhibiting higher pitch (among others, American English: Hirst & Di Cristo 1998; Hausa: Inkelas & Leben 1990; Hawaiian: Murphy 2013; Mandarin Chinese: Shen 1990; Moroccan Arabic: Benkirane 1998; and Vietnamese: Brunelle, Phuong Ha & Grice 2012; cf. Haan 2002, for an overview). This difference in pitch scaling may be expressed in terms of different parameters: Finnish has been reported to exhibit higher initial pitch values in questions than in statements (Iivone 1998). Some languages have higher pitch peaks in questions than in corresponding statements, e.g. Swedish and Moroccan Arabic (Hadding-Koch & Studdert-Kennedy 1964; Gårding 1983; Benkirane 1998). In Hausa, the last lexical high tone in the utterance is raised in questions (Inkelas & Leben 1990). Bengali has been reported to have both raised pitch peaks as well as greater pitch excursions for the corresponding rises in questions (Hayes & Lahiri 1991).

Scaling differences have also been found to be relevant in perception. In their seminal study on English, Hadding-Koch & Studdert-Kennedy (1964) showed that listeners were more likely to rate a sentence as a question where there was higher f0 at three reference points (accent peak, post accentual low, and end of the phrase). Subsequent studies have consistently shown that greater pitch excursion in a rise-fall is more frequently perceived as a question than as a statement for a variety of languages, such as Hungarian (Gósy & Terken 1994), Swedish (House 2003), Russian (Makarova 2007), and Bari Italian (Savino & Grice 2007).

In addition to distinguishing questions from statements, scaling differences may cue different question types, too. In Bari Italian, y/n questions and echo questions are expressed by a rise-fall in pitch at the end of the phrase. Savino & Grice (2011) compared y/n questions with echo questions, which serve as an objection towards the repeated proposition. They found that echo questions exhibit higher pitch peaks than y/n questions.[2] This difference has been attributed to the pragmatically different functions associated with these question types. While echo questions exhibit a strong negative bias towards the questioned proposition in their corpus (listeners do not expect the proposition to be true), y/n questions

---

[2] Typologically, Italian is particularly remarkable because it lacks interrogative morphosyntax in y/n questions.

are rather neutral with regard to the expected answer. In a subsequent perception study, Savino and Grice showed that listeners can reliably make a categorical identification of these two intonational forms.

Apart from differences in scaling, a cross-linguistically common pattern setting questions apart from statements includes a sharp final rise at the end of the utterance in questions (reported for different types of questions, including y/n questions and echo questions; cf. Bolinger 1978). Another pattern that has been found to be relatively common across languages is a final rise-fall. One important parameter in this contour is the 'timing' of the pitch peak and, importantly, the rise up to this peak. In Palermo Italian, for example, the pitch peak occurs at a position in the intonation phrase that is structurally salient: the head of the intonation phrase, where it is part of the nuclear pitch accent that marks the element as pragmatically relevant (Grice 1995). Thus, the rise is on the syllable with the highest metrical strength, rather than at the edge of the phrase. The subsequent fall is realised at the edge. Comparable contours have been observed in other varieties of Italian (for an overview see Grice et al. 2005; Savino & Grice 2011), as well as in other languages such as Bengali (Hayes & Lahiri 1991), Bulgarian (Grice et al. 1995), Greek (Arvaniti 2001; Arvaniti & Ladd 2009), Hungarian (Ladd 1983; Gósy & Terken 1994; Varga 2002), Russian (e.g., Makarova 2007), and Moroccan Arabic (Benkirane 1998).

5.3.2 The intonation of focus

Rise-fall contours flagging questions often resemble tonal events marking focus. A number of discrete as well as continuous prosodic and intonational mechanisms have been found to be used cross-linguistically for marking focus. These include the presence, type, and timing of tonal events, phrasing as indicated by non-tonal boundary phenomena such as pauses and final lengthening, and spatio-temporal expansion of the segments involved (e.g. Buring 2009, for a typological overview of grammatical devices to mark focus). Many languages mark focused constituents using pitch accent type and alignment, including English (Pierrehumbert 1980; Pierrehumbert & Hirschberg 1990; Jun 2005), Italian (Grice et al. 2005), Russian (Meyer & Mleinek 2006), and German (Grice, Baumann & Benzmülller 2005; Grice et al. 2017). For example, Grice et al. (2017) showed that German speakers predominantly use early peak falling pitch accents to mark broad focus, while contrastive focus is predominantly marked by late peak rising pitch accents. In addition to pitch accents position and type, other intonational channels may be exploited to signal focus. Some researchers report on pitch excursion differences (e.g. Pierrehumbert 1980; Liberman & Pierrehumbert 1984;

Braun 2006; Grice et al. 2017) resembling the phonetic parameters described for questions vs. statements. For example, it has been shown that, even when expressed by the same pitch accent type, contrastive focus is realised with tonal movements exhibiting greater pitch excursions than narrow focus (Grice et al. 2017).

Other languages such as Japanese (Beckman & Pierrehumbert 1986), Chicheŵa (Kanerva 1990), Bengali (Hayes & Lahiri 1991), and Korean (Jun 2005) do not use pitch accents to mark focus but encode focus through phrasing. In these languages, phrase boundaries are inserted to the left or the right of focused constituents setting them apart from non-focused constituents. These boundaries may or may not go hand in hand with a perceivable pause, as well as boundary-related spatio-temporal expansion of the segmental material.

Moreover, a focused constituent may come with additional strengthening of the segmental material involved. Research conducted mainly on languages that exhibit pitch accents reports that focused constituents exhibit temporal and spatial expansion. This prosodic strengthening can extend beyond the accented syllable and can affect unaccented syllables within a word. Vowels tend to be longer and hyperarticulated in accented syllables. Harrington, Fletcher & Beckman (2000) show that English high vowels are generally raised when accented. Also for English, Cho (2005) presents data showing that /a/ is consistently lowered and /i/ is consistently fronted when accented. He further shows that vowels in accented position are articulated with faster and longer jaw opening gestures than vowels in unaccented syllables.

In sum, a number of prosodic and intonational mechanisms have been cross linguistically reported to signal that a constituent is focused. These include certain tonal events, phrasing, and spatio-temporal expansion of the segments involved.

5.3.3 Intonational differences between marking questions and marking focus

Some of the phonetic parameters employed to mark focused constituents (especially contrastive focus) resemble those marking questions: rising-falling tonal events with locally increased pitch excursion. Despite their similarities, questions often exhibit greater pitch scaling of the whole contour than corresponding (contrastive) statements. Moreover, focused constituents may exhibit spatio-temporal expansion of the segments involved, setting them locally apart from other elements of the utterance.

In certain constructions, a question and a statement containing a phrase-final contrasted element may have a similar surface form, although there are subtle differences in timing (Gósy & Terken 1994; D'Imperio & House 1997; Makarova 2007). For example, in Neapolitan Italian, y/n questions are characterised by a rise on the accented vowel, followed by a fall marking the end of the phrase. The contour of a statement with narrow focus also has a rise to a pitch peak on the accented vowel followed by a fall. Even though these contours appear to be very similar in certain contexts (i.e. exhibiting the same characteristic rise(-fall)), they have been described as differing in the alignment of the pitch peak. In questions, the pitch peak reaches its target later in the accented vowel than in narrow focus statements.

Most of the above-cited studies have shown that in perception studies listeners are able to use the timing of the pitch peak as a cue to sentence modality. D'Imperio & House (1997) show that in Neapolitan Italian the timing of the peak is an important cue to the underlying function (questions vs. narrow focus statements), when the accented word is final in the phrase. Similarly, Gósy & Terken (1994) showed that in Hungarian later peaks are more often perceived as questions than as narrow focus statements (see also House 2003, for Swedish and Makarova 2007, for Russian).

To sum up, both the pitch scaling and the timing of rising(-falling) tonal events are common phonetic parameters signalling questions and contrastivity across languages. These parameters are exploited by listeners to disambiguate questions from statements. The following sections explore intonational devices employed to mark questions and contrastive constituents in Tashlhiyt. More specifically, y/n questions, taken as a prototypical question type, will be compared to contrastive statements. Based on the cross-linguistic observations discussed above, these sentence modalities may exhibit similar intonation contours, but may differ in pitch scaling and the timing of tonal targets. Furthermore, echo questions will be compared to y/n questions. Since echo questions are usually considered to request confirmation or clarification rather than request new information, they may be distinguished intonationally from y/n questions as for example in Bari Italian (Savino & Grice 2011). Again, pitch scaling and the timing of tonal targets may be relevant parameters that distinguish these two question types.

5.4 Questions and contrastive focus in Tashlhiyt: qualitative observations

The following sections will discuss morphosyntactic devices used to mark questions and contrastive statements in Tashlhiyt. Moreover, the intonational marking of these functions will be discussed based on qualitative observations.

5.4 Questions and contrastive focus in Tashlhiyt: qualitative observations

5.4.1 Questions in Tashlhiyt

Tashlhiyt marks questions morphosyntactically. Y/n questions are canonically characterised by a morphological marker (is-) which cliticises to the verb in clause-initial position (cf. 8).

(8) is=t-sʁa   t-fruχ-t   ddisk?
    INT=3F.SG-bought F-child.BS-F.SG record
    'Did the girl buy a record?'

(9) t-sʁa   t-fruχ-t   ddisk
    3F.SG-bought F-child.BS-F.SG record
    'The girl bought a record.' or 'The girl bought a record?'

In spontaneous speech, declarative questions are used more frequently to request information than y/n questions. Declarative questions do not differ from corresponding declarative statements morphosyntactically (cf. 9).

Both question types (y/n, declarative) are characterised by similar intonation contours: a rise to a pitch peak followed by a fall usually occurring on the last word of the phrase (cf. Figure 5.1).[3]

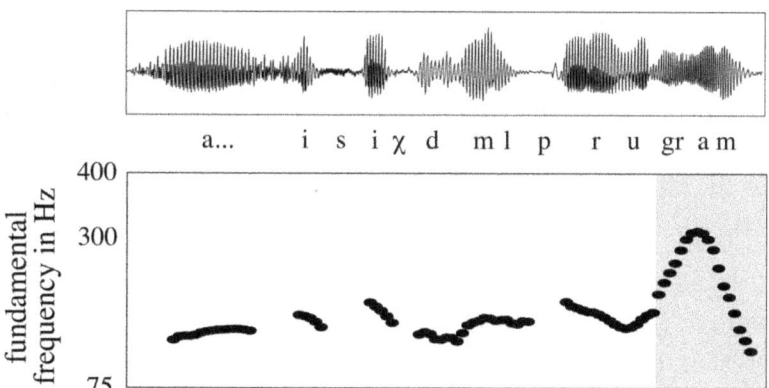

Figure 5.1: Representative waveform and f0 contour of the y/n question /a is iχdm lprugram/ 'Uh...does the program work?' Final syllable highlighted in grey.

Often the phrase-final fall does not reach a low target resulting in different degrees of truncation. In some cases, there is no fall at all. The degree of truncation is prone to both inter-speaker and intra-speaker variation. Figures 5.1 and 5.2

---

[3] This contour is also used for tag questions, in which the rise-fall is located on the tag.

5 The intonation of questions and contrastive focus in Tashlhiyt

illustrate two instances of questions. It is evident from the figures that most of the rise-fall trajectory takes place on the final syllable of the phrase (highlighted in grey).

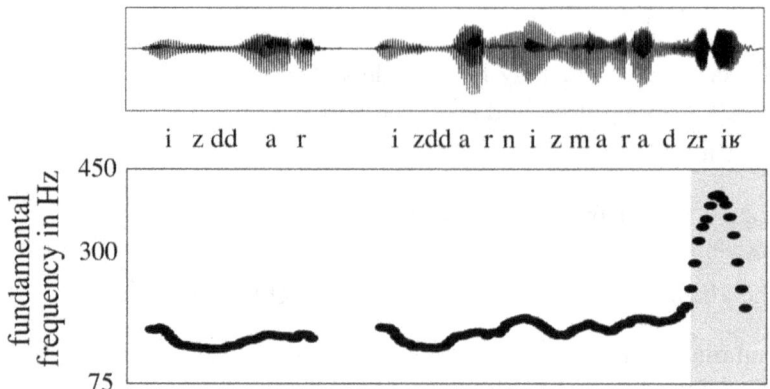

Figure 5.2: Representative waveform and f0 contour of the declarative question /izddar izddar n izm aʁ rad zriʁ/ 'The bottom... the bottom of the lion is it that I will go?' Final syllable highlighted in grey.

5.4.2 Contrastive focus in Tashlhiyt

Contrastive focus can be morphosyntactically expressed using either left dislocation or clefting. In both cases, the contrasted or emphasised element appears in clause-initial position preceding the verb (left dislocation, cf. 10). In clefted constructions the clause-initial constituent is additionally marked morphologically (cleft, cf. 11).

(10) ddisk t-sʁa=t   t-fruχ-t
record 3F.SG-bought=it F-child.BS-F.SG

'A record, the girl bought it.'

(11) ddisk ad t-sʁa   t-fruχ-t
record AD 3F.SG-bought F-child.BS-F.SG

'It is a record that the girl bought.'

Due to the frequent use of morphosyntactic constructions expressing focus, examples of contrastive focus expressed by intonation are only seldom found. In these cases, speakers use a rise-fall to mark contrasted constituents in-situ as illustrated in Figure 5.3. Here, the speaker contrasts /izddar/ 'underneath' with

5.4 Questions and contrastive focus in Tashlhiyt: qualitative observations

/iggi/ 'above' via rise-falls at the end of the respective words. The rise is on the final syllable of each preposition.

This type of contrastive focus can be isolated in elicited speech (cf. Figure 5.4). The rise-fall is located at the right edge of the focused constituent. Similar to the question tune, pitch suddenly falls after reaching the high target and stays low until the end of the utterance. The entire movement is often restricted to one syllable, here the final syllable of the word (highlighted in grey).

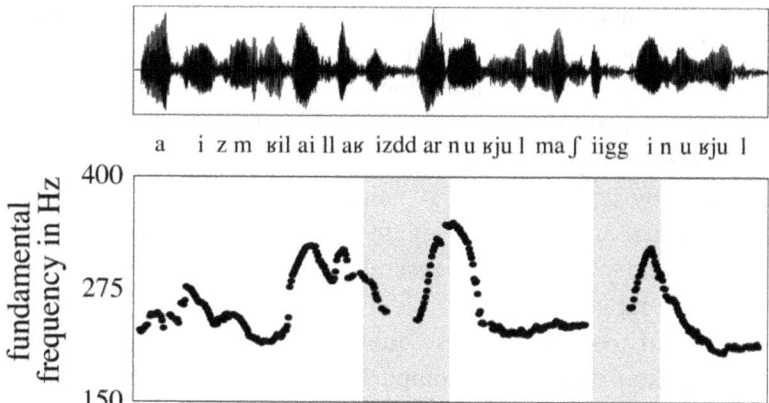

Figure 5.3: Representative waveform and f0 contour of the statement containing contrasted constituents /a izm ʁila illa ʁ izddar n uʁjul maʃi iggi n uʁjul/ 'Uh, the lion, now, he is underneath the donkey, not above the donkey'. Contrasted words highlighted in grey.

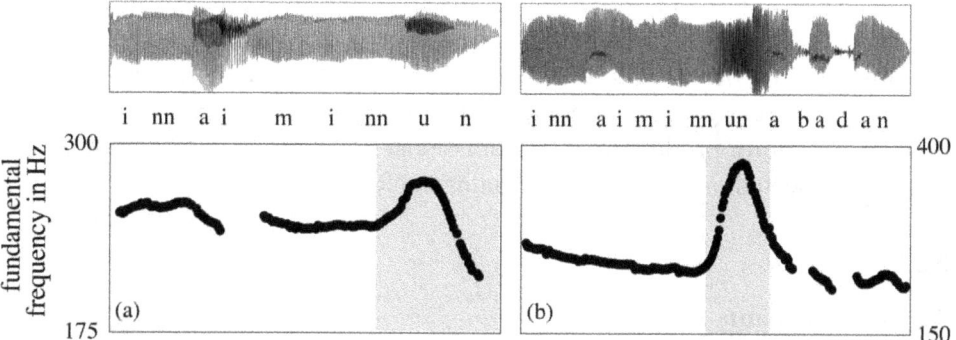

Figure 5.4: Representative waveforms and f0 contours of contrastive statements (a) /inna iminnun/ 'He said 'your mouths'.' and (b) /inna iminnun abadan/ 'He said 'your mouths' always.'. Final syllables of contrasted words highlighted in grey.

5.4.3 Intonational differences between flagging questions and marking contrastive focus in Tashlhiyt

The intonation of questions and contrastive statements are qualitatively similar. Both tunes are characterised by a local rise-fall in pitch. The sentence modalities differ, however, in the position of the rise-fall within the utterance. In contrastive statements, the rise-fall co-occurs with the right edge of the contrasted element. In questions, it co-occurs with the right edge of the phrase. Additionally, the question tune exhibits auditory qualities that distinguish it from the contrastive tune. Comparing the f0 range in questions to the one in statements, it becomes apparent that questions exhibit a higher pitch register, i.e. overall higher f0 values and higher pitch excursion. In fact, speakers frequently change phonation type towards the pitch peak producing a falsetto-like phonation. This is acoustically manifested by strikingly high f0 values of up to 700 Hz and a sudden shift into low vibrational amplitude (Laver 1994). The intonation contours of declarative questions and y/n questions resemble each other in terms of both tonal placement and f0 range.

We now set out to evaluate these qualitative observations quantitatively in a controlled reading experiment comparing questions and corresponding contrastive statements, as well as y/n questions and echo questions.

5.5 Production study

The objective of the present study is to investigate whether the difference between questions and contrastive statements is reflected in global and local scaling differences and/or in the timing of the rise-fall in pitch. Moreover, echo questions are compared to y/n questions to investigate the potential differences between questions requesting information and questions requesting confirmation. In the following sections, production data from a read speech corpus is analysed. Data has been collected on a field trip in Agadir in November 2013.[4]

5.5.1 Method

5.5.1.1 Participants

Ten native speakers of Tashlhiyt (five male, five female, mean age = 22 (20-27)) were recorded. All live in Agadir, Morocco, and are fluent in Moroccan Arabic

---

[4] Parts of the analysis presented in this section have been published in Roettger & Grice (2015).

and have basic command of French. All of them had normal or corrected-to-normal vision. None reported on any hearing impairments. Subjects were paid for their participation (cf. Appendix A2.2 for speaker information).

5.5.1.2 Speech material

The present production data is part of a larger corpus of read speech. The read corpus consisted of short mock dialogues containing target words in four different sentence modalities (y/n question, negation, contrastive statement, and echo question) based on the simple sentence: inna TARGET 'he said TARGET'. Sentences differed with respect to the distance of the target word to the right phrase edge (phrase medial and phrase final). Examples (12a-d) present the layout of the dialogues with the targets in phrase-final position (no adverb).

(12) a. is inna **baba**?
'Did he say 'father'?'

b. ur inna **baba**.
'He did not say 'father'.'

c. inna **dari**.
'He said 'in my house'.'

d. manik? inna **dari**? irwas.
'How? He said 'in my house'? It seems like it.'

In (12a) the target word is in a y/n question. In (b) the same target word is in a negative assertion. Because of the preceding negation, a different target word is explicitly corrected in a contrastive statement in (c). Finally, in (d), the proposition in the contrastive statement is called into question in the counter-expectational echo question. In (13), an example dialogue with the target word in phrase-medial position followed by an adverb is given.[5]

(13) a. is inna **baba** abadan?
'Did he say 'father' then?'

b. ur inna **baba** abadan.
'He did not say 'father' then.'

---

[5] The author is aware of the metalinguistic nature of these context sentences. Exploration of semi-spontaneous and spontaneous speech, however, does not indicate any patterns diverging from the controlled corpus described above. Since target words of different parts of speech were compared, a 'more natural' context sentence for the present question was not available.

5 The intonation of questions and contrastive focus in Tashlhiyt

    c. inna **dari** abadan.
       'He said 'in my house' then.'

    d. manik? inna **dari** abadan? irwas.
       'How? He said 'in my house' then? It seems like it.'

As described above, speakers are expected to produce a rise-fall at the right edge of the phrase in questions (on the target in 12a and 12d, and on the adverb in 13a and 13d). In statements, speakers are expected to produce a rise-fall marking contrastive focus on the target word (phrase final in 12c and phrase medial in 13c). This means that the location of the pitch peak is always either on the target word or on the adverb, in both sentence modalities. The word co-occurring with the pitch peak is henceforth referred to as the 'tone bearing word'. Productions of the negative assertion in (12b) and (13b) are not subject to the present analysis.

The corpus contained 18 different target words. There were ten fully voiced target words and eight target words containing voiceless segments only. For the present analysis only fully voiced target words are considered (cf. Table 5.1). Each target word appeared in each context at least once. Several items appeared twice. This resulted in 54 fully voiced target words for each participant (total 540). The data with target words containing obstruents only will be subject to discussion in Chapter 6.

Table 5.1: Target words and translations of production study.

Word	Translation
ba.ba	'my father'
da.ri	'in my house'
di.ma	'always'
il.di	'he pulls'
i.min.nun	'your mouths'
ma.na.gu	'when'
ʁi.la	'now'
u.dm	'face'

5.5.1.3 Procedure

Participants were seated in front of a computer screen and read out orthographically presented material containing the target words as presented in carrier sentences in (12) to (13) (i.e. in mock dialogues). Participants were asked to enact these dialogues. The materials were presented in a version of the Latin script speakers are used to reading and writing in (see Chapter 3).

Recordings were made in a quiet room at the Ibn Zohr University in Agadir. The production data was recorded using a Marantz PMD 670 solid-state recorder at a sampling rate of 44.1 kHz, and an AKG C420 III head-mounted microphone. Before recordings began, participants were asked to read aloud a word list containing all of the target words to ensure that they were familiar with the words and their meanings. Dialogues were presented in random order.

5.5.1.4 Analyses

All acoustic data was manually annotated employing the following labelling criteria: segment boundaries (and, in turn, syllable and word boundaries) were identified in the acoustic waveform by means of an oscillogram and a wide-band spectrogram. All segmental boundaries of vowels and consonants were labelled at abrupt changes in the spectra at the time at which the closure was formed or released: this was the case for nasals, laterals (especially in the spectra for the intensity of higher formants), and obstruents (at random noise patterns in the higher frequency regions). All acoustic information was automatically extracted via Praat version 5.4 (Boersma & Weenink 2015).

F0 tracks for all utterances were extracted, manually corrected, and smoothed using the Praat script 'mausmooth' (Cangemi 2015). The smoothing algorithm levelled out strong microprosodic effects and enabled the inspection of uninterrupted contours. The smoothed contours were used for automatic extraction of the f0 mean of the word /inna/. Since /inna/ is expected to exhibit a relatively flat f0 over the course of the word in the investigated sentence modalities (cf. Figure 5.4), the mean f0 of /inna/ (in Hz) is taken as a reference level to operationalise 'pitch level'. Any tonal movement following /inna/ can be assessed in relation to this reference level. Additionally, minimum and maximum f0 values of the utterance were extracted. The difference between minimum and maximum was calculated in semitones (ST) to operationalise 'pitch range'. Finally, the timing of the rise-fall was investigated. Due to difficulties in reliably measuring low turning points, it is abstracted away from the actual f0 trajectory and focused on the high turning point for both pragmatic functions. Henceforth the high target is referred to as the pitch peak. Peak timing was calculated as the time lag between the acoustic onset of the final syllable within the word and the f0 maximum in seconds (cf. 14a-c):

(14) a. PITCH LEVEL: mean f0 of the reference word /inna/.
   b. PITCH RANGE: difference between maximum and minimum f0 values in ST.
   c. F0 MAX LAG: lag between the onset of the final syllable of the tone bearing word and the f0 maximum.

5.5.1.5 Statistics

Sentences produced with hesitation or unnatural phrasing patterns, mispronunciations of the segmental material, or instances exhibiting list intonation were excluded from the analyses. Moreover, most echo questions from speaker F5 were excluded. She produced echo questions with a monotonous contour. Native speakers who did not participate in the experiment judged these to resemble bored statements and thus inappropriate realisations of the intended context.

Generally, speakers did well in naturally enacting the dialogues, but they had difficulties with reading aloud. This resulted in an unusually large amount of hesitations and mispronunciations. Overall, acoustic parameters for 471 utterances were submitted to statistical analysis (= 7.8% data loss) and were analysed with generalised linear mixed models, using R (R Core Team 2015), the lme4 package (Bates et al. 2015), and the multcomp package (Hothorn, Bretz & Westfall 2008). Fixed effect specification will be given in the relevant paragraphs below. A term for varying intercepts for speakers and for target words was included. Terms for varying slopes were not included, since the data set is rather small and the factorial design was not balanced (asymmetric exclusion of data points frequently leading to converging issues). Speaker-specific tables will be provided to allow for inspection of consistency across speakers. To determine p-values for the main effects / interactions between factors, a model including the main effect / interaction of interest was compared to the same model with no main effect / no interaction via Likelihood Ratio Tests (LRT).

5.5.2 Results: pitch scaling

First, we will discuss the scaling differences between sentence modalities. Generally, questions exhibit a higher reference pitch level in /inna/ than statements (cf. Figure 5.5, Table 5.2). This is true for the comparison between contrastive statements (CS, 189 Hz) and both echo questions (EQ, 235 Hz) and y/n questions (Y/N, 264 Hz).

The difference between sentence modalities is consistent across all speakers. Interestingly, echo questions reveal an intermediate status, i.e. they are consis-

5.5 Production study

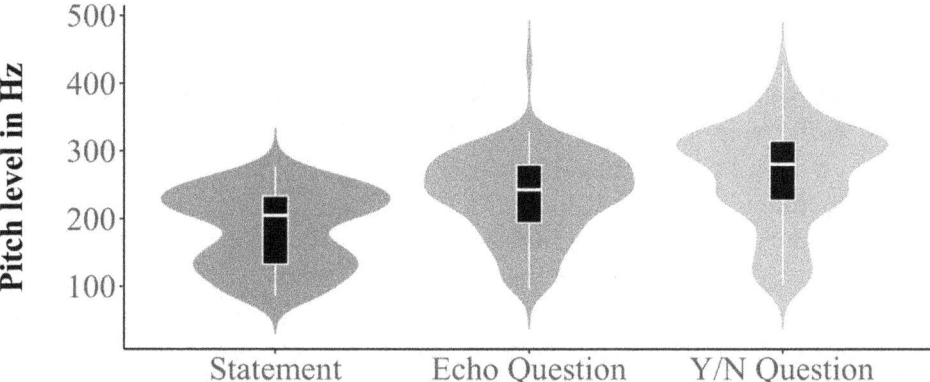

Figure 5.5: Violin plots of the pitch level values of the reference word /inna/ as a function of sentence modality. Inside each plot, the black boxes indicate the inter-quartile range (IQR), the range between the first and third quartile. The solid horizontal line indicates the median. The whiskers indicate the range, up to 1.5 times the IQR away from the median. The overall shape of the violin plots represent kernel density curves of the raw data distribution.

Table 5.2: Mean pitch level (and standard deviation, in Hz) of the reference word /inna/ as a function of sentence modality for each speaker individually averaged over words.

Speaker	Contrastive Statement	Echo Question	Y/N Question
F1	245 (10)	303 (13)	317 (20)
F2	241 (13)	298 (40)	336 (38)
F3	217 (5)	269 (14)	337 (39)
F4	211 (9)	249 (22)	280 (25)
F5	251 (16)	NA	313 (22)
M1	120 (4)	161 (20)	168 (19)
M2	129 (11)	194 (12)	226 (17)
M3	152 (11)	254 (23)	293 (35)
M4	164 (14)	230 (14)	237 (16)
M5	90 (5)	110 (8)	116 (13)
overall	189 (55)	235 (59)	264 (74)

tently higher than statements and consistently lower than y/n questions. A linear mixed effects model was performed including sentence modality as a fixed effect. The model estimated the main effect of sentence modality to be significant ($\chi^2(2)$=496, p<0.00001). Post-hoc Tukey tests reveal that the difference is in fact significant across all comparisons (statement vs. echo question: β=55.7, SE=2.9, z=19.1, p<0.00001; statement vs. y/n question: β=82.1, SE=2.8, z=29.7, p<0.00001; echo question vs. y/n question: β=26.4, SE=2.8, z=9.5, p<0.00001).

We now turn to the pitch range measurements, i.e. the difference between maximum and minimum f0 values within the utterance. Pitch range is numerically rather large with an average of 9 STs across all sentence modalities. In fact, in questions, speakers frequently changed phonation type towards the pitch peak producing a falsetto-like phonation. This is acoustically manifested by very high f0 values of up to 700 Hz and sudden shifts into low vibrational amplitude.

Overall, questions exhibit a greater pitch range than statements. This is true for the comparison between statements (6.8 ST) and both echo questions (10.7 ST) and y/n questions (9.5 ST) (cf. Figure 5.6 and Table 5.3).

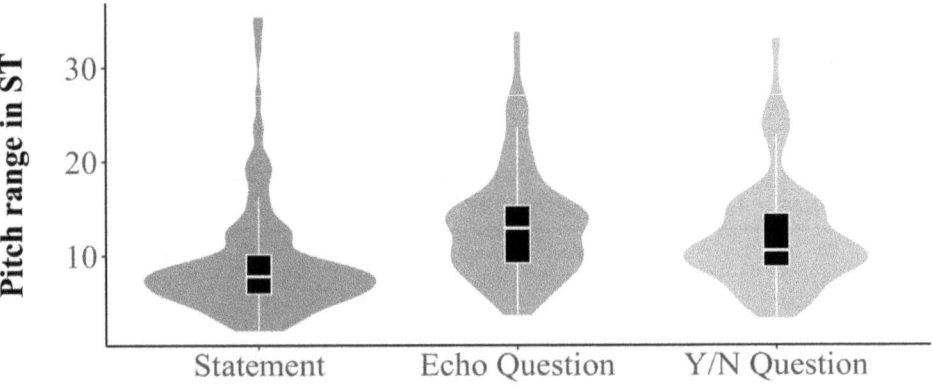

Figure 5.6: Violin plots of the mean pitch range values as a function of sentence modality. Inside each plot, the black boxes indicate the inter-quartile range (IQR), the range between the first and third quartile. The solid horizontal line indicates the median. The whiskers indicate the range, up to 1.5 times the IQR away from the median. The overall shape of the violin plots represent kernel density curves of the raw data distribution.

5.5 Production study

Table 5.3: Mean pitch range (and standard deviations, in ST) as a function of sentence modality for each speaker individually averaged over words.

Speaker	Contrastive Statement	Echo Question	Y/N Question
F1	6.6 (1.7)	8.4 (1.6)	7.3 (1.5)
F2	5.7 (1.6)	13.3 (2.6)	13.2 (2.2)
F3	6.7 (2.7)	8.2 (2.3)	10.8 (2.7)
F4	5.9 (1.2)	10 (2)	7.8 (1.3)
F5	9.1 (3.8)	NA	10.6 (2)
M1	3.1 (1.3)	15.5 (2.5)	7.6 (3.1)
M2	6.9 (1.9)	11.6 (2.1)	9 (2.8)
M3	9.8 (1.5)	14.6 (3.6)	13.3 (3.6)
M4	6.5 (3)	8 (2.3)	9 (3.2)
M5	5 (1.4)	5 (1.8)	5.8 (1.7)
overall	6.8 (2.8)	10.7 (3.9)	9.5 (3.4)

For some speakers, the distinction between statements and questions is very clear (e.g. F2 and M1), while for other speakers, the distinction is more subtle and characterised by heavy overlap (e.g. F1 and M5). With regard to the distinction between echo questions and y/n questions, there is a large amount of individual variation. Some speakers exhibit a greater pitch range in y/n questions (e.g. F3, M4, M5), while others exhibit a greater pitch range in echo questions (F1, F2, F4, M1, M2, M3) (cf. Table 5.3).

A linear mixed effects model was performed including sentence modality as a fixed effect. The model estimated the main effect of sentence modality to be significant ($\chi^2(2)=143.1$, $p<0.00001$). Post-hoc Tukey tests reveal that the difference is in fact significant across all comparisons (statement vs. echo question: $\beta=4.2$, SE=0.3 z=12.6, $p<0.0001$; statement vs. y/n question: $\beta=2.6$, SE=0.6, z=4.5, $p<0.0001$; echo question vs. y/n question: $\beta=1.2$, SE=0.3, z=3.9, $p=0.0003$). Statistically speaking, those speakers that exhibit a greater pitch range in echo questions show a rather strong effect (e.g. speaker M1) which potentially drives the overall mean differences. In light of these inter-individual difference and the fact that the statistical models did not account for varying speaker slopes, generalisations based on the inferential results need to be considered critically here.

5.5.3 Results: pitch peak timing

We now turn to the timing of the pitch peak. On average, pitch peaks occurred around 113 ms after the onset of the final syllable of the tone bearing word (utterance final in questions and focused constituent final in contrastive statements). However, the pitch peak is aligned later in y/n questions (144 ms) and echo questions (159 ms) than in statements in which the pitch peak is reached, on average, close to the syllable boundary between the penult and the final syllable (20 ms). A linear mixed effects model was performed including sentence modality as the critical fixed effect. Additionally, the presence of a coda consonant in the final syllable was added in an interaction with sentence modality. This was done because the presence of a voiced coda consonant might enable the pitch peak to be aligned later while still allowing for the full realisation of the subsequent fall (e.g. Mücke et al. 2009; Niemann & Mücke 2015). Here, the presence of a coda consonant actually confounds with the factor sentence modality because there are more cases of tone bearing words with a coda consonant in questions than in statements. Where target words were phrase-medial, the tonal event for questions is always found on the phrase-final adverb /abadan/.

There is no apparent interaction between the effect of sentence modality and the presence of a coda consonant ($\chi^2(2)$=5.49, p=0.064). The model estimates the main effect of sentence modality to be significant ($\chi^2(2)$=120.41, p<0.00001). Post-hoc Tukey tests reveal that there is a significant difference between statements and questions, but there is no significant difference between question types (statement vs. echo question: β=0.11, SE=0.01 z=10.9, p<0.0001; statement vs. y/n question: β=0.10, SE=0.01, z=10.3, p<0.0001; echo question vs. y/n question: β=0.01, SE=0.01, z=1.1, p=0.5).

It can thus be concluded that the pitch peak in statements is reached earlier in the word than in questions. Echo and y/n questions, on the other hand, appear to have a similar distribution of pitch peak alignment (cf. Figure 5.7).

Looking at the actual distributions of the peak in relation to the onset of the final syllable, it becomes apparent that the averaged values are somewhat misleading (cf. Figure 5.7). First, the alignment of pitch peaks in statements is more variable than in questions, indicated by the wider spread in the distribution. Moreover, the distribution for statements is not unimodal, but bimodal as indicated by the occurrence of two peaks in the distribution. Looking at questions, there is some indication of bimodality here, too. There is a small bump in the distribution left of the syllable boundary (more prominent in y/n questions). These bimodal distributions reflect the auditory impressions of other researchers (e.g. Dell & Elmedlaoui 1985, Ridouane p.c.), as well as the impression of the author.

Although the pitch peak is most often located on the final syllable, it is possible for speakers to produce the pitch peak on the penult as well. The resulting tonal patterns give rise to discretely different auditory impressions rather than to the impression of a continuously variable position of the tonal event.

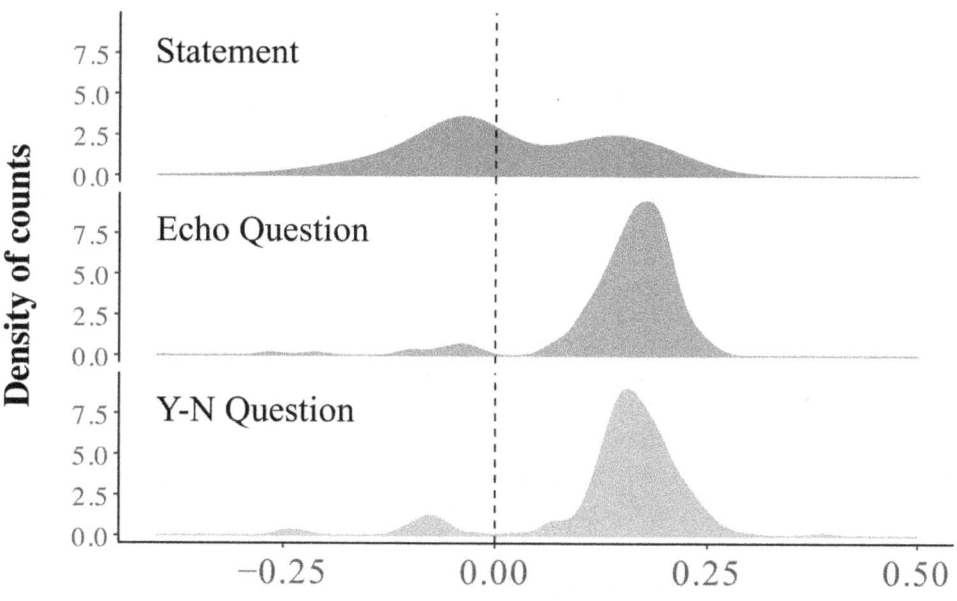

Figure 5.7: Kernel density curves for pitch peak measurements relative to the onset of the final syllable (at final-to-f0 max = 0) for (a) statements, (b) echo questions, and (c) y/n questions. Positive values indicate that the pitch peak occurs in the final syllable, negative values indicate that the pitch peak occurs in the penult. The dashed line marks the onset of the final syllable.

Table 5.4 illustrates the high degree of inter-speaker variability. Generally, there is a strong tendency for individual speakers to produce the pitch peak on the final syllable (most mean values are positive). This trend is stronger for questions than for statements. In fact, some speakers prefer placing the pitch peak on the penult in statements (cf. negative values in M2, M3, and M4). Generally, the pitch peak in statements is found on the penult more frequently than in questions.

5 The intonation of questions and contrastive focus in Tashlhiyt

Table 5.4: Alignment of mean final-to-f0 max (in ms) with respect to final syllable onset (and standard deviations) as a function of sentence modality for each speaker individually averaged over words.

Speaker	Contrastive Statement	Echo Question	Y/N Question
F1	17 (127)	153 (33)	162 (31)
F2	36 (111)	154 (73)	124 (80)
F3	53 (118)	175 (44)	208 (46)
F4	30 (105)	170 (76)	143 (67)
F5	23 (157)	NA	149 (117)
M1	66 (69)	126 (54)	75 (134)
M2	-3 (124)	147 (22)	154 (22)
M3	-31 (55)	147 (71)	146 (82)
M4	-17 (160)	177 (67)	167 (91)
M5	72 (121)	111 (133)	101 (109)
overall	20 (119)	159 (75)	144 (89)

This discretely formulated observation is also reflected in more gradual trends in phonetic alignment. Even if only pitch peaks on the final syllable are considered (f0 max lag > 0), the difference between statements and questions holds with statements reaching the pitch peak 129 ms after the onset of the final syllable while echo questions and y/n questions reach the pitch peak later in the syllable (166 and 167 ms, respectively).

Looking at word-specific distributions, it becomes clear that the mobility of the tonal event appears to be dependent on word-specific properties. Figure 5.8 illustrates the distribution of peak alignment for three representative target words: /i.min.nun/, /ba.ba/, and /u.dm/.

In Figure 5.8a, there is a subtle bimodality but the majority of peaks appears to be on the final syllable (positive values). In Figure 5.8b, there is still a strong bias towards the final syllable but also a noticeable amount of peaks occurring on the penult. In Figure 5.8c, the target /u.dm/ exhibits a strong bimodality with a clear bias towards peaks on the penult. There appears to be something specific about the lexical items that leads speakers to be more likely to produce pitch peaks on the penult or the final syllable.

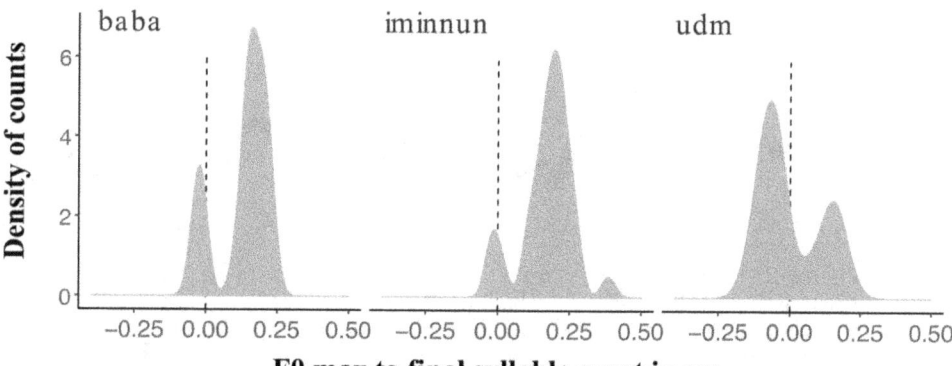

Figure 5.8: Kernel density curve for pitch peak measurements relative to the onset of the final syllable (at final syllable onset to f0 max = 0) for (a) /iminnun/ 'your mouths', (b) /baba/ 'father', and (c) /udm/ 'face'. Positive values indicate that the pitch peak occurs in the final syllable, negative values indicate that the pitch peak occurs in the penult. Values are averaged over subjects and sentence modalities. The dashed line marks the onset of the final syllable.

In addition to potential lexical effects, in many cases, tonal alignment appears to be prone to some degree of free alternation. Figure 5.9 illustrates examples for the pitch peak on the final syllable and the penult, respectively. In Figure 5.9a, the penult of /il.di/ is low before f0 suddenly rises towards the peak on the final syllable. In Figure 5.9b, f0 suddenly drops after reaching its high target on the penult leaving the final syllable low. In most cases, the rise-fall appears to be located exclusively on one syllable.

5.5.4 Discussion

To recapitulate the production results, questions in Tashlhiyt are distinguished from corresponding contrastive statements by all three investigated parameters: compared to statements, questions have an overall higher pitch level, a greater pitch range, and the pitch peak is realised later within the word. The alignment pattern can be described in both discrete as well as continuous terms. In questions, the pitch peak is aligned more often with the final syllable than in statements. Statements have many more instances of pitch peaks aligned to the penult

5 The intonation of questions and contrastive focus in Tashlhiyt

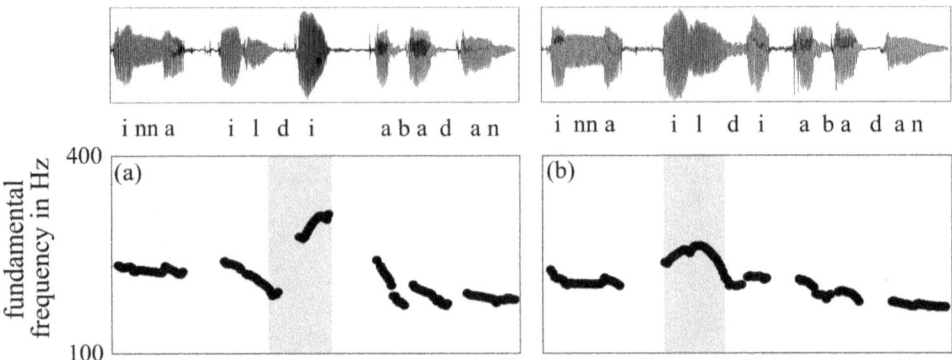

Figure 5.9: Representative waveforms and f0 contours of the contrastive statement /inna ildi abadan/ 'Did he say 'he pulls' always?' with the pitch peak (a) on the final syllable and (b) on the penult. Syllables co-occurring with the pitch peak are highlighted in grey. Both productions are from the same speaker.

than questions. In continuous terms, even if only pitch peaks on the final syllable are considered, questions have later peaks than corresponding statements.

In addition to the distinction between statements and questions, echo questions are distinguished from y/n questions. This distinction is mainly manifested in pitch level with echo questions being lower in pitch than y/n questions. Evidence for echo questions having a greater pitch range is weak at best and the two question types exhibit comparable alignment patterns of the pitch peak.

Generally, there is a high degree of variability both across and within speakers with regard to the position of the pitch peak. While some variability can be explained by functional factors like sentence modality, there remains a substantial amount of unexplained variance. A recent study by Grice, Ridouane & Roettger (2015) shed more light on the factors that determine tonal placement in Tashlhiyt. Their results will be reviewed here briefly.

Grice et al. recorded Tashlhiyt speakers living in Paris. Four native speakers of Tashlhiyt, originally from Morocco but permanently living in Paris, participated in the experiment. Even though the speakers did not live in Morocco anymore, they were frequently in contact with friends and family there. According to the author's impression (and according to Rachid Ridouane, p.c.), their intonational patterns did not diverge from those speakers recorded in Agadir.

Speakers read out short mock dialogues (15-17) similar to the corpus described in the production study above (§5.4.1). Twenty-eight pairs of disyllabic target words were recorded. Target words varied in the sonority of the syllable nucleus and in the weight of the final syllable.

5.5 Production study

(15) is inna **tugl**?
'Did he say 'she hung'?'

(16) ur inna **tugl**.
'He did not say 'she hung'.'

(17) inna **tmdl**.
'He said 'she buried'.'

In line with the findings presented above, Grice et al. observed that the phrase-final word bears a pitch peak in both y/n questions and contrastive statements. They described the distribution of the pitch peak as a bimodal pattern, with the pitch peak being aligned either with the penult or with the final syllable of the target word. This discrete pattern coincided with the auditory impression of prominence, i.e. the syllable on which the peak occurred sounded louder and longer to the authors. They explicitly state that the position of the pitch peak was unambiguously identifiable when listening to the utterances. In the following, we will focus on the discrete placement patterns of the pitch peak reported by Grice, Ridouane & Roettger (2015).

In target words with only one sonorant nucleus (i.e. a sonorant consonant, e.g. /r/ in /tṛ.kẓ, tḅ.dṛ/ 'she danced, she mentioned'), the pitch peak was almost exclusively located on that syllable. When both syllables had a sonorant nucleus (i.e. a sonorant consonant or vowel, e.g. /tiri, tm̩.dl̩/ 'she wanted, she buried') there was no clear preference for a peak on the penult or final syllable. Here, the placement of the peak for both statements and questions was highly complex and subject to the influence of a number of interacting factors. Compared to statements, they found a preference for pitch peaks on the final syllable in questions. Orthogonal to that, they identified two independent factors relevant for determining the location of the pitch peak:

First, the pitch peak was more likely to co-occur with more sonorous syllable nuclei than with less sonorous syllable nuclei. For example, in a word like /tu.gl̩/ 'she hung', the vowel, which has a higher sonority than the liquid, was more likely to attract the pitch peak to the penultimate syllable. Conversely, in a word like /tn̩.za/ 'it was solved', the final syllable was more likely to attract the pitch peak. The sonority asymmetry was not only relevant for the distinction between vowels and sonorant consonants, but for the distinction between consonants with differing degrees of sonority, e.g. a liquid was preferred over a nasal (e.g. /tm̩.dl̩/ 'she buried' vs. /tṛ.km̩/ 'she rotted'). Overall, the effect of sonority was stronger for vowels than for sonorant consonants, i.e. vowels were stronger attractors for the pitch peak than consonants.

Second, the pitch peak was more likely to co-occur with heavy syllables than with light syllables. In /tu.glṭ/, the pitch peak was more likely to co-occur with the final syllable than in /tu.gl̩/.

The weighting and interaction of these factors was to some degree speaker-specific, although they generally appeared to be additive and systematic throughout the sample (cf. Tables 5.5–5.9). There was a general preference for the pitch peak to occur on the final syllable indicated by the high overall proportional values. Questions were generally more likely than statements to be produced with a final pitch peak, resulting in ceiling effects for several cells. Heavy syllables systematically attracted a final pitch peak more often than corresponding light syllables and more sonorous nuclei attracted a pitch peak more often than less sonorous nuclei.

The above-identified factors do not explain, however, the entire variance. In many cases, tonal placement was prone to some degree of free alternation. There were numerous cases where the same speaker produced pitch peaks in different locations within the same target word across different repetitions. Figure 5.10 illustrates a minimal quadruplet with statements and y/n questions.

Table 5.5: Results of Grice, Ridouane & Roettger (2015: 250f.): mean proportion (in %) of pitch peak location on the final syllable in words containing vowels in contrastive statements for each speaker separately. Results are ordered according to the syllable nuclei of the penult and final syllable (V = vowel, S = sonorant consonant) and syllable weight of the final syllable (light or heavy)

	Contrastive Statements Words Containing Vowels)				
	F1	F2	M1	M2	Overall
V.S	58.3	0	66.7	75	51.1
V.V	75	0	100	10	47.8
S.V	100	81.8	100	100	95.8
light	61.1	29.4	79	55.6	56.9
heavy	94.4	23.5	100	75	73.9

5.5 Production study

Table 5.6: Results of Grice, Ridouane & Roettger (2015: 250f.): mean proportion (in %) of pitch peak location on the final syllable in words containing consonants only in contrastive statements for each speaker separately. Results are ordered according to the syllable nuclei of the penult and final syllable (L = Liquid, N = Nasal) and syllable weight of the final syllable (light or heavy).

	Contrastive Statements (Words Containing no Vowels)				
	F1	F2	M1	M2	Overall
L.N	41.7	0	58.3	50	37.5
N.N / L.L	66.7	0	75	100	61.7
N.L	100	41.7	100	100	84.8
light	55.6	5.9	64.7	83.3	52.9
heavy	82.4	22.2	88.9	83.3	69

Table 5.7: Results of Grice, Ridouane & Roettger (2015: 250f.): mean proportion (in %) of pitch peak location on the final syllable in words containing vowels in y/n questions for each speaker separately. Results are ordered according to the syllable nuclei of the penult and final syllable (V = vowel, S = sonorant consonant) and syllable weight of the final syllable (light or heavy).

	Y/N Questions (Words Containing Vowels)				
	F1	F2	M1	M2	Overall
V.S	76.9	63.6	50	91.7	70.8
V.V	100	100	100	100	100
S.V	100	100	100	100	100
light	84.2	76.5	66.7	94.4	80.6
heavy	100	100	100	100	100

5 The intonation of questions and contrastive focus in Tashlhiyt

Table 5.8: Results of Grice, Ridouane & Roettger (2015: 250f.): mean proportion (in %) of pitch peak location on the final syllable in words containing consonants only in y/n questions for each speaker separately. Results are ordered according to the syllable nuclei of the penult and final syllable (L = Liquid, N = Nasal) and syllable weight of the final syllable (light or heavy).

	Y/N Questions (Words Containing no Vowels)				
	F1	F2	M1	M2	Overall
L.N	72.7	45.5	75	75	67.4
N.N / L.L	83.3	83.3	83.3	91.7	85.4
N.L	100	100	100	100	100
light	72.2	61.1	72.2	77.8	70.8
heavy	100	94.1	100	100	98.6

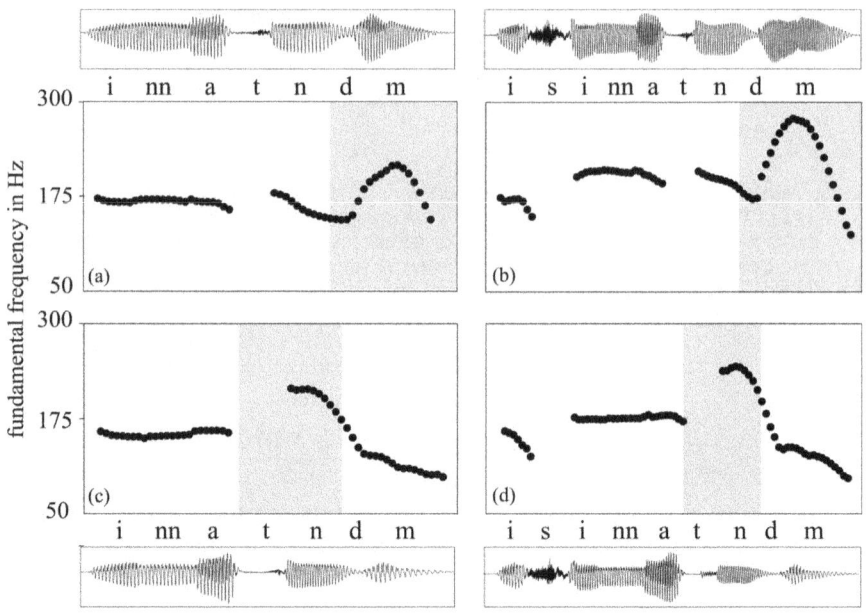

Figure 5.10: Representative waveforms and f0 contours of two realisations of the contrastive statement /inna tndm/ 'he said 'she regretted'' (a,c) and the y/n question /is inna tndm/ 'did he say 'she regretted'?' (b,d): the two different realisations for each sentence modality illustrate variation in pitch peak placement. All utterances are from the same male speaker. Tone bearing syllable is highlighted in grey.

Grice et al.'s findings put the results of the production study presented in this chapter into perspective. As opposed to Grice et al., there was an even stronger preference for final pitch peaks in the present data set. This might be due to the nature of stimuli employed, i.e. most words had a light final syllable with a vowel in syllable nucleus position. In line with Grice et al., these structures generally attract the pitch peak to the final syllable. Across sentence modalities, the word /u.dm̩/ 'face' exhibits an exceptionally large number of pitch peaks on the penult (overall 64% of all cases across sentence modalities). This may be a reflex of the sonority asymmetry in udm. The vowel in the penult is more sonorous than the nasal in the final syllable and attracts the pitch peak to the penult syllable. The word /i.min.nun/ 'your mouths', instead, exhibits mainly final pitch peaks. This is possibly a reflex of the final syllable being heavy. So even though Grice, Ridouane & Roettger (2015) and the present production study had different speaker samples and different speech materials, comparable tonal placement regularities can be observed.

To sum up, Tashlhiyt exhibits a remarkable amount of variability in tonal placement. However, this variability has a particular structure, i.e. it is bimodal. The occurrence of a particular tonal event can only be stated as a probabilistic distribution affected by multiple interacting factors. The question arises if, and if so, how, these probabilistic patterns are used to distinguish sentence modalities perceptually.

5.6 Perception study

In the preceding section, it has been shown that statements and questions differ in terms of pitch register according to pitch level and pitch range. Moreover, sentence modalities differ with respect to the timing of the tonal event involved. The timing of the pitch peak common to both statements and questions, showed variation in both discrete and continuous terms. The pitch peak co-occurred either with the penult or with the final syllable of the tone bearing word, with more instances of the pitch peak on the final syllable in questions. Moreover, even if only pitch peaks aligned with the final syllable are considered, questions still exhibited a later peak alignment within the syllable. The following perception study investigates whether, and if so, how, Tashlhiyt listeners use these pitch parameters to interpret morphosyntactically ambiguous sentences.

5 The intonation of questions and contrastive focus in Tashlhiyt

5.6.1 Method

5.6.1.1 Participants

Nine native speakers of Tashlhiyt (four male, five female, mean age = 21 (20–23)) participated in the experiment. None of them had participated in the previous production experiment. All live in Agadir, Morocco, are fluent in Moroccan Arabic, and have basic command of French. All of them had normal or corrected-to-normal vision. None reported on any hearing impairments (cf. Appendix A2.3 for participant information).

5.6.1.2 Speech materials and procedure

In order to control for pitch register and pitch peak placement, stimuli were resynthesised. As base stimuli, four fully voiced phrases were recorded: /inna baba/, / inna bibi/, / inna dima/, and / inna ʁila/ 'He said ('father, turkey, always, now')' all produced by a phonetically trained native speaker of Tashlhiyt (Rachid Ridouane). For each phrase, the speaker produced two contours corresponding to two discretely different pitch peak positions resulting in two sets of stimuli: one set contained the pitch peak on the final syllable (F) of the target word and the other set contained the pitch peak on the penult (PU). The speaker was instructed to produce the two sets in the same register. Subsequent inspections of the contours confirmed that this was the case.

Both sets were resynthesised using PSOLA in Praat version 5.4 (Boersma & Weenink 2015). F0 was manipulated resulting in two different pitch register conditions: the low register condition started with a baseline of 130 Hz, the high register condition started 4 semitones higher (~164 Hz). The difference is comparable to values obtained for male speakers in the production study above.

Generally, f0 was manipulated such that the start of the pitch rise was located at the offset of /inna/ towards two different f0 maximum locations for each set. In the early peak condition, f0 reached its maximum at 1/3 of the way into the vowel (penult vowel in set PU and final vowel in set F). In the late peak condition, f0 reached its maximum at 2/3 of the way into the respective vowel. Note that the alignment differences exceed those typically found in the production study above in order to maximise a potential effect of alignment within the syllable. The maximum f0 value was set to be four semitones higher than the baseline (164 Hz for low register and 206 Hz for high register, respectively). These values are comparable to the typical rise excursions obtained for male speakers in the

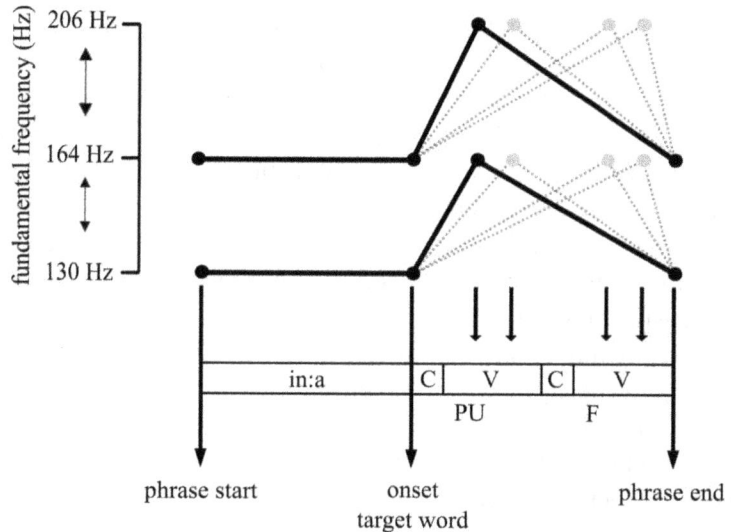

Figure 5.11: Schematised representation of the manipulation conditions displaying the differences in pitch register, discrete peak alignment (penultimate = PU, final = F), and gradual peak alignment: small arrows indicate early and late alignment within the syllable, respectively.

production study above. After reaching its maximum, f0 fell towards the baseline located at the end of the target word.[6]

These manipulations resulted in 32 stimuli (4 target words * 2 pitch registers (low vs. high) * 2 peak alignments in discrete terms (penult vs. final) * 2 peak alignments in gradual terms (early vs. late)) (cf. Figure 5.11).

Participants were seated in front of a computer screen in a quiet room at the Ibn Zohr University in Agadir. They were told that they were going to listen to a robot that speaks Tashlhiyt reasonably well, but has difficulties with producing the difference between statements and questions. Participants were asked to decide whether they would consider the sentences produced as statements or questions by pressing one of two buttons.

The experiment was run using Superlab (Haxby et al. 1993). At the beginning of each trial, a fixation stimulus consisting of a '+' was presented in the centre of

---

[6] Since the start of the rise and the end of the fall were not identifiable in the production data in a reliable way, the start of the rise and the end of the fall have been fixed to the offset of /inna/ and the end of the utterance accordingly. The potential implications of this methodological choice will be discussed below.

the screen for 1500 ms during which participant heard the stimulus. Following this, two sentences appeared on the right and left side of the screen. On one side the statement was displayed in blue (e.g. inna baba !), on the other side the question was displayed in red (e.g. inna baba ?). Both were presented in Latin script. The position of the question and the statement was kept constant within participants, but was counterbalanced across participants. Participants had to press the left or right button on the computer keyboard matched with the respective sentence modalities displayed on the screen. After response delivery, a blank screen appeared for 500 ms.

Each participant started with a training session, in which all combinations of pitch registers and peak alignments (discrete and continuous) were presented once. In subsequent test blocks, each target word in each of the manipulation conditions was repeated five times and presented in randomised order resulting in 160 data points per participant.

5.6.1.3 Statistics

All data was analysed with generalised linear mixed models, using R (R Core Team 2015) and the lme4 package (Bates et al. 2015). To analyse responses categorically, mixed logistic regression models were used with rating (question or statement) as the dependent measure. Pitch register (low vs. high), discrete peak alignment (PU vs. F), and gradual peak alignment (early vs. late), word, and mean-centred repetition were included as fixed effects. Additionally, a term for random intercepts for participants was included, which quantifies by-participant variability, as well as random slopes for the fixed effects pitch register, discrete peak alignment, and gradual peak alignment for each participant. Models including the main effect / interaction of interest were compared to the same models with no main effect / no interaction via Likelihood Ratio Tests (LRT) to determine p-values.

5.6.2 Results and discussion

Overall, participants rated the stimuli as corresponding to questions in 43% of the cases indicating a slight bias towards rating the stimuli as statements. This may be due to the declarative syntactic structure of the utterance (no interrogative marker). Regardless of this bias, there was a significant effect of pitch register ($\chi^2(1)=7.5$, p=0.006), such that items with a high pitch register were significantly more often rated as questions (58% vs. 28%). There was a significant effect of discrete peak alignment ($\chi^2(1)=8.9$, p=0.003), as well, such that items with the f0

5.6 Perception study

peak on the final syllable were significantly more often rated as questions than statements (61% vs. 25%). Gradual peak alignment did not have a significant effect on ratings. F0 peaks early in a respective syllable were rated as corresponding to questions comparably as often as f0 peaks late in the respective syllable (44% vs. 41%) ($\chi^2(1)$=1.16, p=0.28, cf. Table 5.9).

Table 5.9: Mean proportions of question ratings as a function of pitch register (low vs. high) and peak alignment (discrete and gradual).

Register	Discrete Alignment	Gradual Alignment	Responses		
Low	PU	early	0.16	0.15	0.28
		late	0.14		
	F	early	0.46	0.40	
		late	0.33		
High	PU	early	0.31	0.36	0.58
		late	0.41		
	F	early	0.82	0.79	
		late	0.77		

Figure 5.12 illustrates the overall results (left panel) and the listener-specific results (right panels) for pitch register and discrete peak alignment. As can be seen, the overall effects of register and discrete alignment appear to be additive, with a final pitch peak in a high register being the preferred question type, and a penultimate pitch peak in a low register being the least preferred question type.

However, there appears to be no clear-cut distinction between questions and statements. Even the least preferred intonational pattern for questions (low register and pitch peak on PU) shows a considerable amount of question ratings (14%). Even though these general trends are statistically generalisable, there is a considerable amount of variation across listeners. Consider the listener-specific patterns in Figure 5.12 (right panels). Most listeners show a clear bias towards rating the high register condition as more likely to be a question (black lines are above the grey lines). In fact, some listeners show almost no question ratings when the register is low (listeners 2 and 5). Listeners 6, 8, and 9, however, seem to show a much weaker effect of pitch register. With regard to timing differences, most listeners show a clear bias towards rating sentences with the pitch peak

5 The intonation of questions and contrastive focus in Tashlhiyt

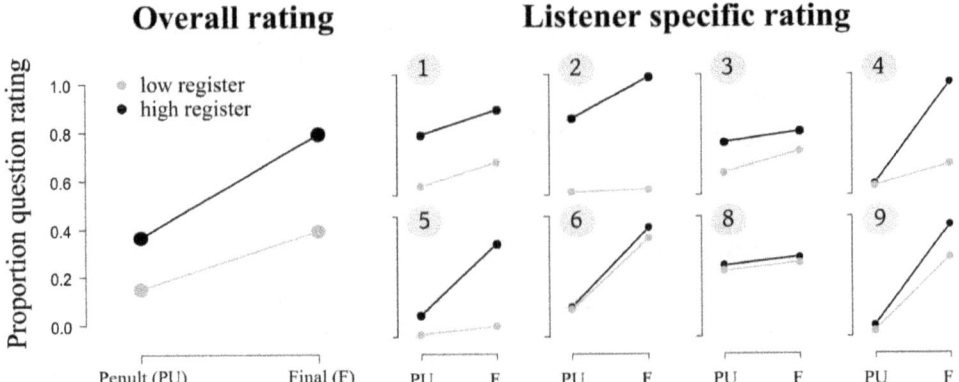

Figure 5.12: Ratings as a function of pitch register (low vs. high) and discrete peak alignment (in PU and F, respectively). Left panel displays overall results. Right panels display results for each listener individually (listener 7 was excluded as mentioned above).

aligned within the final syllable more likely to be a question than statements. Some listeners show almost no question ratings for pitch peaks aligned with the penult and, conversely, almost no statement ratings for pitch peaks aligned with the final syllable (listeners 4, 5, and 9). This effect appears to interact with register: the preference for questions with a pitch peak in the final syllable is stronger for the high register condition, as is very clearly illustrated by the patterns displayed by listeners 2, 4, and 5.

To sum up, two main factors are identified that affect the perception of morphosyntactically ambiguous sentences. First, contours in a high pitch register are perceived more frequently as questions than contours in a low register. This matches the strong pitch register differences found in the production study discussed in §5.4. Second, contours with pitch peaks on the final syllable are perceived more frequently as questions than contours with pitch peaks on the penult. However, even contours with a pitch peak on the penult appear to be acceptable contours for questions, reflecting the variation in pitch peak placement found in the production experiment. More gradual differences in tonal alignment within the syllable did not affect ratings. This null result could be due to the nature of the experimental design. Since both pitch register and discrete alignment are perceptually very prominent and represent sufficient cues to perform the task, listeners may not pay attention to subtle alignment differences. The present results are clear evidence for the rather discrete nature of peak alignment in our data. The relative peak delay is not as relevant as the position of the peak in a particular syllable.

As has been acknowledged, the low pitch target preceding the peak was set at the offset of /inna/, and the low pitch target after the peak was set to the end of the utterance. This alignment results in asymmetries in the steepness of rises and falls, across alignment conditions, with shallow rises and steep falls in peaks on the final syllable and steep rises and shallow falls in peaks on the penult. This potentially confounds the manipulation of the actual peak position (cf. Figure 5.11). Thus, the results could be interpreted as shallow rises and steep falls being more likely to be interpreted as questions than steep rises and shallow falls. The present investigation cannot rule out that the shape of the rise-fall affects listener ratings, but there are two arguments counter to this interpretation. This interpretation is not in line with the production results: rises in questions are consistently produced with substantially larger pitch excursions than statements. At the same time, the rise in pitch appears to start roughly at the same time across questions and statements. Taken together, these patterns result in substantially steeper rises in questions than in statements. Moreover, since falls are frequently truncated, the perceptual relevance of the fall is generally questionable.

5.7 Summary

The present chapter has explored the acoustic parameters associated with the distinction between contrastive statements and questions on the one hand, and information-requesting y/n questions and confirmation-seeking echo questions on the other. Production data revealed that, compared to statements, questions (a) had a higher pitch level and a greater pitch range, and (b) were more often realised with the pitch peak on the final syllable. In statements, the pitch peak occurred more often on the penult. Furthermore, there was a tendency for (c) the pitch peak in questions to be realised later within the syllable than in statements. Comparing questions types, echo questions were found to have a lower pitch level than y/n questions and a higher pitch level than corresponding statements. Other than that, the two question types revealed comparable pitch ranges and comparable peak alignment patterns.

The pitch register differences were consistent within and across speakers and appear to be a robust cue for disambiguating questions from statements, in both production and perception. In terms of pitch peak alignment there was a significant difference across sentence modalities in production. The perception results showed that listeners use pitch peak alignment in discrete terms (i.e. syllable-based alignment) to guide their perception of sentence modality, although pitch peaks in both syllable positions (on penult or final syllable) are acceptable locations for the pitch peak in both questions and statements.

5 The intonation of questions and contrastive focus in Tashlhiyt

Apart from this systematic correlation of tonal placement and sentence modality, there was considerable variation in peak alignment, both within and across speakers. Additional evidence presented by Grice, Ridouane & Roettger (2015) revealed that lexically determined segmental factors such as syllable weight of the final syllable and the sonority of syllable nuclei were relevant determinants of tonal placement. The investigated tones prefer to be realised on heavy syllables and sonorous elements. While syllables in other languages such as German or English usually contain at least a sonorant consonant, Tashlhiyt allows any type of segment in syllable nucleus position. The question arises as to how tones align with the segmental material when there are no sonorants available in the tone bearing word. The following chapter will explore these cases in detail.

6 Tonal placement in adverse phonological environments

6.1 Introduction

Tonal placement in words containing vowels and sonorant consonants is to some extent systematic, but, at the same time, characterised by a high degree of variability. On the one hand, the data suggest a systematic alignment of the pitch peak with a certain structural unit (here the syllable nucleus). On the other hand, the choice of which syllable nucleus the pitch peak co-occurs with is prone to a vast amount of variability. Beyond words containing vowels and sonorant consonants, Tashlhiyt offers the rare possibility to look at tonal placement in absence of voiced material. Although there is much cross-linguistic work on tonal placement in contexts that are impoverished in terms of voiced material (cf. Chapter 2), these contexts usually contain at least a short vowel to carry parts of the tonal movement. The present chapter will explore tonal placement in words where sonorant material is completely absent, i.e. in words that are comprised of obstruents only.

The chapter is structured as follows. First, we will present a qualitative exploration of tonal placement in words containing obstruents only based on Grice et al.'s findings (2015) (§6.2). We will show that there are three different patterns: the pitch peak either remains unrealised (no noticeable pitch movement), occurs on the vowel of the preceding word, or, crucially, occurs on a non-lexical central vowel. This central vowel will be henceforth referred to as schwa. In the last two decades, schwa in Tashlhiyt has been subject to extensive debates with regard to its linguistic status (or the lack thereof). After reviewing the literature surrounding the debate on schwa (§6.3), we will present evidence that sheds new light on schwa and its role within Tashlhiyt's linguistic system (§6.4). Finally, we will discuss the results in light of the available literature and conclude with a revised evaluation of the status of schwa in Tashlhiyt (§6.5).

6 Tonal placement in adverse phonological environments

6.2 Tonal placement in absence of sonorants

Grice, Ridouane & Roettger (2015) report on tonal placement on target words containing neither a lexical vowel nor a sonorant consonant (e.g. /tḅ.dġ/ 'she was wet'). These words exhibited an exceptional degree of variability resulting in tonal placement patterns that diverged considerably from words with sonorants. Three patterns were observed: first, in some utterances the pitch peak remained unrealised (no noticeable pitch movement). This is henceforth referred to as 'no surfacing tone'. Second, the pitch peak was produced on the vowel in the previous word, i.e. on /a/ of /inna/. This pattern is henceforth referred to as 'anticipated tone'. Thirdly, the pitch peak was sometimes realised on a schwa-like non-lexical vowel in word-medial or word-final position. This pattern is henceforth referred to as 'tone on schwa'. Which pattern was used was to some extent speaker dependent. However, all speakers showed instances of all three patterns and all three patterns were found for both questions and contrastive statements. The schematic representation of these strategies is displayed in Figure 6.1 and production examples are illustrated in Figure 6.2 and Figure 6.3.

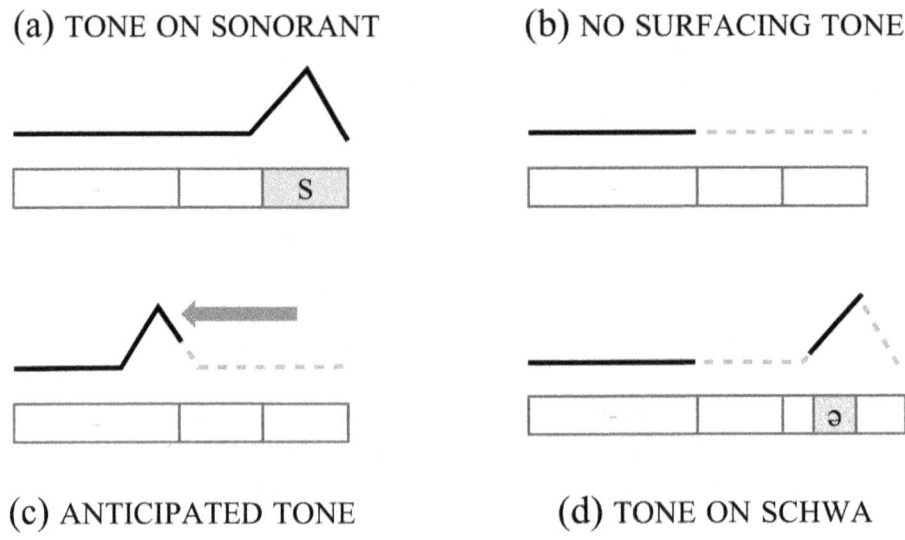

Figure 6.1: Schematic representation of tonal placement patterns observed in phrase-final words with a sonorant nucleus (a) and with obstruent nuclei only (b-d). In (b) the pitch peak is not realised; in (c) the pitch peak is realised on the final vowel of the preceding word; and in (d) the pitch peak surfaces on a schwa.

6.2 Tonal placement in absence of sonorants

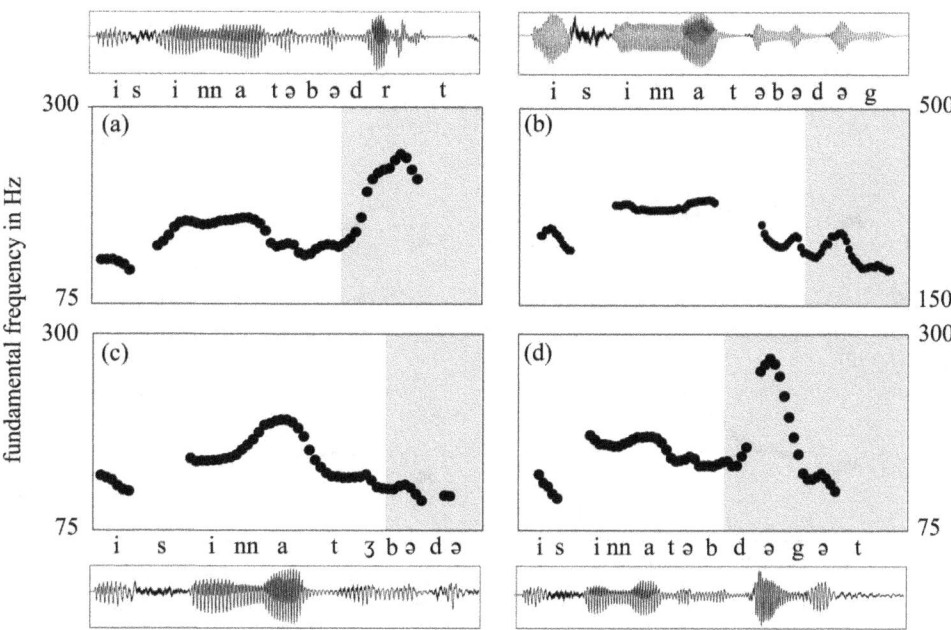

Figure 6.2: Representative waveforms and f0 contours of y/n questions /is inna (a) tbdr, (b) tbdg, (c) tjbd, (d) tbdgt/ 'Did he say 'she mentioned', 'she was wet', 'she pulled', 'you were wet'? (a) illustrates an utterance with a sonorant nucleus (/r/); (b) illustrates a production without any residual of the pitch peak; (c) illustrates a production of the pitch peak being anticipated and realised on the preceding word; (d) illustrates a production of the pitch peak being realised on a schwa. Final syllables are highlighted in grey.

As can be seen in Figure 6.2b, when the phrase-final word does not contain a sonorant, the pitch peak can remain unrealised exhibiting no noticeable pitch peak (no surfacing tone). Importantly, the target word (/tḅ.dġ/ 'she was wet') contains voiced segments and it even surfaces frequently with schwa-like elements between consonants. Thus, phonetically, the word is able to carry a tonal movement.[1]

In the anticipated tone pattern, the tone was shifted to the left resulting in the pitch peak occurring on the final vowel of /inna/. Similar to the no surfacing tone pattern, the target word (/tj.bḍ/ 'she pulled') exhibits clear voicing, but does not bear the pitch peak (Figure 6.2c). The no surfacing tone pattern and the anticipated tone pattern were only found in utterances containing target words

---

[1] Note that the small bumps in f0 on /tbdg/ are caused by microprosodic perturbations. They do not give rise to the perception of a tonal movement (cf. respective sound files).

6 Tonal placement in adverse phonological environments

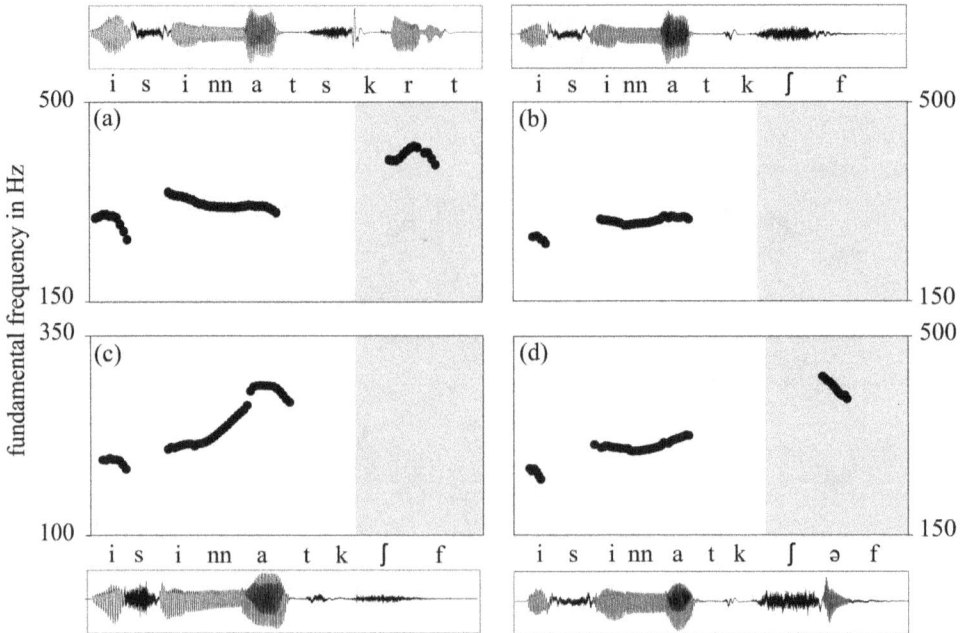

Figure 6.3: Representative waveforms and f0 contours of y/n questions: /is inna (a) tkʃf, (b-d) tskrt?/ 'Did he say 'it dried', 'you did'? (a) illustrates an utterance with a sonorant nucleus in a voiceless environment (/r/); (b) illustrates a production without any residual of the pitch peak; (c) illustrates a production of the pitch peak being anticipated and realised on the preceding word; (d) illustrates a production of the pitch peak being (partly) realised on a schwa. Final syllables are highlighted in grey.

comprised of obstruents only. It is never observed in utterances with target words containing sonorants.

In the tone on schwa pattern, the pitch peak was realised on a schwa-like non-lexical vowel (Figure 6.2d). Although it is not the final vocoid in the word, schwa between /d/ and /g/ carries significant parts of the rise-fall in pitch. The same patterns of tonal placement are found for phrase-final words containing voiceless obstruents only, as illustrated in Figure 6.3.

Most importantly, in words containing only voiceless obstruents, the anticipated tone and the presence of a schwa were mutually exclusive, i.e. when the pitch peak was anticipated, no schwa occurred in the target word; and vice versa, if there was a schwa in the target word, it carried the pitch peak. Thus, tonal placement in voiceless environments exhibits a discrete alternation dependent on the availability of a schwa. This suggests a structural function of this schwa.

However, as certain authors have argued, the phonological status of schwa in Tashlhiyt is questionable. The placement of tones on schwa and, in turn, its linguistic status appears to be a key in understanding tonal placement in its entirety. Thus, the following section will summarise the literature on this topic.

6.3 The status of schwa in Tashlhiyt: a review

Schwa and its role in the phonological system of Tashlhiyt has sparked a heated debate lasting for over two decades. Coleman (1996; 1999; 2001) considers schwa as a phonological element epenthesised by the phonological component to repair illicit syllable structure. This account will be referred to as the 'epenthetic vowel account'. Contrary to this approach, several authors have claimed that schwa has no phonological relevance for the linguistic system whatsoever (Dell & Elmedlaoui 1985; 1996; 2002; 2008; Ridouane 2008; Fougeron & Ridouane 2008; Ridouane & Fougeron 2011). These authors treat these vocalic elements as transitional vocoids – phonetic artifacts caused by the dynamics of speech articulation. The occurrence of schwa is assumed to be largely predictable from the laryngeal and supralaryngeal specification of its consonantal environment. This account will be referred to as the 'transitional vocoid account'. The two mentioned views correspond roughly to the typology of inserted vowels proposed by Hall (2006) which assumes a clear-cut division between inserted vowels that are phonological units and those that are not. This assumption is based on traditional linguistic models that consider 'phonetics' and 'phonology' as separable subsystems. More recent models incorporate distributions of variation that do not require such a categorical distinction between phonetics and phonology. For the sake of discussing the relevant literature, we will stick to the categorical view put forward by the involved authors. The epenthetic vowel account and the transitional vocoid account differ mainly in their predictions with regard to schwa's interaction with phonological patterns and its distribution within the word. In the following, both accounts will be discussed and compared.

6.3.1 The epenthetic vowel account

Coleman (1996, 1999, 2001) treats interconsonantal schwas as epenthetic segments, interpreting syllabic consonants in Dell and Elmedlaoui's model (e.g., /b̩/ and /g̩/ in /tb̩.dg̩/ 'she was wet') as sequences of a phonological schwa plus consonant (/təb.dəg/). In his model, epenthetic schwas are expected to occur in any syllable nucleus position that is not occupied by one of the lexical vowels /a, i, u/.

6 Tonal placement in adverse phonological environments

Schwa is argued either to acoustically surface as a central vowel (as in the case of [təbdəg]), or not to surface due to articulatory overlap of adjacent consonantal gestures. According to Coleman, the assumed underlying schwa in the first syllable in /təs.ti/ 'she selected' does not surface because it is completely overlapping with the surrounding consonants resulting in [tsti]. This leaves differing acoustic realisations to variability in the phonetic implementation of the epenthetic vowel.

The most important arguments in favour of this analysis come from the acoustic study presented in Coleman (2001). He analysed recordings of one Tashlhiyt speaker producing 654 target words in a carrier phrase (/ini za TARGET tklit ad'n'i(n')/ 'please say TARGET again'). He counted the occurrences of schwa and measured duration and the first three formants (among other parameters). First, Coleman compared how well his account predicted the presence of schwa in comparison to a phonetic account (concretely referring to Dell & Elmedlaoui 1996). Comparing the goodness-of-fit between the observed distribution of schwa and their expected occurrence according to the two models, Coleman reports on slightly better fits of his model compared to Dell and Elmedlaoui's model. Coleman further discusses cases of schwa that are problematic for Dell and Elmedlaoui's account. For instance, he reports on productions of a schwa in word-final position (e.g. [tbdgə]). This word-final schwa can obviously not be considered as a mere transition between consonantal gestures but, according to Coleman, can be considered as a realisation of a syllable nucleus in word-final position. In addition to distributional arguments, he claims that the quality of schwa is, while highly dependent on its consonantal context, not entirely predictable by adjacent consonants.

To summarise Coleman's position in this debate, he considers neither the presence of schwa nor its acoustic properties as entirely predictable from the consonantal environment. Even though he admits that Tashlhiyt has syllabic consonants at the phonetic surface, he considers it as not necessary to treat them as phonological syllable nuclei. He concludes that schwa elements are better explained as acoustic reflexes of syllable nuclei not occupied by lexical vowels.

6.3.2 The transitional vocoid account

Opposed to Coleman's view, a number of authors have argued that schwa is not a phonological element but a mere epiphenomenon of the coordination of oral and laryngeal gestures. Support for this view can be subsumed under two types of arguments, phonological and distributional in nature.

6.3 The status of schwa in Tashlhiyt: a review

6.3.2.1 Phonological arguments

Tashlhiyt Berber has a strong musical tradition. One particular type of verse form is the 'Rrways' (cf. Schuyler 1979). One characteristic of Rrways is the uniformity of lines, in other words, all lines are sung to the same tune, resulting in lines with identical metre. A metre is defined as a specified sequence of two types of syllables: light syllables, defined as syllables lacking a coda consonant (e.g. /ma/) and heavy syllables, defined as syllables with a coda consonant (e.g. /mat/).

(1) a. tʃ ʃit tswit
        tʃ. ʃi.(t)ts.wit
        'you have enough to eat and to drink'
     b. tlsit dʒin
        tl.si.td.ʒin
        'you wear Jean's trousers'
     c. tasit lquq
        ta.si.tl.quq
        'you have a girlfriend'
     d. ma ssul trit
        ma.(s)su.lt.rit
        'what else do you want?'

The four lines in (1) have the same meter characterised by a sequence of three light syllables followed by one heavy syllable (cf. Table 6.1, taken from Ridouane 2008). If one compares the syllables across the first column of Table 6.1, it becomes apparent that syllables containing two consonants such as in line (a) and (b) (/tʃ/ and /tl/) pattern with CV syllables such as in line (c) and (d) (/ta/ and /ma/). In other words, a sequence of two consonants, analysed by Dell and Elmedlaoui as an open syllable with a consonant in nucleus position, is considered metrically equivalent to a sequence of a consonant plus vowel, constituting a light syllable. On the other hand, consider the possibility that syllables containing two adjacent consonants contain a schwa, illustrated in line (a2) and (b2) (cf. Table 6.1).

Syllables like /t(ə)ʃ/ and /t(ə)l/ cannot be counted as heavy syllables because they pattern metrically with CV syllables like /ta/ and /ma/ and the insertion of an actual heavy syllable at this position would lead to the ill-formedness of the tune. Instead, these syllables have to be treated as light syllables. Alternatively, in Coleman's account, schwa has to be considered the only phonological element that does not contribute to syllable weight in the context of versification. As

6 Tonal placement in adverse phonological environments

Table 6.1: Metrical analysis of the verses in (1) as described in Ridouane (2008: 352) and the corresponding analysis based on Coleman's account (a2-d2) which assumes a schwa in nucleus position. Cells a2-b2 (indicated by a an asterisk) in the first columns and cells a2-d2 in the third columns illustrate mismatches of assumed phonological structures and meter in the epenthetic vowel account.

		light	light	light	heavy
according to DE (2002)	a	tʃ	ʃi	(t)ts	wit
	b	tl	si	td	ʒin
	c	ta	si	tl	quq
	d	ma	su	lt	rit
according to Coleman (2001)	a2	təʃ*	ʃi	(t)təs*	wit
	b2	təl*	si	təd*	ʒin
	c2	ta	si	təl*	quq
	d2	ma	su	lət*	rit

opposed to consonants and the bona fide vowels /i, u, a/, schwa would be an element to which the versification is blind (cf. Dell & Elmedlaoui 2002; Ridouane 2008).

Similar evidence for the lack of metrical visibility of schwa comes from the causative formation in Tashlhiyt (Jebbour 1996; 1999). The causative is formed by prefixing either /s-/ or /ss-/ to the verb stem. According to Jebbour, the choice between the singleton and the geminate prefix depends on the moraic structure of the word. He proposes that every monomoraic verb base receives /ss-/ and every polymoraic base receives /s-/. Monomoraic bases consist of either one open syllable (e.g. /nu/ 'to cook' or /fl/ 'to leave') or one closed syllable with a consonantal nucleus (e.g. /rġl/ 'to lock'). Polymoraic bases consist of one closed syllable with a vowel in nucleus position (e.g. /mun/ 'to accompany') or more than one syllable. Again, assuming a schwa in nucleus position for e.g. /fl/, i.e. assuming /fəl/ (following Coleman 2001), schwa would not contribute to the number of moras. Note that Jebbour's account to prosodic structure of words is somewhat incompatible with the rather simple account to versification proposed above, in which no distinction is made between syllables with a consonant and a vowel in nucleus position.

These metrical arguments, however, are not necessarily conclusive arguments against the epenthetic vowel account. As Hall (2006: 397) acknowledges, metrical evidence is the least reliable evidence for or against the phonological status of

6.3 The status of schwa in Tashlhiyt: a review

an inserted vowel. She discusses cases in which an inserted vowel exhibits prototypical properties of a phonological vowel while, at the same time, it is invisible to the metrical system with regard to stress assignment.

In addition to metrical arguments, there are phonological alternations that provide further evidence for the non-phonological status of schwa (Ridouane 2008). In a variety of Tashlhiyt spoken in the Anti-Atlas, the coronal stops /t, d/ surface as [s, z] when separated by one of the lexical vowels /i, a, u/ (Boukous, 1994, /tir.ʁi/ [sirʁi] 'heat'). This alternation does not occur when the coronal stop immediately precedes another coronal consonant (e.g. /tr.ʁa/ *[srʁa] 'it is hot', examples from Ridouane 2008: 352f.). If schwa is a phonological entity, it should interact with this process. According to the epenthetic schwa account (Coleman 2001), /tr.ʁa/ should be phonologically represented as /tər.ʁa/ resulting in /t/ and /r/ not being adjacent and, in turn, enabling the assibilation process. This is not the case. Again, as opposed to the lexical vowels /i, u, a/, assibilation would be blind to schwa.

In sum, both metrical patterns in versification, metrical patterns in causative formation, and assibilation processes do not treat schwa like lexical vowels.

6.3.2.2 Distributional arguments

The second type of argument for the non-phonological nature of schwa is based on the distribution of schwa within the word. In a direct response to Coleman, Dell & Elmedlaoui (2002) give two important arguments counter to his account (pp. 178-187). First, there is a general disparity of observed schwa and predicted schwa in Coleman's account. Dell and Elmedlaoui discuss the example /ts.bʁt/ 'you painted', which sometimes surfaces acoustically as [tsəbʁt]. The position of schwa, however, is not compatible with Coleman's analysis in which schwas are expected between /t/ and /s/ as well as /b/ and /ʁ/, respectively (/təs.bəʁt/). Second, Coleman predicts less schwa than is actually observed. Take for example the word /tbdgt/ 'you were wet'. According to native speakers, this word is disyllabic, thus Coleman would assume this word to be represented phonologically as /təb.dəgt/. However, in careful speech, it surfaces often as [təbədəgət]. Coleman therefore must assume two different types of schwa: one phonological schwa that occupies the syllable nucleus position and one phonetic schwa with no relevance for the phonological component. We will come back to this assumption below.

Following up on these arguments, Ridouane (2008) conducted production experiments in order to instrumentally substantiate earlier claims made by Dell and Elmedlaoui. He reports on a production study, in which six native speakers read entirely voiceless words produced either in isolation (e.g. /ftχt/ 'roll it') or in the carrier sentence /inna jas TARGET jat twalt/ 'he told him TARGET once'. Counting the number of occurrences of schwa in his corpus, he observed 18% instances of schwa in voiceless words produced in isolation (79/432) and 4% instances of schwa in voiceless words produced in the carrier phrase (19/432). Interestingly, the majority of observed schwas were word-final schwas (84/98, e.g. [ftχtə]) as opposed to word-medial ones (14/98, e.g. [ftəχt]). The distribution and position of these schwas were highly variable both within- and across speakers. Crucially, Ridouane argued that the distribution of these schwas is largely incompatible with Coleman's account. In addition to the fact that there are generally few schwas to start with, he argued that those few schwas that do occur are mostly not adjacent to assumed nuclei positions in which Coleman would predict them.

Ridouane concluded that schwa is merely an epiphenomenon of the dynamics of speech articulation exhibiting no phonological status. This conclusion was further corroborated by subsequent experiments: Ridouane & Fougeron (2011) recorded five native speakers reading 31 words of the form C_1C_2VC, varying in the laryngeal specification (voiced vs. voiceless) and the manner of articulation (stop vs. fricative) of both C_1 and C_2. Stimuli were embedded in the carrier phrase /inna TARGET jat twalt/ 'he said TARGET once'. Results showed that at least two conditions should be met for what they refer to as a voiced transitional vocoid to surface acoustically: (1) the vocal tract has to be sufficiently open during the transition from one consonant configuration to the next, and (2) at least one of the consonants in the sequence should be voiced.

These studies have demonstrated that the investigated transitional vocoids are highly predictable from the laryngeal and supralaryngeal specification of the consonantal environment. The authors consider schwa to be a result of gestural underlap, i.e. adjacent consonantal gestures are not entirely overlapping. Consider, for example, the cluster [dg] illustrated in Figure 6.4.

The articulation of the [dg] cluster is characterised by two constriction gestures: the tongue tip reaches its constriction target at the alveolar ridge for [d], after which the constriction is released and the tongue body moves towards the velar region reaching a new constriction target for the [g]. The release of the first constriction has to be timed with respect to the second constriction. If the release of the first constriction takes place well before reaching the second constriction target at the velar region (cf. Figure 6.4a), there is a gestural underlap. The tongue tip has moved away from the alveolar ridge and the tongue body has not yet reached the target at the velar region. During a short period of time the

6.3 The status of schwa in Tashlhiyt: a review

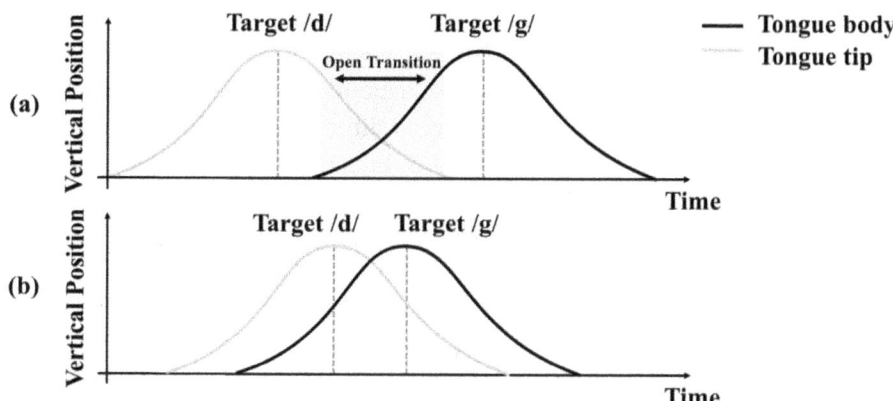

Figure 6.4: Schematic representation of the time course of articulating the cluster [dg]. In (a) there is a large lag between the constriction target of /d/ and the constriction target of /g/ resulting in an open transition. In (b), there is no open transition because the constriction targets are reached shortly after each other.

vocal tract is relatively open, i.e. air can flow through the vocal tract without hindrance. The resulting open transition is accompanied by vocal fold vibration resulting in an articulatory configuration that is characteristic for vowels. The acoustic consequence is a short vowel-like articulation.[2]

Alternatively, the consonants can overlap substantially (Figure 6.4b). The second constriction target is reached shortly after the first constriction target leaving not enough space for an open transition. Consequently, no vowel-like articulation is observed. This articulatory account is further supported by Ridouane & Fougeron's (2011) reanalysis of articulatory data presented in Fougeron & Ridouane (2008). In words with an acoustic schwa, they found less overlap of consonantal gestures than in words without a schwa. The discussed articulatory account is able to capture the distributional constraints discussed in Ridouane & Fougeron (2011). However, their account is not able to explain certain aspects of the observed data. First, it does not explain the occurrence of schwa in entirely voiceless words as reported by Ridouane (2008; see also Louali & Puech 2000).

---

[2] The reason for gestural underlap in Tashlhiyt might lay in the need of perceptual recoverability. In a consonant-heavy language like Tashlhiyt, consonants bear a high functional load and many acoustic cues to e.g. the place of articulation are found in the release of the consonant (Householder Jr. 1956; Malécot 1958; Wang 1959; Fujimura, Macchi & Streeter 1978; Ohala 1990). Overlapping constriction gestures decrease the number of acoustic cues available to distinguish the segments and, in turn, lead to diminished perceptual recoverability.

6 Tonal placement in adverse phonological environments

If schwa was only an epiphenomenon of the laryngeal and oral specification of adjacent consonants, a voiced transitional vocoid is not expected to surface in voiceless environments. Second, from an articulatory point of view which only considers the timing of oral gestures, it is difficult to explain the presence of schwa in absolute final position (Louali & Puech 2000; Ridouane 2008). Third, this account does not explain the observed asymmetry between target words produced in isolation and target words produced in carrier phrases (Ridouane 2008).

In sum, even though some of the arguments for one or the other account appear to capture some facts about schwa, neither account can explain all distributional properties of those vocalic elements. The epenthetic vowel account cannot account for certain phonological regularities that are blind to the proposed epenthesised vowels. The transitional vocoid account has to face unresolved distributional anomalies that cannot be accounted for straightforwardly by a phonetic view that is based on supralaryngeal gestural coordination only.

6.4 Production study

While the accounts presented above took only segmental and lower prosodic domains into account, aspects of higher prosodic domains were so far ignored. Yet, aspects of phrase-level prosodic organisation may be able to shed some more light on schwa and its role in Tashlhiyt's phonological system. In the following, additional data from the reading task corpus introduced in Chapter 5 is analysed. The presence, distribution, and acoustic salience of schwa is explored as a function of prosodic and intonational context.

6.4.1 Method

Four sentence modalities were elicited in a reading task as discussed in detail in Chapter 5. For more details about the participants and the procedure, see section §5.4. Relevant details of the speech material, the procedure, and the analysis are repeated here. A mock dialogue was produced with the target word in phrase-final position (2) and phrase-medial position followed by an adverb (3).

(2)   a.   is inna **tfsχt**?
             'Did he say 'you cancelled'?'
       b.   ur inna **tfsχt**.
             'He did not say 'you cancelled'.'

c. inna ʃtf.
   'He said 'crush'.'

d. manik? inna ʃtf? irwas.
   'How? He said 'crush'? It seems like it.'

(3) inna ʃtf abadan
    'He said 'crush' always.'

In (2a) the target word is in a y/n question. In (b) the same target word is in a negative assertion. Because of the preceding negation, a different target word is explicitly corrected in a contrastive statement in (c). Finally, in (d), the proposition in the contrastive statement is called into question in the counter-expectational echo question. Eight different target words consisting exclusively of voiceless obstruents were embedded in these sentences (see Table 6.2) resulting in overall 72 data points per speaker (overall 720).

Table 6.2: Target words and translations of production study.

Target word	Translation
ʃʃ	'eat'
ʃtf	'crush'
ftχ	'roll'
tctft	'you crushed'
tfss	'she is quiet'
tfsxt	'you cancelled'
tkʃf	'it dried'
tsxf	'she fades away'

All acoustic materials were manually segmented and annotated as described in 5.4.1. The present analysis focuses on the presence of schwa. In most cases, this element was acoustically straightforward to identify (cf. Figure 6.5, Figure 6.6, and Figure 6.7, as well as corresponding sound files). In fact, it resembled acoustic realisations of lexical vowels with regard to duration and intensity. In less straightforward cases, a liberal approach of operationalising schwa was adopted. Schwa was labelled as any interval presenting periodic vibrations accompanied by a local increase in the signal energy at the consonantal release, and/or any interval after the consonantal release with formant structure or energy in the F2/F3 region characteristic of vowels.

6 Tonal placement in adverse phonological environments

As described in 5.4.1, productions with hesitation, unnatural phrasing patterns, and mispronunciations of the segmental material were excluded from the analyses. The amount of excluded data was substantially higher than in cases of target words containing vowels and sonorant consonants. As mentioned earlier, Tashlhiyt speakers are not used to reading aloud in their language. While care was taken to familiarise speakers with the words before the experiment, they still produced a substantial amount of mispronunciations. Only 573 of 720 utterances could be included in the statistical analysis corresponding to a data loss of 20.4%.[3]

Data was statistically analysed using R (R Core Team 2015). Besides descriptive exploration of the data, the following aspects of the data set determined the choice of statistical method used here. First, the data was not intended to investigate schwa. Schwa was not expected in voiceless environments and the large number of words containing schwa came as a surprise. Second, the design was not entirely balanced (and became even less balanced due to the large amount of asymmetric data loss). Taking these factors together, it is refrained from applying statistical methods concerned with hypothesis testing. Instead, a data exploration account is taken to shed light on patterns underlying the data.

To that end, random forests analyses are applied (Breiman 2001), implemented by the party package (Hothorn et al. 2006; Strobl et al. 2007; 2008) in R (R Core Team 2015). For a discussion of these techniques in the context of linguistics, see Tagliamonte & Baayen (2012). Random forests analysis is a data mining technique used for classification. It is a so-called "ensemble method". A multitude of decision trees is constructed (500 in this case). Each tree takes a set of variables and determines which variable best splits the data according to a particular criterion. Each tree is built on a random subset of variables and data. The final classification is based on the overall ensemble of trees.

6.4.2 Results and discussion

6.4.2.1 General observations

Overall, there was an unexpectedly large amount of schwas, with 57% of all voiceless words containing schwa. In words with schwa, there was almost exclusively only a single schwa. Schwa further occurs in all sentence modalities. Figure 6.5

---

[3] Despite methodological efforts, the relatively large number of exclusions is probably still an artefact of speakers being unpractised readers of Tashlhiyt. The remaining productions, however, were judged to be natural-sounding utterances expressing the intended communicative function by independent Tashlhiyt speakers who did not participate in the experiments.

illustrates schwas in phrase-final words for y/n questions, negative assertions, and contrastive statements. Figure 6.6 illustrates schwas in phrase-medial words for contrastive statements and corresponding echo questions.

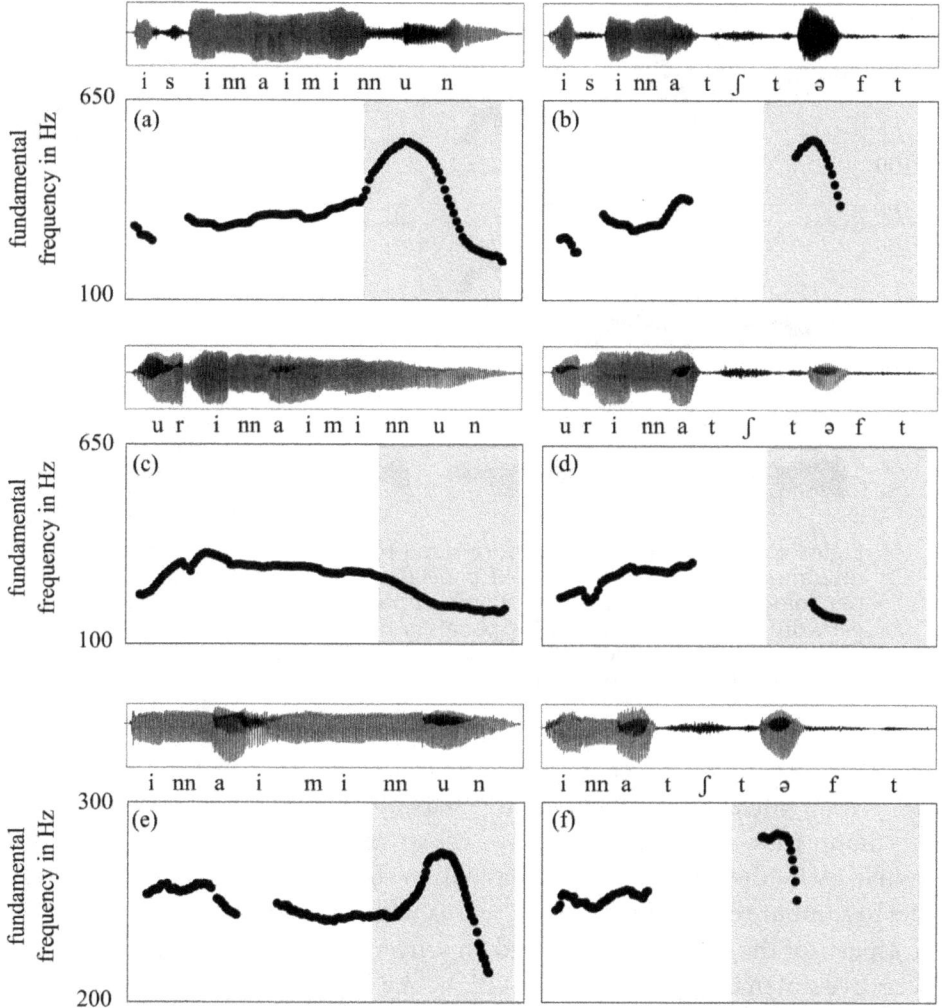

Figure 6.5: Representative waveforms and f0 contours of fully voiced utterances (target word /iminnun/, left panels) and utterances containing phonologically voiceless target words in phrase-final position (target word /tʃtft/, right panels). Top panels (a-b) display y/n questions, middle panels (c-d) display negative assertions, and bottom panels (e-f) display contrastive statements. Final syllables are highlighted in grey.

6 Tonal placement in adverse phonological environments

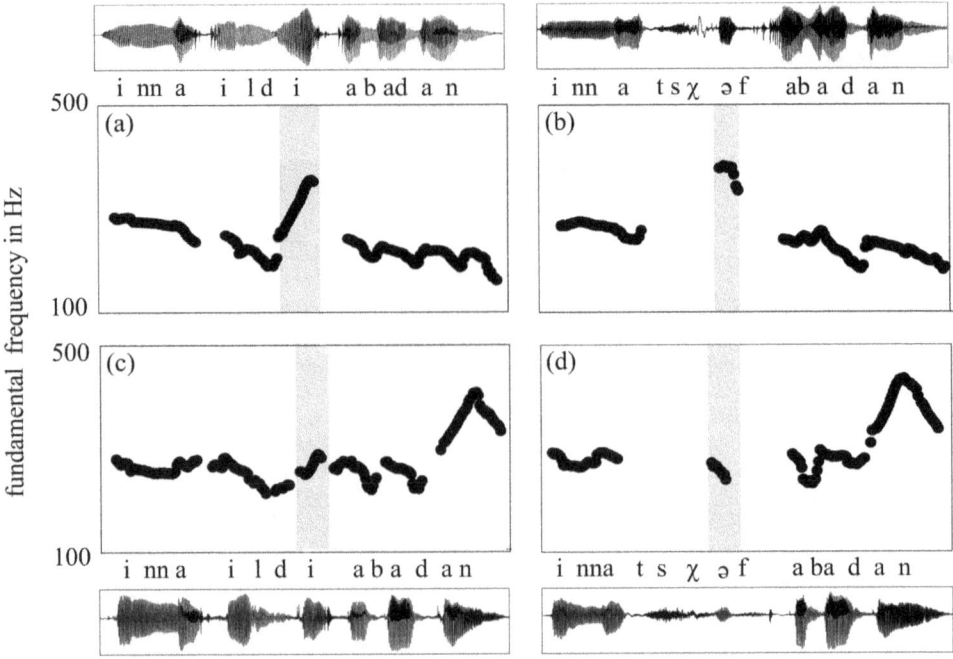

Figure 6.6: Representative waveforms and f0 contours of fully voiced utterances (target word /ildi/, left panels) and utterances containing phonologically voiceless target words in phrase-medial position (target word /tsχf/, right panels). Top panels (a-b) display contrastive statements and bottom panels (c-d) display echo questions. Final syllables of the target word are highlighted in grey.

The contours of utterances with fully voiced words and corresponding utterances with a voiceless word containing schwa sound remarkable similar. Auditory impressions of utterance pairs as illustrated in Figure 6.5 and Figure 6.6 resemble each other concerning the intonation contour. Even though large parts of the f0 contour remain unrealised in words with voiceless segments, characteristic aspects of the contour are realised on schwa. For example, in questions and contrastive statements, schwa carries a high tone often accompanied by residuals of the rise-fall. In negative assertions, schwa carries a falling movement towards a low target.

Interestingly, schwa can be realised either in word-medial position between consonants or in word-final position. When it is in word-medial position, it always occurs between the syllable onset and syllable nucleus (see also Gordon & Nafi 2012). Irrespective of its position in the word, schwa appears to carry the same characteristic aspect of the intonation contour (cf. Figure 6.7).

6.4 Production study

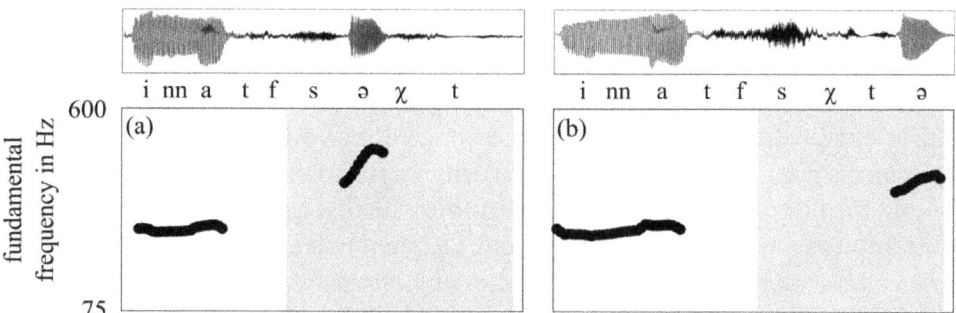

Figure 6.7: Representative waveforms and f0 contours of echo questions containing phonologically voiceless target words in phrase-final position (target word /tfsχt/). (a) illustrates schwa in word-medial position and (b) illustrates schwa in word-final position. Final syllables are highlighted in grey.

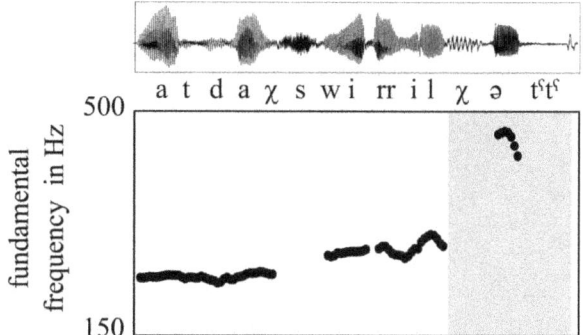

Figure 6.8: Representative waveform and f0 contour of the declarative question /ad d daχ swirriχ lxtˤtˤ/ 'I make the line go back?' The final syllable is highlighted in grey.

Before considering the quantitative aspects of this phenomenon, it is important to note that schwas carrying functionally relevant pitch movements are not restricted to elicited speech but they are also found in natural data. Figure 6.8 illustrates a declarative question ending on voiceless segments. A schwa is found between /χ/ and /tˤtˤ/ and it carries high pitch. Such patterns are quite frequently observed, especially in phrase-final position of phrases marked for non-finality.

6.4.2.2 Exploratory analysis

Random forest analyses enable us to identify which factors contribute to predicting the presence vs. absence of schwa independently, thus, accounting for

6 Tonal placement in adverse phonological environments

collinearity between factors. The following factors were included in the analysis: factors capturing idiosyncratic properties of speakers in addition to speaker origin and speaker gender, factors capturing idiosyncratic properties of words, a factor capturing differences in sentence modality (y/n question, echo question, statement, negative statement), and a factor capturing the position of the word within the utterance (phrase medial vs. phrase final). Figure 6.9 displays the variable importance estimated by the model, i.e. the relative relevance of the factors. The factors are ranked from top to bottom by importance. As can be seen, all of the factors capture some of the variance. Tables Figure 6.3 and Figure 6.4 display the observed proportions with respect to the relevant factors.

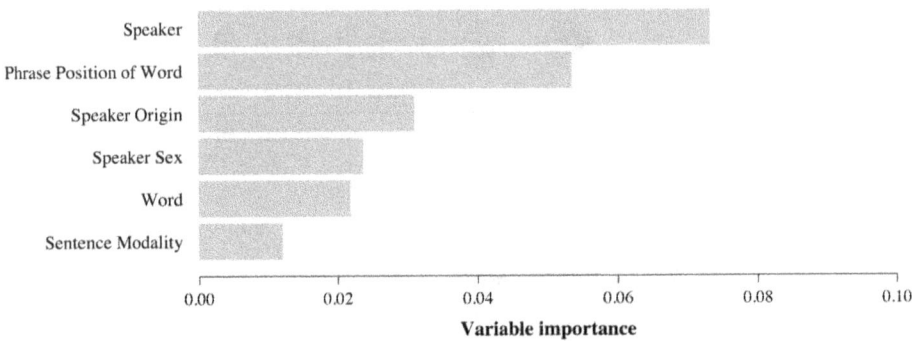

Figure 6.9: Variable importance for the prediction of schwa presence generated by the random forest analysis for all utterances containing phonologically voiceless words.

The factor capturing idiosyncratic properties of the speakers themselves is the highest ranked predictor. There are two speakers that showed no schwa (M3 and M4) while F3, for example, almost always produced a schwa. Additionally, both the area in which the speaker was brought up and the gender of the speaker explain additional variance. There is a general trend for speakers coming from rural areas (Anti-Atlas) to produce less schwa (33%) than those from urban areas (Agadir and Taroudant: 67%). Furthermore, women produce generally more schwa (77%) than men (36%) (cf. Table 6.3). According to the random forest analysis, these factors explain observed variability independently of each other. The other source of potential idiosyncratic variability is the lexical word in which schwa surfaces. As can be seen in Table 6.4, there are large differences across

6.4 Production study

Table 6.3: Mean proportions of productions exhibiting schwa averaged over words. The proportion of word-medial (CəC) and word-final schwa (Cə#) is given in relative terms.

Speaker	Schwa	Position in Word	
		CəC	Cə#
F1 (Agadir)	0.54	1.00	-
F2 (Taroudant)	0.76	0.98	0.02
F3 (Agadir)	0.97	0.98	0.02
F4 (Agadir)	0.75	0.07	0.93
F5 (Anti-Atlas)	0.87	1.00	-
M1 (Agadir)	0.44	0.04	0.96
M2 (Taroudant)	0.70	1.00	-
M3 (Anti-Atlas)	-	-	-
M4 (Anti-Atlas)	-	-	-
M5 (Agadir)	0.48	1.00	-
mean	0.57	0.67	0.33

Table 6.4: Mean proportions of productions exhibiting schwa averaged over speakers. The proportion of word-medial (CəC) and word-final schwa (Cə#) is given in relative terms.

Word	Schwa	Position in Word	
		CəC	Cə#
ʃʃ	0.20	-	1.00
ʃtf	0.56	0.60	0.40
ftχ	0.50	0.44	0.56
tʃtft	0.67	0.74	0.26
tfss	0.42	0.38	0.63
tfsχt	0.70	0.71	0.29
tkʃf	0.54	0.66	0.34
tsxf	0.53	0.68	0.32
mean	0.57	0.67	0.33

6 Tonal placement in adverse phonological environments

words. Some words are produced with schwa in two thirds of all productions (/tʃtft/ and /tfsχt/), while others are barely produced with schwa (e.g. /ʃʃ/).

Apart from idiosyncratic factors of speakers and words, phrase position has been estimated to have the second highest variable importance. Target words in phrase-final position exhibit schwa more often (64%) than target words in phrase-medial position (41%). This pattern is consistent across speakers, words, and sentence modalities. This proportional trend is reflected by durational patterns with schwa being generally longer in phrase-final words than in phrase-medial words. (cf. Table 6.5).

Table 6.5: Mean proportions of schwa and duration of schwa (in ms) for sentence modality and phrase position of the word it occurred in averaged over words and speakers.

Sentence Modality	Phrase Position	Schwa Presence		Schwa Duration	
Y/N Question	Medial	0.43	0.66	50 (12)	82 (30)
	Final	0.78		91 (28)	
Echo Question	Medial	0.33	0.55	50 (12)	83 (27)
	Final	0.64		89 (24)	
Contrastive Statement	Medial	0.67	0.73	62 (4)	81 (22)
	Final	0.76		88 (21)	
Negative Statement	Medial	0.34	0.51	55 (13)	78 (2)
	Final	0.57		82 (19)	

Even though it is the least important variable in the model, sentence modality is estimated to independently explain some of the variance. Contrastive statements exhibit the highest proportion of schwa, followed by questions, and negative statements.

Having explored potential aspects affecting the presence of schwa, we now turn to the curious divergence between schwa in word-medial and word-final position. The same factors used for the random forest analysis above were included predicting the position of schwa within the word (cf. Figure 6.10).

This model estimates that speaker information is by far the most important predictor. Apart from some indications of speaker gender and speaker origin playing a role (women = 18% word-final schwa, men = 68%; Agadir = 33% word-

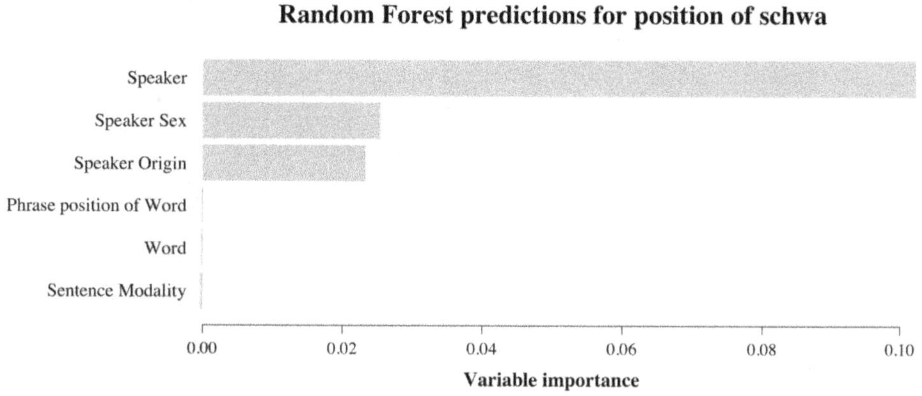

Random Forest predictions for position of schwa

Figure 6.10: Variable importance measure for the position of schwa within the word generated by the random forest analysis for all utterances containing schwa in phonologically voiceless words.

final schwa, Taroudant = 50%, Anti-Atlas = 0%), most variance is explained by speaker specific behaviour irrespective of gender and origin. Other linguistic factors appear to have no impact on the position of schwa within the word.

6.4.2.3 Summary

To sum up, the present exploration has revealed a large number of schwa in phonologically voiceless environments. Schwa appears in two particular positions in the word. It is either between the onset and nucleus of the final syllable (e.g. [tkʃəf], [tsχəf]) or in word-final position (e.g. [tkʃfə], [tsχfə]). As opposed to earlier studies (that used speakers who had lived in France for a significant amount of time), schwa is not found between syllables or between the nucleus and the coda (Grice et al. 2011; Grice, Ridouane & Roettger 2015). This rather strict appearance of schwa in a specific structural position, irrespective of the supralaryngeal properties of the consonantal environment, is remarkable and should be considered when evaluating the status of schwa in Tashlhiyt (also highlighted by Gordon & Nafi 2012). When schwa is present, it carries characteristic aspects of the tonal contour, e.g. parts of the rise-fall in questions and contrastive statements. This is the case regardless of the position of schwa, i.e. the same characteristic aspect of the contour is realised on word-medial and on word-final schwas.

6 Tonal placement in adverse phonological environments

Explorative statistical analyses reveal that the presence of schwa was to some degree predictable from the phrase position of the word in which schwa surfaced (phrase medial vs. phrase final) and sentence modality of the utterance. In addition to these linguistic factors, both the presence of schwas and the position of schwa within the word are strongly affected by properties of the speaker sample. In addition to idiosyncratic properties of each individual speaker, speaker origin, and speaker gender played a role.

6.5 The status of schwa revisited

6.5.1 Schwa as a sociolinguistic marker

Both the presence of schwa and the position of schwa within the word is prone to a large amount of both within and across speaker variation. This variation is to some degree accountable by demographic factors like the area in which the speaker was brought up and his / her gender. This is in line with the discussion of the sociolinguistic dimension of schwa by Boukous (2012). He recognised that in urban areas, children are more likely to produce a schwa between consonants, which, according to Boukous, occupies the syllable nucleus position. He attributes this feature to the strong influence of Moroccan Arabic on Tashlhiyt.

> Nous remarquons que dans les formes réalisées par les sujets appartenant au groupe des enfants ruraux, les syllabes n'ont pas de noyau vocalique alors que dans celles performées par les enfants citadins il y a insertion d'une voyelle de type schwa (ə) pour constituer le noyau de la syllabe. Cette habitude articulatoire est probablement acquise avec l'arabe dialectal car l'insertion du schwa correspond à une nécessité de la phonotaxe de l'arabe marocain [...]." (Boukous 2012: 83)[4]

Boukous already acknowledges a potential phonological status of schwa in the speech of Tashlhiyt speakers in urban areas. However, instead of being a native phenomenon, it is attributed to the contact with Moroccan Arabic. In addition to the three cardinal vowels /i, a, u/, Moroccan Arabic has a phonological schwa, the position of which can be distinctive (compare /həbs/ 'prison' and

---

[4] "We notice that in the forms realised by the subjects belonging to the group of rural children, the syllables do not have a vocalic nucleus whereas in the ones performed by the urban group of children there is an insertion of a schwa type vowel (ə) forming the nucleus of the syllable. This articulatory habit is probably acquired with dialectal Arabic because the insertion of the schwa corresponds to a phonotactic requirement of Moroccan Arabic [...] (my own translation)

/hbəs/ 'imprison'). This stands in contrast to Tashlhiyt, which does not exhibit such minimal pairs. Therefore, one should exercise caution when attributing a phonological status to schwa in Tashlhiyt simply due to the assumption that it is borrowed from a language in which schwa is a phonological element.

While Boukous does not explicitly discuss the position of schwa within the word, Ridouane (2008: 337) attributes word-medial schwas in his data to language contact with Moroccan Arabic. In light of its sociolinguistic context, it might be objected that the observed variability in the present production data is due to a heterogeneous sample, i.e. speakers from different subvarieties of Tashlhiyt (see Table 6.3 and Appendix A2.2 for an overview of speaker origins). In defence of considering the recorded speakers together as representing a single variety (see also Bruggeman, Roettger & Grice 2017) one could argue that differences between speakers from geographically distant areas do not supersede the differences between speakers with the same birthplace. Speakers who grew up in Agadir do not behave more uniformly than any other grouping of speakers. Thus, it can be concluded that the observed variability is not solely caused by the heterogeneous sample. Other demographic or sociolinguistic properties of the speakers beyond the present investigation might account for these different production patterns.

It is noteworthy that this potential contact phenomenon goes against other sociolinguistic trends. Tashlhiyt speakers (at least the educated speakers that were recorded in the present sample) are highly self-conscious of schwa not being a phoneme in Tashlhiyt. However, they are clearly aware of schwa being a phonological element in other Berber varieties and Moroccan Arabic. In other words, Tashlhiyt speakers have a high awareness of schwa being a linguistic feature that distinguishes their own language from other languages in the area. Despite this awareness, they do produce schwa in the majority of utterances. This tension between language contact and language identity may cause a high degree of variability within and across studies and might be one of the reasons why the literature was unable to settle on any consensus regarding the status of schwa.

6.5.2 Schwa as reflecting gestural reorganisation

Irrespective of schwa being to some degree dependent on speaker-specific properties, schwa is determined by prosodic and intonational properties of the utterance. Schwa occurs more often in words in phrase-final position than in phrase-medial position, irrespective of sentence modality. This is in line with Ridouane (2008) reporting on more schwa in words produced in isolation than in words inserted in carrier sentences with the target word in phrase-medial position. Additionally, looking at schwa occurrences in phrase-medial words only, one sentence modality stands out: words in contrastive statements exhibit a substantially higher proportion of schwa (67%) than questions (43/33%) and negative assertions (34%) (cf. Table 6.4). Questions are characterised by a pitch peak at the right edge of the phrase. Negations are characterised by a pitch peak at the beginning of the utterance (on /ur-/, the negative marker). In both questions and negations, there is no tonal event on the phrase-medial target word. As opposed to questions and negative assertions, contrastive statements are characterised by a tonal event on the target word in phrase-medial position. This suggests a correlation between the proportion of observed schwas and the occurrence of communicatively relevant tonal events. This correlation can be accounted for by dynamics of speech production. It is well known that elements in certain prosodically privileged position are spatio-temporally adjusted (introduced in Chapter 2 and 5). This adjustment refers either to edge-induced strengthening, e.g. final lengthening, or to prominence-induced strengthening.

For example, it has been shown that the syllable rhyme is longer in final position of prosodic constituents than in non-final position for English (e.g. Turk & Shattuck-Hufnagel 2007). In addition to temporal adjustments, elements in phrase-final position have been shown to exhibit increased jaw movement duration and decreased velocity of oral closing gestures (Beckman & Edwards 1990; Edwards, Beckman & Fletcher 1991).

Similarly, articulatory gestures may be adjusted due to prominence-induced strengthening. In many languages, certain elements of the utterances can be emphasised by intonational events. In languages with lexical word stress, pragmatically highlighted words can co-occur with a pitch accent. Research conducted mainly on languages that exhibit such pitch accents (e.g. English, French, Italian, and German) reports that the co-occurrence of a pitch accent with a syllable results in temporal and spatial expansion of the articulatory gestures involved.Cho & Keating (2009) found longer durations for /n/ and higher burst intensities for the alveolar plosive /t/ in accented position. Alongside, longer vowels, Cho & McQueen (2005) found evidence for a strengthening of fricatives and stops in accented syllables in Dutch (e.g. closure / frication duration, voicing duration, VOT). With respect to spatial properties, vowels tend to be hyperarticulated in accented position. For example, in his work on English, Cho (2005) showed that vowels in accented position were articulated with longer jaw opening gestures than respective vowels of unaccented syllables. He further showed that /a/ is consistently lowered and /i/ is consistently fronted when accented. Similarly, Harrington, Fletcher & Beckman (2000) showed that English high vowels are generally raised when accented.

6.5 The status of schwa revisited

While not explicitly tested for in the present study,[5] several indirect arguments indicate that there are similar spatio-temporal adjustments of segments as a function of their co-occurrence with a tonal event. First, several phoneticians working with the data sets presented here (the author, Grice, Bruggeman, Ridouane) perceived the syllable the tone co-occurs with as more prominent than other syllables. Of course, one has to exercise great caution when interpreting such impressionistic observations made by analysts speaking languages that have prominence-lending pitch accents.

Second, Gordon & Nafi (2012) found evidence for duration and intensity asymmetries across syllables as a function of the co-occurrence with a tone. As has been argued in Chapter 4, these asymmetries cannot be attributed to lexical stress, but can be related to the postlexical tonal events with which the segmental material co-occurs.

Third, there is some anecdotal evidence that a vowel is spatio-temporally extended when it co-occurs with a pitch peak. Grice et al. (2011) investigated the nature and distribution of phrase-medial pitch peaks in contrastive sentences for three Tashlhiyt speakers (similar to Chapter 5). In line with the findings reported on here, the contrasted element co-occurred with a rise-fall in pitch. When there was no sonorant available, the authors obtained highly variable tonal placement. They observed patterns equivalent to the anticipated tone pattern and the tone on schwa pattern discussed in section §6.2. Grice et al.'s (2011) data was recorded for an independent articulatory experiment (Hermes et al. 2011). This allowed Diercks (2011) to take a closer look at both acoustic and articulatory patterns of segments as a function of their co-occurrence with the pitch peak. Diercks looked at the productions of one speaker who revealed a high degree of variation between the anticipated tone pattern and the tone on schwa pattern. Acoustic analyses revealed that the word /inna/ was longer and that the vowel /a/ exhibited lower F1 values when co-occurring with the pitch peak (Figure 6.11, left panel). The acoustic results were reflected in the kinematic data. When /a/ co-occurred with the pitch peak, the tongue body was lower than when the vowel did not occur with the pitch peak (cf. Figure 6.11, right panel).

In line with the literature on prominence-induced strengthening (e.g. Harrington, Fletcher & Beckman 2000; Cho & Keating 2009; Mücke & Grice 2014), the rise-fall in Tashlhiyt caused spatio-temporal expansion of the segments it co-occurred with. Here the open vowel /a/ is lowered.

---

[5] Note that spatio-temporal asymmetries as a function of co-occurrence with a tonal event are empirically difficult to evaluate in Tashlhiyt, since the co-occurrence of a tone with a specific syllable is not deterministically predictable. In both Grice, Ridouane & Roettger (2015) and the present production corpus, pitch peaks on the penult and the final syllable were distributed in a very unbalanced way making a statistical assessment based on such a small sample impossible.

6 Tonal placement in adverse phonological environments

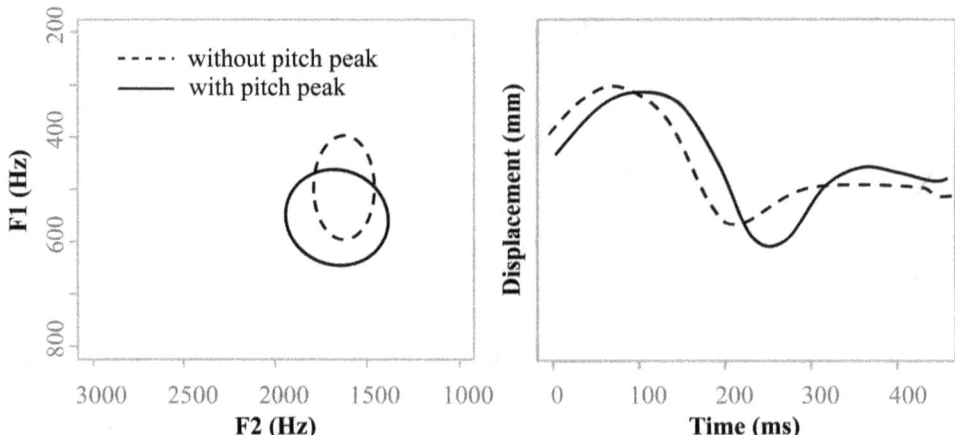

Figure 6.11: Left panel displays F1 and F2 of /a/ in /inna/ dependent on the presence of the pitch peak. Right panel displays averaged vertical trajectories of the tongue body in /inna/. Figures taken from Diercks (2011). Note: Diercks does not provide a y-axis for the displacement values.

Both edge-induced strengthening and prominence-induced strengthening can be conceptualised as a local slowing down of articulatory gestures resulting in less gestural overlap and more precise achievement of articulatory targets (Byrd & Saltzman 2003; Saltzman et al. 2008). This slowing down mechanism may explain the phrase-position dependent presence of schwa in Tashlhiyt. In both phrasal positions in which less gestural overlap is expected (phrase-final position and in those positions where a tonal event occurs phrase medially), we observe an increased proportion of schwa and an increased duration of schwa when it is present.

Prosodically triggered gestural adjustments may not only affect oral gestures, but laryngeal gestures, too. According to Ridouane, Hoole & Fuchs (2007), voiceless consonant clusters in Tashlhiyt have to be considered as sequences of multiple glottal opening gestures. Using transillumination, they measured the degree of glottal adduction during voiceless consonant clusters. They showed that in words made up of voiceless obstruents only, the glottis does not simply remain open. The glottal aperture is modulated by the segments with which it co-occurs. This is interpreted as evidence for separate glottal opening gestures that are coupled to supralaryngeal gestures. Given these findings, a slowing down of the articulation might result in less overlap of both oral and glottal opening gestures. If glottal opening gestures are sufficiently apart, glottal adduction can occur. This,

6.5 The status of schwa revisited

in turn, would lead to an articulatory configuration that gives rise to a vowel-like element, i.e. an open oral transition accompanied by glottal adduction (Goldstein 2011; 2014).

Based on these mechanisms, a voiced interval within a voiceless cluster could be attributed to a gestural reorganisation reflecting a prosodically triggered adjustment. The proposed interpretation can be considered a purely phonetic one, i.e. schwa is an artefact of the dynamic interaction of individual articulatory gestures and higher prosodic relationships. It is thus highly compatible with the transitional vocoid account. This articulatory model might even be able to account for word-final schwas: if the release of the final consonant is slowed down and remains active beyond the glottal opening gesture of the consonant, the glottis will achieve its default position in speech (adducted) before the end of the release, resulting in a voiced interval (Goldstein 2014).[6]

Importantly, the discussed model and its articulatory predictions are not only interpretable in terms of the transitional vocoid account; they are also compatible with Coleman's epenthetic vowel account. The latter explicitly assumes that a phonological schwa can be obscured by surrounding articulatory gestures. Its phonetic variability would be accounted for by the degree of gestural overlap as a function of prosodic position. According to Coleman, the assumed underlying schwa in the first syllable in /təs.ti/ does not surface acoustically because it is completely overlapped by the surrounding consonantal gestures. Similarly, one could argue that schwa usually does not surface in voiceless clusters because the glottal opening gestures of the surrounding consonants overlap heavily, which disables the voicing of schwa to surface. However, in certain prosodic positions these glottal opening gestures are pulled apart, enabling schwa to surface acoustically. The epenthetic vowel account could thus capture the asymmetries found in the present corpus just as well as the transitional vocoid account.

Neither the original epenthetic vowel account nor the original transitional vocoid account were able to explain the observed schwa asymmetries related to the phrasal context (Ridouane 2008; Gordon & Nafi 2012; the present study). However, some of those anomalies can be accounted for with the presented gestural organisation model taking into account that articulatory gestures are modulated by prosodic and intonational factors (Byrd & Saltzman 2003; Saltzman et al. 2008; Goldstein 2014). This model is compatible with schwa in voiceless environments. Even though schwa is traditionally not expected to occur in voiceless clusters, gestural reorganisation in prosodically privileged positions may lead to an un-

---

[6] It is important to note that this account is speculative and based on indirect evidence, since laryngeal gestures were not investigated directly.

6 Tonal placement in adverse phonological environments

derlap of glottal opening gestures and, in turn, may result in voicing in both word-internal and word-final position. This account, however, does not provide conclusive evidence in favour of either the epenthetic vowel account or the transitional vocoid account. To a certain degree, both accounts are compatible with the idea of gestural underlap.

Even though prosodically triggered gestural reorganisation in combination with both the epenthetic vowel account and the transitional vocoid account may explain some observations, there remain unresolved issues: neither can explain why there is a robust alternation between word-medial and word-final schwa. Crucially, these schwa locations are mutually exclusive, i.e. when a schwa occurs in word-medial position, it does not occur in word-final position and vice versa. Moreover, throughout the reading experiment, speakers use either one pattern or the other with very few exceptions. The epenthetic vowel account would have to assume that speakers differ with respect to their lexical representations. For example, while speaker F1's production [tkʃəf] would be a reflection of /tək.ʃəf/, speaker F4's production [tkʃfə] would be a reflection of /təkʃ.fə/. The alternation in this case would be at the lexical level of phonological representation rather than at the level of phonetic instantiation.

Alternatively, this alternation could be due to variable gestural reorganisation. Similar to discrete tonal alignment patterns observed in words with more than one sonorant nucleus (see Chapter 5), speakers might probabilistically produce schwa in either word-medial or word-final position dependent on sentence modality. However, individual speakers have a clear preference for either one or the other position. As the random forest analysis suggests, sentence modality does not have an impact on the choice between the two patterns at all. This alternation, therefore, is fundamentally different from the one observed for tonal placement in words containing vowels and sonorant consonants, where there is more within-speaker variation.

The production data presented in section §6.3 suggest that the alternation between word-medial and word-final schwa may be due to demographic characteristics such as gender and place of upbringing. This suggests a sociolinguistic component to schwa (see also Boukous 2012) which is not covered by any of the above discussed accounts.

In addition to speaker variability, proponents of the transitional vocoid account have criticised the epenthetic vowel account for predicting the occurrence of more schwas than actually attested as well as the occurrences of schwas in positions where they are not attested at all (see §6.3). However, the transitional vocoid account has also problems accounting for distributional facts. In the

6.5 The status of schwa revisited

present study, word-medial schwa is always found between the onset and the nucleus consonant of the final syllable (see also Gordon & Nafi 2012). This preference for a particular structural position does not follow from the transitional vocoid account, which assumes that the presence of schwa is predominantly determined by laryngeal and supralaryngeal properties. In the epenthetic vowel account, schwa is considered a phonological element that occupies an empty syllable nucleus position in syllables with no lexical vowels. This model predicts an epenthetic schwa in exactly this structural position, between the onset and the nucleus (according to Dell and Elmedlaoui's syllabification algorithm). However, one may ask the question as to why schwa in the present data only appears in the final syllable (e.g. /tk.ʃəf/) and not in the penult (e.g. /tək.ʃf/) or in both syllables (e.g. /tək.ʃəf/).

6.5.3 Schwa as a prosodic marker

In the following, we introduce a way to resolve some of the conflicts between these competing accounts: Tashlhiyt may exhibit two different types of schwa: one schwa is merely a transitional vocoid with no relevance for any phonological component whatsoever; the other is at least relevant for the alignment of intonational tones (Gordon & Nafi 2012). This dichotomy roughly matches the typology of inserted vowels proposed by Hall (2006). She has argued that there are two distinct kinds of inserted vowels (see also Harms 1976; Levin 1987; Warner et al. 2001; Silverman 2011). On the one hand, there are intrusive (or excrescent) vocoids, i.e. phonetic transitions between two consonantal gestures that do not exhibit any phonological status and are thus invisible to the phonological system. On the other hand, there are epenthetic vowels, i.e. segments that have stable forms and distributions and are visible to the phonological system.

Different types of schwa within the same language have been proposed for Ath-Sidhar Rifian, a variety of Tarifiyt Berber spoken in North-Eastern Morocco (Dell & Tangi 1985; Dell & Elmedlaoui 2002). One type of schwa in Ath-Sidhar Rifian has to be considered a transitional vocoid. This vocoid is never observed between homorganic and voiceless consonants. The other type of schwa in Ath-Sidhar Rifian is conceived of as phonologically inserted in order to syllabify sequences of consonants, similar to Coleman's proposal for Tashlhiyt. The position of such epenthetic vowels may be the only feature that distinguishes two words from each other. Moreover, they are not constrained by the consonantal environment, i.e. they can occur between homorganic and voiceless consonants. Thus, non-phonological transitional vocoids co-exist with phonological epenthetic schwas across varieties of Berber.

6 Tonal placement in adverse phonological environments

In Tashlhiyt, the presence and form of intrusive vocoids is predictable from the laryngeal and supralaryngeal consonantal environment, their presence does not add duration to the syllable, and they play no role in any aspect of the phonological system, including versification, morphological processes, and intonation (e.g. Dell & Elmedlaoui 2002; 2008; Ridouane 2008; Ridouane & Fougeron 2011). These transitional vocoids are illustrated in Figure 6.2, where there are clear instances of schwas in the target word. These elements, however, do not carry the expected tonal event. It is likely that instrumental studies on schwa such as Ridouane & Fougeron (2011), which led to convincing empirical arguments for the non-phonological status of schwa, investigated mainly these types of intrusive vocoids.

In addition to intrusive vocoids, Tashlhiyt exhibits something that may fall under the umbrella term of an 'epenthetic vowel'. To distinguish it terminologically from the elements referred to in the epenthetic vowel account, it is referred to as a 'postlexically triggered epenthetic vowel' (PTEV). Neither its form nor its presence is fully predictable from its consonantal environment. However, note that it is still determined by the consonantal environment to some degree. In the data presented here, there was no schwa in homorganic clusters and schwa did not break up geminate consonants. Despite this, the phonological system –at least the intonation system– does refer to it. The present corpus provides strong arguments for schwa being an element that bears functional load, i.e. it enables the production of a functionally relevant tonal movement. Moreover, a pitch peak before the target word is incompatible with a PTEV within the target word, indicating a strong relationship between the presence of the PTEV and the location of the tone. However, the PTEV cannot be an epenthetic vowel that is always eligible for tonal alignment; it is rather occasionally inserted to serve as a landing site for a communicatively relevant tone. Interestingly, there are several reports on similar phenomena in neighbouring languages. Dell and Elmedlaoui's description of Moroccan Arabic mentions a similar pattern, formulated as a grammatical rule.

> In the last syllable of an Intonational Phrase, if the nucleus does not contain a sonorant, make it complex by inserting e before the nuclear consonant. (Dell & Elmedlaoui 2002: 300)

They describe a type of schwa epenthesis in Moroccan Arabic that takes place near the end of the intonation phrase. More specifically, schwa is inserted between the onset and the nucleus consonant of the final syllable. The authors explicitly state, that this schwa enables a tonal event to be realised. Heath (1987:

184) describes the mirror image of this pattern for the same language. He notes, that schwa deletion in word-final voiceless clusters can be blocked when there is the necessity to realise a high tone attributed to list intonation. Dell & Tangi (1985) report on a respective pattern in Ath-Sidhar Rifian, in which schwa is usually devoiced between voiceless consonants but remains voiced "under an intonation which requires a final high pitch [...]" (ibid: 154).

These patterns strikingly resemble what is found in Tashlhiyt. While phenomena like the vowel insertion in Moroccan Arabic and the blocking of devoicing in Ath-Sidhar Rifian are formulated in a way that suggests consistent patterns, the present data exhibits many degrees of freedom: first, the PTEV is not obligatory in tone bearing contexts. There is a lot of variation within and across speakers. Second, the PTEV is not only found in intonation phrase-final position, but also in phrase-medial position. Third, the PTEV not only surfaces between the onset and nucleus of the final syllable but also in word-final position, i.e. after the final consonant. Despite this variability, the proposed epenthetic schwa in Tashlhiyt can be considered to be phonological to the extent that it is necessary for a structural description of the intonation system. Therefore, the PTEV should be considered a relevant aspect of the intonational system of Tashlhiyt.

It has to be noted, however, that the amount of unexplained variance makes a discrete phonological formalisation difficult. As described earlier, when there is no sonorant in the target word, the no surfacing tone and the anticipated tone patterns appear to freely alternate with the tone on schwa pattern. Further, the present data does not make any statement about the phonological status of PTEV at a lexical / syllabic level. Coleman claims that schwa is epenthesised into an empty nucleus when the syllable does not contain a lexical vowel. In that vein, the question arises as to whether the PTEV in the present data is occupying the syllable nucleus position or not. There is indeed a clear preference for the PTEV to occur in the position between onset and nucleus of the final syllable. However, as discussed above, assigning the PTEV to the nucleus position is somewhat difficult to uphold for cases with word-final schwas if one does not want to propose different lexical representations for different speakers.

As of now, it appears empirically justified to refer to this element as a postlexical rather than a lexical phenomenon, introduced by the requirements of tune-text-association. This account shares aspects with Dell and Elmedlaoui's account of Tashlhiyt's text-setting in singing. They present evidence that schwa can align with musical notes (Dell & Elmedlaoui 2002):

6 Tonal placement in adverse phonological environments

[...] schwas may not be metrically relevant [...], but they are nonetheless relevant in singing, as they participate in the mapping of the text onto the melody. (Dell & Elmedlaoui 2002: 152).

Consider a disyllabic word (e.g. /ad.rar/ 'mountain') produced in a song with a sequence of two musical notes X and Y. The musical notes are aligned to the two vowels in a one-to-one mapping. However, in words with no vowel but with sonorant consonants, the musical notes can either be realised on the sonorant consonants or on a schwa within the consonant cluster (e.g. /n.ʃr̩k/ 'we share': [nʃr̩k] or [nəʃrək]). Dell & Elmedlaoui (2008) report free alternation between these two forms. Furthermore, if the word contains a syllable with neither a lexical vowel nor a sonorant consonant (such as the second syllable of /tn̩.dbt̩/ 'you regret'), they report on three patterns: (i) The second musical note can be left unrealised; (ii) it can be realised earlier, resulting in two notes aligned to the first syllable /tn̩/; (iii) it can be realised on a schwa. These strategies are strikingly similar to what has been found in the present speech corpus. Dell and Elmedlaoui argue that schwas serve as carriers of musical notes in singing and are thus relevant for a description of musical form. However, Dell and Elmedlaoui maintain that despite their role in singing, they do not need to be considered as phonological entities (2008: 177-182), since they do not play a role in syllabification or in metre (ibid: 55). Accordingly, one could argue that schwa serves as a carrier of intonational tones and is, thus, relevant for a description of the intonation. Without the need to propose any role of schwa for syllabification, the PTEV should be considered phonological nevertheless.

The fact that such a divergence of lexical and postlexical functions has not been reported on in the world's languages, invites one to speculate on the reasons for this typological gap. It could be argued that a vowel element as evident in Tashlhiyt is an unstable state for a sound system, eventually leading to sound change. PTEVs are louder and longer than other instances of schwa resulting in perceptually salient acoustic events. Listeners may reanalyse these salient elements as context-dependent prosodic markers (Browman & Goldstein 1990: 318). Consequently, speakers may start to insert these elements at certain prosodic positions systematically. Being exposed to these frequent occurrences of schwa in certain constructions, speakers may eventually reanalyse PTEVs as lexical schwas, even outside of these prosodic contexts. If this is a valid evolutionary path for the emergence of phonological vowels, the question arises as to where the schwa in Tashlhiyt currently stands on this path, a question that can only be answered by historical records or cross-generational comparisons, both fruitful avenues for future research.

6.6 Summary

Tonal events in Tashlhiyt appear to be attracted to certain prosodically privileged positions. Apart from sentence modality and a general preference for the right edge, more sonorous segments are stronger attractors than less sonorous segments. The present chapter has demonstrated that obstruents can be considered as no attractors at all. In case of an obstruent-only word, tonal events can either be produced on a sonorant of the preceding word or remain unrealised. A third option is the realisation of a schwa within the target word. In this case, the tonal event (or a significant part of it) can be realised on the target word.

It has been argued here that the observed schwas are neither mere phonetic artefacts of articulatory timing nor phonological elements that are lexically inserted by default. These elements are best considered postlexical elements that are able to bear functionally relevant tonal movements. Schwa could therefore be interpreted as a prosodic unit with which intonational tones can align. This structural element has been argued to co-exist with transitional vocoids that play no role in the linguistic system of Tashlhiyt. The proposal of two co-existing non-lexical vowel phenomena sits well with observations in related languages and resolves some aspects of the long-standing disagreement in the literature. However, the observed alternation between word-medial and word-final schwas cannot be accounted for with the present model. It is likely that sociolinguistic factors orthogonal to prosodic structure play a crucial role here.

It is concluded that even though schwa is not necessarily relevant for syllabification, it is certainly relevant for tonal placement and therefore for a phonological description of Tashlhiyt.

7 Towards an intonational analysis

7.1 Introduction

This chapter proposes an abstract formalisation of the phonetic observations discussed in the preceding chapters. The proposed formalisms serve a descriptive purpose in the tradition of structuralism and theoretical phonology and may be an informative departure point for models of how language users represent given patterns cognitively. The observations are formalised within the Autosegmental-Metrical (AM) model to enable the comparison to other intonation systems. As we will show, particular aspects of the phonological analyses either do not yield an unambiguous analysis or cannot be implemented into available formalisms. We will discuss possible consequences of these modelling difficulties accordingly.

The structure of the chapter is as follows: First, we will recapitulate the phonetic observations (§7.2). We will then compare the tonal events under discussion to similar patterns in other languages. Based on these comparisons, the rise-falls in Tashlhiyt turn out to be best described as edge tones with a primary association to a prosodic edge and a secondary association to a specific tone bearing unit. Different possibilities are evaluated as to which prosodic edge the tonal events primarily associate to, which symbolic representation and internal structure is most appropriate to represent the tonal events, and to which tone bearing units the tonal events secondarily associate (§7.3). While the resulting analysis captures general trends, there remains unexplained variability, which we will subsequently turn to. We will discuss two types of variability found in the present study, both of which pose a problem to the AM model: discrete variability and gradient variability (§7.4). Finally, we will summarise the results of the proposed analysis (§7.5).

7.2 Recapitulation of observations

The previous chapters presented data that yielded a number of observations based on qualitative and quantitative phonetic analyses as well as a perceptual

7 Towards an intonational analysis

evaluation for a subset of these observations. The relevant findings are summarised here.

Chapter 4 presented an instrumental investigation on word stress. There was no compelling evidence that one syllable within a word is phonetically enhanced in comparison to other syllables. Supported by a number of qualitative arguments, these findings were interpreted as evidence for the absence of lexically determined strength relationships. We concluded that there is no word stress in Tashlhiyt.

Chapter 5 presented qualitative observations revealing that questions were characterised by a rise to a pitch peak followed by a fall usually occurring on the last word of the phrase. This pattern was found for yes-no questions and echo questions. Contrastive statements were characterised by a similar tonal contour, i.e. a rise to a pitch peak followed by a fall, usually occurring on the contrasted word. In both contours, the entire trajectory of the rise-fall was realised on a single syllable either on the penult or on the final syllable. The co-occurrence with a syllable indicated a phonetically enhancing function of the tonal event, i.e. the syllable the rise-fall co-occurred with sounded longer and louder.

Quantitative analyses of production data showed that compared to statements, questions had a higher pitch level and a greater pitch range. Echo questions were found to have a lower pitch level than y/n questions and a higher pitch level than corresponding statements. Statements and questions differed not only in scaling, but also in the tendency to place the tonal event on the penult or final syllable within the word. The rise-fall was more often realised on the final syllable in questions than in statements. Importantly, this was only a probabilistic trend. Both sentence modalities exhibited rise-falls that occurred on either the penult or the final syllable. Mirroring these probabilistic differences, there was a tendency for the pitch peak in questions to be realised later within the syllable than in statements, independent of which syllable it occurred on.

A subsequent perceptual experiment revealed that listeners made use of both the pitch scaling cues and the discrete location of the tonal event to distinguish questions from statements. Utterances with a higher pitch level were more likely to be rated as questions than utterances with a lower pitch level. Utterances with a pitch peak on the final syllable were more likely to be rated as questions than utterances with a pitch peak on the penult. Alignment differences within the syllable did not affect ratings, however.

Irrespective of sentence modality, the location of the tonal event was dependent on several interacting factors. Generally, the pitch peak was more likely to occur on the final syllable than on the penult. Additionally, syllables with more sonorous nuclei were more likely to co-occur with the pitch peak than syllables with less sonorous nuclei, and heavy syllables were more likely to co-occur with the pitch peak than light syllables. These factors influenced the distribution of pitch peaks significantly, but could not account for all observations by themselves, leaving a certain amount of unexplained variation. There were a number of cases in which a speaker produced two distinctly different pitch peak locations in two different repetitions of the same target word with the same sentence modality.

Finally, Chapter 6 explored the alignment of pitch peaks when the target word did not contain a vowel or a sonorant consonant. Results showed three different possible realisation patterns: the pitch peak either remained unrealised (no noticeable pitch movement), occurred on the vowel of the preceding word, or occurred on a non-lexical schwa, word-medially or word-finally. The tone-carrying schwa in the latter pattern was shown to exhibit distributional and phonetic properties that are difficult to reconcile with what has been claimed in the literature. The observed schwa is neither a purely phonetic artifact nor a lexically inserted phonological element. It has been argued that schwa is a postlexical unit that enables the realisation of intonational tones.

7.3 Analysis of the rise-falls

We first turn to the descriptive category into which the investigated tonal events fall. Tashlhiyt exhibits a rise to a local high pitch target followed by a fall in pitch to flag questions and signal contrastive focus. This resembles patterns found for well-documented languages such as Bengali, Greek, Italian, and Moroccan Arabic, among others. Differences in the location of this tonal event have been analysed in different ways for different languages. In the following, we will review how the patterns in Tashlhiyt compare with similar tonal events in other languages. Subsequently, we will explore possible phonological representations.

In the Autosegmental-Metrical model, there are different representations for a rise-fall, depending on the regularities of the tonal contour across different contexts with which it co-occurs. In varieties of Italian that have a rise-fall question contour (cf. Grice et al. 2005; Savino & Grice 2011), the pitch peak is taken to be part of the rising pitch accent (represented as an L+H* tone). The pitch accent associates with the head of the intonation phrase, i.e. the stressed syllable of the most relevant unit. The subsequent fall is attributed to a low edge tone (L%, resulting in a L+H* L% sequence). In other languages, such as Standard Hungarian (Ladd 1983; Varga 2002) and Cypriot Greek (Arvaniti 1998), a rise to a pitch peak is analysed as an edge tone and is taken to be associated with the edge of the intonation phrase. Its placement can be represented in two ways, either it is specified as simply aligning with prosodic constituents without an association to a tone bearing unit (e.g. with the right edge of a prosodic phrase, following Pierrehumbert & Beckman 1988) or it has a secondary association to the penult or final syllable (Grice, Arvaniti & Ladd 2000). In Standard Greek and Romanian, the pitch peak is placed even further away from the edge, typically on a post-focal lexically strong syllable. It is analysed as a phrase accent, an edge tone of a prosodic constituent smaller than the intonation phrase, secondarily associated to a TBU (represented as H-, see Grice, Arvaniti & Ladd 2000). In this case, the pitch peak is neither on the strongest syllable in the phrase, nor close to the edge of the phrase. It marks the head of a post-focal constituent but not of the entire phrase. This high tone is preceded by a low nuclear pitch accent (L*) and followed by a low intonation phrase edge tone (L%, resulting in a L* H- L% sequence).

The preceding recapitulation identified three descriptive categories (see also Chapter 2): pitch accents, edge tones, and edge tones with an additional association to a TBU. The choice of which descriptive category represents a tonal event best is mainly informed by the temporal alignment of tonal targets with certain segmental landmarks. Patterns of alignment are often taken as direct evidence for a proposed phonological association (Arvaniti, Ladd & Mennen 2000).

Proposing the association of a tone to an edge is justified by the consistent alignment of the tone with that edge. Proposing the association of a tone to a TBU is justified by the consistent alignment of the tone with (or close to) that TBU. The analysis of secondarily associated edge tones is often justified by an alternation between a tone aligned with the edge of the phrase and a tone aligned to a structural unit dislocated from the edge. For example, in Grice's analysis of Palermo Italian (1995), a rise-fall in pitch consists of a rising pitch accent (L+H* in Grice's annotation) followed by low boundary tone (L-). When the final syllable is accented, the subsequent fall does not fully reach a low target. If the accented syllable is not final, however, there is a complete fall towards a low pitch target. This is analysed as an edge tone that additionally associates to the final syllable.

7.3.1 Rise-falls in Tashlhiyt: primary association to prosodic constituents

The question arises as to which descriptive category characterises rise-falls in Tashlhiyt best. Generally, the high target of the rise exhibits a rather discrete alignment pattern, i.e. it aligns either with the penult or with the final syllable. Crucially, in the presented data, the peak was seldom found somewhere

7.3 Analysis of the rise-falls

in-between. This discrete alignment is accompanied by the auditory impression of prominence, i.e. the syllable the tone co-occurs with sounds longer and louder. This impression is further supported by quantitative evidence for durational and articulatory adjustments (Diercks 2011; Gordon & Nafi 2012; Grice, Ridouane & Roettger 2015). Segments exhibit greater duration and higher intensity, vowels are articulated more peripherally, and articulatory gestures exhibit larger displacement difference when co-occurring with tones. The consistency in alignment of the pitch peak and the accompanied phonetic enhancement are analysed as phonological association of tones to tone bearing units (as already assumed by Dell & Elmedlaoui 1985).

The tonal events cannot be pitch accents in the sense of a tone or tonal complex associating to metrically strong syllables because Tashlhiyt has been shown to lack lexically determined metrical structure. Moreover, there is systematic variation with regard to the discrete association of the tonal complex under investigation across and within words. This further underlines the conclusion that metrical strength is something that is determined at the postlexical rather than the lexical level. The tonal events can neither be simple edge tones that are only primarily associated to the periphery of a prosodic constituent. While the tonal events are somehow attracted to the right edge of the phrase, they are not aligned at a fixed distance from its edge. The tonal events are edge seeking and, at the same time, associated to a tone bearing unit. This resembles phrase accents, as proposed by Grice, Arvaniti & Ladd (2000). The analysis of the tonal events as hybrid tones is compatible with findings on Moroccan Arabic, a language in close contact with Tashlhiyt. Hellmuth et al. (2015) discuss a rise-fall contour in y/n questions. The high target of the rise is neither consistently aligned with a stressed syllable nor consistently aligned at a fixed distance from the utterance edge. They analysed this contour as an "edge-aligned pitch accent" which associates to the final foot of the rightmost word in the phrase.

The following analysis for questions in Tashlhiyt can be tentatively proposed: there is a phonologically specified tonal event, which will be preliminarily referred to as a LHL tonal complex. The LHL sequence can be analysed as an intonation phrase edge complex with a secondary association to the penult or final syllable, similar to Standard Hungarian and Cypriot Greek (Grice, Arvaniti & Ladd 2000). Which of these two syllables the tonal complex is associated with is, unlike in other languages, not dependent on lexically determined metrically strong syllables. Similar to questions, contrastive statements exhibit an LHL tonal complex, too. Unlike questions, this tonal complex is located on the contrasted word. Again, this tonal event is edge seeking, i.e. it exhibits a general

7 Towards an intonational analysis

preference for the final syllable. It can be considered as secondarily associated to either the penult or final syllable.

The question as to which prosodic constituents the rise-falls in questions and contrastive statements are primarily associated with, still remains. This is related to the question as to whether the LHL complex has to be decomposed into smaller primitives that are potentially associated to different prosodic constituents. Bengali exhibits tonal placement patterns comparable to what has been found for Tashlhiyt (Hayes & Lahiri 1991) and its analysis may be insightful for an evaluation of rise-falls under investigation. Hayes and Lahiri's discuss two intonation contours in which the combination of pitch accents and edge tones of different prosodic constituents combine to form a rise-fall pattern. Y/n questions and statements with utterance-final narrow focus are both characterised by a rise-fall in pitch. In y/n questions, the pitch peak is achieved later in the syllable and has a greater pitch excursion than in corresponding statements. The authors account for this difference by means of edge tones associated with different constituents in the prosodic hierarchy. Hayes and Lahiri propose two levels of prosodic phrasing above the word: a focused element constitutes a phonological phrase (φ), a phrase larger than the word and smaller than the intonation phrase. In addition to the phonological phrase, they propose an intonation phrase (ι) which contains one or multiple phonological phrases.

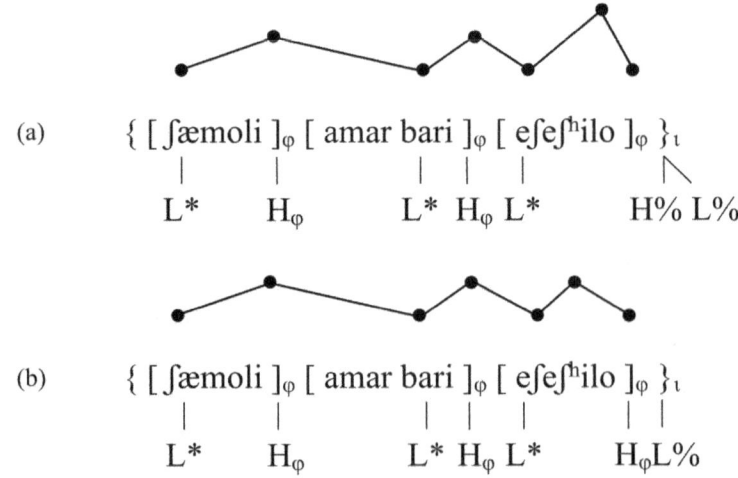

Figure 7.1: Schematic representation of (a) a y/n question and (b) a statement with intonation phrase-final narrow focus in Bengali (Hayes & Lahiri 1991), adapted from Gussenhoven (2002: 136).

7.3 Analysis of the rise-falls

In y/n questions, the fall in pitch is represented as a HL complex associated with the right edge of the intonation phrase (H% L%, Figure 7.1a). In corresponding statements, the H is an edge tone associated to the phonological phrase and the L is an edge tone associated to the intonational phrase (Hφ L%, Figure 7.1b). This analysis allows them to capture the phonetic similarity of the tonal events by proposing the same sequence of tones. At the same time, it accounts for the phonetic differences in terms of alignment and scaling by assuming different association patterns with the prosodic structure.

Analogously, a very simple prosodic structure can be proposed to account for tonal placement in Tashlhiyt. We propose an intonation phrase which is characterised by certain edge tones (here L% in statements and LHL% in questions), a clear pause following the right edge of the phrase, and lengthening of the segments at the right edge. Similar to Bengali, one may propose that a focused constituent in Tashlhiyt constitutes its own phonological phrase. This would resonate with the preliminary analysis of phrase-medial tones in Tashlhiyt proposed by Grice et al. (2011). Such an analysis may also account for the anticipated tone pattern discussed in Chapter 6. Recall that when no sonorant consonant or vowel is available in the contrasted word (e.g. /inna tkʃf/ 'Did he say 'it dried'?'), the tonal complex can be found on a syllable in the preceding word (final syllable of /inna/), i.e. outside the contrasted word. The tonal complex would be analysed as associating with the rightmost available TBU within the same phrase. However, as opposed to the intonation phrase, there is no independent acoustic evidence for a phrase boundary after focused constituents. There is neither an audible pause nor lengthening of segments at the right edge. In fact, vowel coalescence across the proposed edge can be frequently observed. These findings raise doubts as to whether the proposal of a prosodic boundary is phonetically justified. Moreover, proposing a phonological phrase is not necessary to account for the present observations.

Alternatively, one could analyse the tonal complex in contrastive statements as an edge tone of the phonological word, which is a well-defined prosodic domain in Tashlhiyt (e.g. Dell & Elmedlaoui 2002). In light of the anticipated tone pattern, the tonal complex must be permitted to surface outside of its word-domain. This is in line with Pierrehumbert and Beckman's analysis of Japanese (1988), in which they allow for the association of a right edge tone of the accentual phrase with the first TBU of the following accentual phrase (cf. Chapter 2).

We proceed by postulating an association of the LHL with the phonological word. Regardless of the constituent the tone is associated with, the proposed analysis assumes that questions and contrastive statements are expressed by the same

7 Towards an intonational analysis

tonal sequences (LHL), which are associated to different prosodic constituents. Similar to Hayes and Lahiri's analysis for Bengali (1991), the present account allows one to capture the phonetic similarity of the tones by proposing the same sequence of tones. At the same time, it accounts for the phonetic differences in terms of alignment and scaling by proposing different association patterns with the prosodic structure. Recall that the LHL in question reaches its high target later within the syllable than the LHL in statements. This difference is captured by the analysis of the tone as associated with the intonation phrase in questions and with the phonological word in contrastive statements. Crucially, this analysis avoids the introduction of additional phonological primitives to account for subtle alignment differences like 'alignment features' (Remijsen 2013) or 'supplementary association of tones' (Prieto, D'Imperio & Gili Fivela 2005; Face & Prieto 2007).[1]

7.3.2 The internal structure of the rise-fall

So far the rise-fall in pitch has been analysed as a LHL tonal complex that is either associated to the right edge of the intonation phrase in questions or to the right edge of the phonological word in contrastive statements. Even though the symbolic representation of the discussed tonal events are descriptively well justified by its form (sharp rise to a high target followed by a sudden drop towards a low target), a parsimonious representation may not need this maximal specification. It may be possible, to reduce and/or decompose the tonal complex into separate tonal events.

To evaluate this possibility, an additional intonation contour of Tashlhiyt is considered. A recent study by Bruggeman, Roettger & Grice (2017) investigated the intonational marking of question words in Tashlhiyt (henceforth referred to as the 'question word tune'). Question words in a direct interrogative construction co-occurred with a rise-fall in pitch (represented as a LHL sequence). In these contexts, Bruggeman et al. measured the alignment of the high target. While the high target was consistently produced somewhere on the question word, there was no stable alignment with any specific segmental landmark within the word. The onset of the rise consistently occurred in utterance-initial position and was

---

[1] Prieto, D'Imperio & Gili Fivela (2005) use the term 'secondary association'. However, as Arvaniti, Ladd & Mennen (2006) pointed out, their mechanism differs significantly from the original usage of the term by Pierrehumbert & Beckman (1988) and Grice, Arvaniti & Ladd (2000). In accordance with Arvaniti, Ladd & Mennen (2006), the term supplementary association is used here to avoid confusion.

7.3 Analysis of the rise-falls

not necessarily located on the question word. The trailing low target was found after the high target near the right edge of the question word. Bruggeman et al. analysed this as an intonation phrase initial %L and a HL tonal complex marking narrow focus on the question word. They interpreted the HL to be associated with the question word (cf. Figure 7.2).

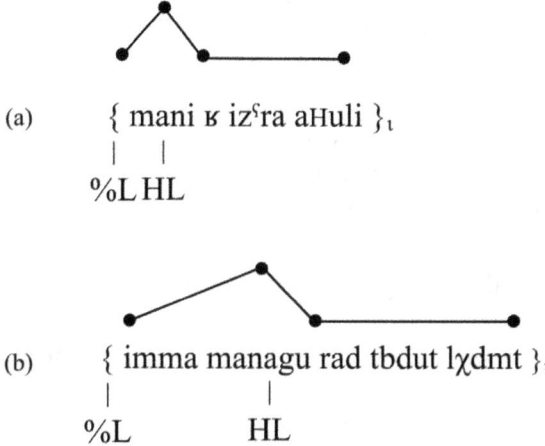

Figure 7.2: Schematic representation of tonal association for the question word tune as proposed by Bruggeman, Roettger & Grice (2017) (a) /mani ʁ izˤra ahuli/ 'Where does he see the sheep?'. (b) /imma managu rad tbdut lχdmt/ 'So when will you start working?'. Note that the HL is analysed as loosely associated with the question word exhibiting no further association to a syllable.

In contrast to the question word tune, the low leading tone of the LHL marking contrastive statements, echo questions, and y/n questions cannot easily be accounted for by an intonation phrase-initial low boundary tone (%L). The rise to the pitch peak is a sharp rise with the low target located immediately before the pitch peak realised within the same syllable.

While a decomposition of the tonal complex appears to capture distributional observations in the question word tune (Bruggeman, Roettger & Grice 2017), it is not an attractive formalism for the rise-falls of questions and contrastive statements discussed in Chapter 5. The rise-fall in the question word tune and rise-fall events investigated in this book differ with respect to their tune-text-association. Bruggeman et al. did not find any evidence for an association of the H tone to a constituent below the word level. Distribution of variance was unimodal and there was no indication of phonetic enhancement correlated with peak position.

139

7 Towards an intonational analysis

This stands in sharp contrast with the data discussed in Chapter 5 as well as with the data discussed in Grice, Ridouane & Roettger (2015), where the pitch peak was reached on either the penult or the final syllable and its location was accompanied by phonetic enhancement. The former phenomenon has been analysed as a tonal event loosely associated to the question word, the latter phenomena have been analysed as tonal events associated with tone bearing units. We can thus conclude that the descriptively most justified representation is a tritonal complex (LHL) for both questions and contrastive statements.

This analysis might be extended to other focus types exhibiting larger focus domains than just single words as well as neutral statements. It is very likely that Tashlhiyt exhibits mechanisms to express different focus types in addition to the contrastive focus investigated in the present work. Impressionistic observations indicate that non-contrastive elements of the utterance are tonally marked by less prominent rise-fall movements, an observation that resembles high pitch accents in Germanic languages: they do not have a large pitch excursion but sound prominent. Besides these impressionistic observations, there are no further insights on focus marking in Tashlhiyt. Speakers reliably use morphosyntax to express information structure, which involves fronting of the focused constituent (cf. Chapters 2 and 5). This fronting often comes with a prosodic break as well as a very prominent rising pitch movement (Sadiqi 1997; Dell & Elmedlaoui 2002; Mettouchi & Fleisch 2010). Speakers were rather resistant to traditional methods of eliciting different focus types in absence of morphosyntactic devices. If tonal events indeed mark less prominent focus types (e.g. broad or narrow focus), the present analysis can be taken as a baseline from which future analyses can depart. Less prominent tonal events may be formalised with less complex tonal representations (e.g. H, LH, HL). This would resemble pitch accent distinctions in well-described intonation systems. For example, the distinction between rising peaks and high rising late peaks in German is communicatively relevant and reflected in their phonological representations (H* and L+H* in GToBi, see Grice, Baumann & Benzmülller 2005).

Ultimately, the most adequate analysis of intonation in Tashlhiyt can only be proposed in light of the full inventory of intonational events. It may turn out that certain analytical decisions need to be revised in light of more available data. Leaving these analytical decisions for future research, all discussed representations conceptually share that tones are attracted to certain positions defined by prosodic constituents and their edges, specific structural units, and specific tonal targets in the tonal sequence. This appears trivial in light of the consistent and stable attraction of tonal events towards prominent positions in other languages. However, Tashlhiyt exhibits an intricate interaction between association requirements. This results in an unusual degree of variability and, in turn, makes a phonological analysis of the tune-text-association challenging.

7.3.3 Secondary association to tone bearing units

While the LHL complexes in questions and statements consistently co-occur with certain prosodic constituents (the final word of the intonation phrase for questions, the contrasted word in contrastive statements), the actual location within these constituents is prone to variability. When there is only one sonorant nucleus in the word (a vowel or a sonorant consonant), the tone is consistently located on this element. If there are multiple sonorants, the tone can be realised either on the penult or on the final syllable.

These findings are in line with impressionistic observations made by Dell & Elmedlaoui (1985): they provide an analysis of optional syllabification in intonation phrase-final position that goes hand in hand with the placement of intonational tones. For example, when the word /igidr/ 'eagle' is at the end of a phrase with question intonation, they report a rising f0 contour occurring on the final /r/. In this case, it is analysed as a syllable nucleus which functions as a tone bearing unit (TBU, resulting in /i.gi.dr̩/). Alternatively, the final consonant can "lose" its syllabic status and, in turn, be "annexed" to the previous syllable (resulting in /i.gidr/). In this case, the pitch peak is aligned with the second vowel /i/. They propose an optional rule of prepausal annexation, turning trisyllabic /i.gi.dr̩/ into disyllabic /i.gidr/ with a final complex coda. This analysis is supported by Elmedlaoui's intuitions about syllable count and acceptability of tonal placement. According to Dell and Elmedlaoui, this alternation is only observable when the word has a final sonorant consonant, which could either form the nucleus of a light syllable or be part of a complex coda. They state that "similar observations can be made with other intonations" (Dell & Elmedlaoui 1985: 119f.).

Under this assumption, a word such as /tugl/ would be monosyllabic if the pitch peak is on /u/ and disyllabic if the pitch peak is on /l/. Even though this analysis may reflect Elmedlaoui's native speaker intuitions about syllable count, it is not sufficient to explain some of the observations made by Grice, Ridouane & Roettger (2015) and the production corpus presented in Chapter 5. First, disyllabic words with two vowels have also been observed to alternate with respect to the pitch peak position. For instance, in /ba.ba/ 'father', the peak can occur on either of the vowels, at least in contrastive statements. For native speakers, words with two vowels are disyllabic regardless of the position of the pitch peak. Thus, there appear to be cases in which the position of the peak cannot be accounted

7 Towards an intonational analysis

for by the syllabification of the word. Second, disyllabic words with a final heavy syllable (e.g. /tu.glt/) showed pitch peak alternations, too. According to Dell & Elmedlaoui (1985: 120), prepausal annexation "requires the prepausal syllable to be an open one". A closed syllable showing this alternation of pitch peaks would make a super complex syllable coda necessary with /glt/ in the coda of monosyllabic /tuglt/. This level of complexity of syllable structure is not supported by any native speaker intuition reported on in the literature. It is concluded that resyllabification cannot account for the spectrum of evidence coherently. Although Dell and Elmedlaoui's impressionistic observations reflect strong tendencies, the placement of tones is not as clear-cut as they propose. Moreover, their account does not capture tonal placement in words without sonorants.

When there is no sonorant available, tonal placement for both functions exhibit a high degree of variability, with at least three possible realisation patterns: the pitch peak either remains unrealised (no noticeable pitch movement = no surfacing tone), occurs on the vowel of the preceding word (anticipated tone), or occurs on a non-lexical schwa word-medially or word-finally (tone on schwa). These patterns were only found in target words containing neither lexical vowels nor sonorant consonants. These observations suggest a representational difference between syllables with sonorants and syllables without sonorants. This is achieved either by appealing to Dell and Elmedlaoui's syllabification algorithm (1985, 1996, 2002) or by appealing to alternative syllabification models, such as the epenthetic vowel account proposed by Coleman (2001). In the former, the difference is captured by differentiating between syllables with sonorant nuclei and those with obstruent nuclei (/tn̩.dm̩/ vs /tḅ.dġ/). In this case, the no surfacing tone pattern and the anticipated tone pattern are only permitted when the word contains no sonorant nuclei. In the latter account, the epenthetic vowel account, schwa vowels are assumed to occupy syllables that do not contain lexical vowels. The words /tən.dəm/ and /təb.dəg/ only differ in the identity of the coda consonant. In this case, the no surfacing tone and the anticipated tone patterns are only permitted in words with empty nuclei (or schwa nuclei) and obstruents in the coda. Regardless of the underlying subsyllabic analysis, distinctions between sonorants and obstruents have been made for other intonation systems. In their analysis of Japanese, Pierrehumbert & Beckman (1988) propose that sonorants but not obstruents can serve as TBUs.

Grice, Ridouane & Roettger (2015) accounted for the tonal placement patterns in Tashlhiyt with the following phonological analysis. They assume that the tone bearing unit is a syllable containing a sonorant (either a vowel or a sonorant consonant). The LHL tonal complex (in their analyses the H tone) under discussion

7.3 Analysis of the rise-falls

is an edge tone seeking secondary association to a TBU in the edge-final word. If there is no TBU in the edge-final word, the tone does not have a secondary association and is only primarily associated to the edge itself. In the absence of a sonorant, the tone simply aligns with an element with enough voicing or energy to make it audible. In this approach, a target word with no lexical vowel or sonorant would require the LHL to align with voiced material as close to the edge as possible. This may result in the no surfacing tone pattern with the LHL tonal sequence not being realised at all. Alternatively, the tone can align with an element with enough voicing or energy to make it audible. This is achieved by an alignment with the rightmost available sonorant in the preceding word or to a schwa, an element that is phonetically prominent enough to bear a pitch movement. This account captures the distribution of tones and does not have to assign any phonological status to schwa co-occurring with the tone.

While this is a parsimonious analysis with respect to the available data in Grice, Ridouane & Roettger (2015), it does not account for three observations presented in this book.

First, there is evidence that the tone in the anticipated tone pattern phonetically strengthens the syllable it co-occurs with, i.e. it exhibits spatio-temporal enhancement of the segments.

Second, schwas co-occurring with tonal events exhibit distributional properties that are difficult to reconcile with a purely phonetic analysis. The anticipated tone pattern and the presence of schwa in a voiceless target word are mutually exclusive. Either there is a schwa and it carries the tone, or the tone is anticipated and there is no schwa. This observation suggests a structural function of schwa.

Third, the choice of tonal placement strategy in the absence of sonorants appears to be somewhat independent of the actual phonetic material available to carry the tonal movement. In a substantial number of cases, the tone is anticipated even though the final word contains voiced obstruents. These voiced obstruents often surface with vowel-like elements, that are, phonetically speaking, well suited to carry tonal movements from both a production and a perceptual point of view. Moreover, words like /tb̩.dġt/ usually surface with multiple schwas (e.g. [təbədəgət]). If the tone is really aligned with the last phonetic element that is able to carry the tone, one would expect the tone to be aligned with the last available schwa. This is not the case. If the tone occurs on a schwa, there is a strong tendency for the tone to co-occur with the schwa between the onset and nucleus of the final syllable (e.g. between /d/ and /g/ in /tb̩.dġt/), irrespective of whether there is another schwa following. The alignment of tones in these cases is systematically dislocated from the edge and not as close to the edge as possible.

7 Towards an intonational analysis

Given these three observations, the analysis for tonal placement in cases of obstruent-only words as simple edge tones (Grice, Ridouane & Roettger 2015) should be revised. The phonetic enhancement of elements occurring with tones should be taken as evidence for the association of tones to TBUs. In that vein, it is proposed that both the anticipated tone and the tone on schwa are instances of tonal association to TBUs (similar to sonorant syllables). In the absence of a lexical TBU in the word (syllable with a sonorant), the tone either associates with a TBU of the preceding word (anticipated tone), or associates with a postlexically triggered schwa (tone on schwa). Alternatively, the tone can be deleted (no surfacing tone).

To sum up, the rise-falls in questions and contrastive statements are analysed as LHL tonal complexes that are associated to the intonation phrase (questions) and to the phonological word (contrastive statements). The tone is analysed as an edge tone that is secondarily associated to a tone bearing unit in the phrase-final word. The tone bearing unit is identified as a syllable with a sonorant, or a schwa element that is inserted into the consonantal string to bear a functionally relevant tonal movement. Consider Figure 7.3 for a schematic illustration of the analysis.

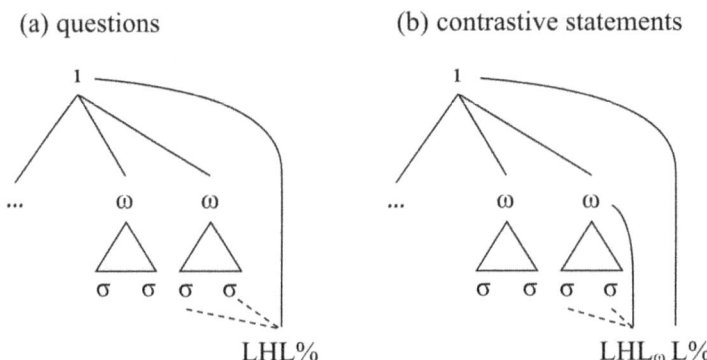

Figure 7.3: Schematised analysis of prosodic structure and tune-text-association for a simple sentence with the focused constituent at the right edge of the intonation phrase (ı). (a) illustrates a question with a LHL intonation phrase edge tone secondarily associated to either the penult or the final syllable. (b) illustrates a contrastive statement with a LHL word edge tone secondarily associated to either the penult or the final syllable.

While the phonological analysis proposed here captures our observations in a parsimonious way, it does not offer an account for the vast amount of variability with regard to the association of the LHL to a specific TBU. It does not account for global pitch scaling distinctions between sentence modalities, either. In the following section, these two remaining issues are discussed.

7.4 Formalising variability

There are two types of variable form-function mappings that pose some difficulties for formal intonational analyses: 'discrete variability' and 'gradient variability'.

'Discrete variability' refers to the variability in the frequency of occurrence of mutually exclusive, categorically definable events. Functions can be expressed by different phonetic events that occur with varying probabilities. The intonation system of Tashlhiyt exhibits discrete variability in tonal placement, i.e. categorically definable tonal events (tone on penult or final syllable) are associated with specific structural positions probabilistically (i.e. in x% of cases the tonal event is associated to the penult, and in y% of cases the tonal event is associated to the final syllable).

'Gradient variability' refers to gradual modulations of a phonetic parameter that may go hand in hand with a gradual modulation in meaning. For example, in English certain phonetic dimensions such as pitch scaling can be modulated to signal emphasis in that small differences in scaling correspond to small differences in emphasis (Bolinger 1961; Ladd 2014). In addition to signalling gradual meaning differences, they may also signal more discrete meaning differences, e.g. the distinction between questions and statements (see Chapter 2). Often it remains unclear where to draw the line between gradual and discrete distinctions. Tashlhiyt illustrates gradient variability in terms of pitch scaling.

7.4.1 Discrete variability in intonation

The presented data suggests that it is not possible to predict the occurrence of an intonational event deterministically. The occurrence of a particular event can only be stated as a probabilistic distribution affected by multiple interacting factors rather than a deterministic rule (or mapping) that applies across the board.

Most phonological models, including the Autosegmental-Metrical model, assume a rigid mapping of form and function. For example in German, a high rising pitch accent with a late peak is described as signalling contrastive focus or new information, while a falling pitch accent with an early peak is described as signalling broad focus or given information (cf. Grice, Baumann & Benzmülller

7 Towards an intonational analysis

2005; Kohler 2006; Féry & Kügler 2008; Ritter & Grice 2015). These statements suggest a one-to-one mapping of form and function. Such a one-to-one mapping cannot account for discrete variability as it is found, for example, for pitch accent categories in German. Baumann, Röhr & Grice (2015) investigated the intonational encoding of information status in German. Their results revealed that there are specific pitch accents that are often used to encode specific information status. For example, when in nuclear position, new referents are prototypically realised with a high rising accent, and given referents with a falling accent. Most importantly, these form-function mappings were found to be only probabilistic preferences, in that speakers used a certain pitch accent category in the majority of cases, but not always (see also Schafer et al. 2000; Mücke & Grice 2014; Cangemi & Grice 2016; Grice et al. 2017).

Variable tonal placement in more general terms is not new to phonologists in general and intonational phonologist in particular. For example, Hayes & Lahiri (1991) explicitly mention the high degree of variability in tonal placement for Bengali:

> Although the generalization that H_p links to the right edge of the focused P-phrase seems secure to us, we must note that phonetically, there is some variation: the phonetic location of the H_p peak often occurs one or two syllables before, and occasionally a syllable or two after the $]_p$ boundary to which H_p is linked phonologically. Similar variation in the placement of H_p has been noticed for Swedish by Bruce (1977). Where differences of focus are to be made precise, the alignment of H_p can be controlled carefully to do this. But in less guarded speech, there is variation. (Hayes & Lahiri 1991: 65)

The authors abstracted away from the observed variability by proposing a single underlying association. In order to make such a leap to a unifying level of abstraction, convincing arguments need to be made. For example, such a proposal can be put forward if variation is gradual in nature, i.e. the tone is located somewhere around the edge with a unimodal distribution of variance. Alternatively, certain factors like tonal crowding or the segmental context may account for the variation in a predictable way (for a discussion, see Chapter 2).

In Tashlhiyt, however, distributions of tonal alignment are clearly multimodal. Moreover, there appear to be no clear distributional or contextual parameters accountable for some of the variance, i.e. speakers alternate between tonal events on the penult and the final syllable within exactly the same lexical and pragmatic

7.4 Formalising variability

context. A unifying abstraction away from this variability is not empirically justified. Even though, there are statistically preferred mappings (e.g. LHL on the final syllable in questions, LHL on the penult in statements), there is no a priori reason to formalise these mappings in a way that ignores their probabilistic nature. However, in terms of model-theoretical reasons, a deterministic mapping of form and function enables a parsimonious phonological description. In this case, questions could be described as exhibiting a rise-fall on the final syllable and contrastive statements as exhibiting a rise-fall on the penult. Despite it being economic and simple, this description is empirically not adequate.

While not prominently discussed in the domain of intonation research, discrete variability has been discussed with regard to phenomena of the segmental domain. A prototypical phenomenon that has been argued to exhibit discrete variability is the /t/ deletion in English.[2] In English, /t/ is variably deleted in complex codas (e.g. Guy 1980). This deletion has been argued to apply probabilistically dependent on multiple linguistic (and non-linguistic) factors such as its segmental context and its prosodic position. Labov (1969) formalised these phonological patterns as ordinary rules that can be marked to be optional and can encode the contextual factors that promote or inhibit their application. While Labov's model only accounted for relative differences (deletion is more likely than no deletion), subsequent authors offered more elaborate mathematical implementations that allow for quantitative predictions. For example, Sankoff, Tagliamonte & Smith (2005) used multivariate stepwise logistic regression to predict application of a specific rule as a function of multiple independent variables.

Alternatively, 'Optimality Theory' (OT, Prince & Smolensky 1993) proposes that the observed patterns of language are a result of interacting competing constraints. OT offers a formalism that allows the evaluation of alternatives based on ranked preferences. However, as opposed to traditional rule-based models, it allows for the violation of these preferences. The general OT architecture, which assumes non-probabilistic output, has been extended to enable the modelling of discrete variability (see Anttila 2012, for an overview). For example, 'Stochastic Optimality Theory' introduces numerically weighted constraints that predict discrete outcomes probabilistically (Boersma 1997; Boersma & Hayes 2001). A different approach is taken by the 'Multiple Grammars Theory' (Kroch 1989; Kiparsky 1993) which proposes that the linguistic system of an individual is defined by multiple competing grammars that themselves refer to different rankings of compet-

---

[2] For exposition purposes, we ignore here that deletion phenomena are most likely not discrete alternations but should rather be conceived of as continuous modulations of gestural coordination with differing degrees of overlap (Browman & Goldstein 1986).

ing constraints. The interaction of these grammars results in discrete variability. The probability of a certain event to occur (e.g. the /t/ being deleted or the tone being associated to the penult) is defined by the number of grammars predicting this particular event divided by the total number of grammars (see e.g. Reynolds 1994, and Anttila 1997, for an extension of these ideas).

In sum, several phonological formalisms explicitly address probabilistic form-function mappings. In addition to models that evaluate the contribution of competing factors with traditional mathematical inference, there are variants of OT that can model probabilistic variation. The Autosegmental-Metrical model, however, does not offer any mechanism to model variable form-function mappings.

The observed discrete variability poses a threat to those phonological models that assume a rigid one-to-one mapping of form and function. It has to be stressed that Tashlhiyt is not an exception to the norm. Well-studied languages such as German exhibit similar probabilistic mappings of different tonal events expressing the same function (e.g. H+!H* and L+H* expressing given referents, Baumann, Röhr & Grice 2015). What makes Tashlhiyt seemingly different from the German case is that it shows a probabilistic association of arguably the same tonal event to different structural units in the utterance.

7.4.2 Gradient variability in intonation

After we have explored possible formalisms to capture discrete variability, we now turn to instances of gradient variability. Tashlhiyt uses raised pitch level and greater pitch range to flag questions. This has been observed for other languages such as Bengali (Hayes & Lahiri 1991) and Moroccan Arabic (Benkirane 1998) among others (see Chapter 5 for an overview). There are generally two ways global scaling differences have been treated in the past. Either these differences were considered phonological or they were considered paralinguistic, and therefore not incorporated in a phonological analysis. We will discuss these in turn. Building on the AM model, there are two different approaches to this issue, which roughly correspond to what Ladd (2008) identifies as 'intrinsic' and 'extrinsic' factors affecting pitch scaling.[3]

Intrinsic factors refer to pitch scaling differences encoded in the tonal specifications relative to the tonal space (Beckman & Pierrehumbert 1986; Sosa 1999).

---

[3] Ladd (2008) also discusses a third factor affecting pitch scaling: the 'metrical' factor. Since the metrical approach models scaling relations across multiple tonal events within the same utterance, it does not contribute to the present analysis which is based on simple utterances containing one intonational event only.

7.4 Formalising variability

For example, in his work on Spanish, Sosa (1999) argues for incorporating pitch-scaling differences in the tonal string itself. He proposes H+H* for an extra high nuclear accent in questions, as opposed to a L+H* in corresponding statements. Certain local tonal events may trigger the lowering or raising of following tones. For example, Sosa analyses y/n questions as having an initial high boundary tone (e.g. %H) which triggers 'up scaling' of the rest of the tonal string, i.e. the pitch height of all subsequent tones in the utterance is raised.

Extrinsic factors refer to overall modifications of the tonal space that can be incorporated by adding representation, for example, a 'register tier'. This register tier is orthogonal to the tonal tier, i.e. H and L tones can be in an upper or a lower register. Yip (1989) proposed such a register tier to account for contrasts between high falls and low falls in Mandarin and Cantonese. Snider (1999) similarly introduced it to account for up scaling in different tone languages. Inkelas & Leben (1990) applied a register tier to capture the extra high tone at the end of questions in Hausa. Similarly, Ladd (1983) proposed scaling features (e.g. [raised peak]) that are associated to the tones to account for scaling asymmetries in English.

As Ladd discusses (2008: 308f.), intrinsic and extrinsic factors should not be seen as mutually exclusive or applicable across the board. The question is not which analysis is best suited cross-linguistically and across different phenomena. The question is which analysis is most parsimonious and empirically adequate for the linguistic system under investigation. In Tashlhiyt, pitch scaling appears to be a relevant parameter in production. Y/n questions exhibit overall higher pitch values than echo questions which exhibit higher values than statements. In perception, listeners make use of this information to distinguish questions from statements. Pitch scaling should therefore be considered a meaningful phonetic parameter and should be incorporated into any phonological analysis.

An intrinsic account can capture the observed differences between statements and questions by proposing an initial high edge tone that raises following tones (%H). For the distinction of questions types, an additional level must be assumed. A tripartite distinction could be formalised by two different initial high edge tones that raise following tones to different degrees (%H and %^H). The model-theoretical advantage of an intrinsic account is that the phonological specification does not have to be enriched by additional primitives (register tier or features). The description would solely rely on a tonal tier including left edge tones triggering different degrees of pitch scaling. However, this account increases the inventory of tonal events significantly. An extrinsic account, on the other hand, would add either orthogonal register features ('high' for echo questions and 'super high' for y/n questions) or an additional register tier with two different register specifications for questions. The model-theoretical advantage of an extrinsic account is that the inventory of tonal events remains small and no additional up scaling mechanisms need to be proposed.

Given the amount of symbolic representations necessary to account for a simple observation, both accounts appear to be cumbersome. If new data uncovers evidence for even more levels of global pitch scaling, the formalism needs to be adjusted accordingly, inflating the inventory of functional elements.

To circumvent the enrichment of phonological primitives, pragmatic differences between echo and y/n questions could be outsourced and treated as paralinguistic, i.e. not phonological (e.g. Pierrehumbert 1980; Bolinger 1989). Paralinguistic aspects of speech are considered to deal with interpersonal interaction and the speaker's current emotional state (Ladd 1983). The distinction between an echo question and a y/n question could thus be conceived of as a paralinguistic distinction referring to the speaker's level of surprise towards the proposition (among other things). However, as is discussed in detail by Ladd (2008; 2014) and others, the distinction between paralinguistic and linguistic meaning in intonation is not clear-cut. One argument for a contrast being a linguistic contrast lies in the quantitative nature of its form-function mapping. Paralinguistic contrasts are considered to scale linearly with the function they express. If raising pitch level can signal emphasis, raising the pitch level even higher can signal even more emphasis. Linguistic contrasts, on the other hand, are considered to have a non-linear mapping of form and function with instances of the contrast falling in either one or the other category. This distinctions is, however, empirically difficult to uphold. Gussenhoven & Rietveld (2000) have shown that high rises and low rises in Dutch are non-linearly perceived as discretely different contours. This distinction is used to signal surprise, a function clearly related to aspects of interpersonal interaction and therefore traditionally associated with paralinguistic functions. As opposed to that, unambiguous linguistic contrasts, such as the distinction between questions and statements, have been shown to exhibit linear, non-categorical properties as demonstrated experimentally by e.g. Ladd & Morton (1997).

It can be concluded (e.g. Ladd 2008) that there is no clear boundary between language and paralanguage when dealing with intonational phenomena. Shifting the contrast signalled by pitch scaling into the domain of paralanguage is not empirically justified. Such an exclusion can be motivated by model-theoretical consideration and the desire to have a parsimonious model, i.e. a model with a small inventory of symbolic primitives. Based on statistical distributions of acoustic parameters, however, no such choice can be vindicated.

Similar to discrete variability, gradient variability in terms of pitch scaling is difficult to incorporate into the AM framework in a straightforward way. Even though these types of variability are ubiquitous in intonational systems, their formalisation remains a problem in intonational phonology.

7.5 Summary

The present chapter discussed the phonological analysis of intonational patterns in Tashlhiyt within the Autosegmental-Metrical model. The tonal events in questions and contrastive statements have been analysed as LHL tonal complexes that are associated to the intonation phrase (questions) and to the phonological word (contrastive statements). The tones have been analysed as edge tones that are secondarily associated to a tone bearing unit in the respective domain. The tone bearing unit has been identified as a syllable with a sonorant nucleus or a schwa that is inserted into the consonantal string to bear a functionally relevant tonal movement. While these analytical choices resemble analyses of comparable phenomena in other languages, certain aspects of it turned out to remain ambiguous and open for alternative interpretations. Some of these aspects of the analysis may become disambiguated by further observations in the future. Other aspects may remain ambiguous since they are mainly determined by model-theoretical considerations of parsimony and simplicity.

Yet other aspects of the analysis could not be accounted for within the AM model. The investigated intonation contours are characterised by discretely definable tonal events that are probabilistically associated to structural units. This type of discrete variability cannot be incorporated within an AM analysis. Orthogonal to that, Tashlhiyt exhibits multiple functionally relevant levels of pitch scaling. Even though the AM model offers different formalisation mechanisms for scaling distinctions, the available formalisms appear rather cumbersome. In these cases, the number of analytical primitives chosen by the analyst is mainly informed by model-theoretical considerations.

8 Concluding remarks and future directions

This book presented a first investigation into stress and intonation in Tashlhiyt Berber. The analysis contributes to the small but steadily growing body of available phonetic descriptions and phonological analyses of Tashlhiyt in particular and Berber in general. In addition to its descriptive contributions, the analysis of tonal events contributes to phonological typology by supplementing our knowledge of intonation systems with data from a Berber language. Moreover, Tashlhiyt proved to be a case study of particular relevance for intonational theory. The linguistic system of Tashlhiyt exhibits two structural properties that make it especially interesting in view of cross-linguistic prosody research: Tashlhiyt does not have word stress and it allows for phonotactic patterns that are adverse to the production and perception of pitch.

8.1 Tonal placement without word stress

In well-investigated word stress languages, such as West Germanic languages, tonal events often align with lexically stressed syllables. Tashlhiyt lacks word stress, which raises the question as to how intonational events are aligned with the segmental string.

Most of the (few) languages that are postulated not to have word stress have been described in terms of predetermined tonal strings associating sequentially within a domain like the accentual phrase or phonological phrase (Jun 2005, for Korean; Jun & Fougeron 2002, for French; Karlsson 2014, for Mongolian). To my knowledge, the only language which has been instrumentally studied with regard to tonal alignment and which exhibits comparable patterns to Tashlhiyt is Ambonese Malay (Maskikit-Essed & Gussenhoven 2016). Maskikit-Essed and Gussenhoven reported on a sparse distribution of tonal events in Ambonese Malay. They investigated two tunes characterised by a rise-fall and a rise, respectively, both occurring at the end of a intonation phrase. The alignment of the high target of the rise-fall was prone to a large amount of variability. This vari-

8 Concluding remarks and future directions

ability appeared to be of gradual nature, i.e. tonal events were variably aligned with the phrase-final word. These tonal events were interpreted as edge tones that are approximately timed to occur with the phrase-final word, rather than associated to a specific syllable.

This variability resembles the tonal placement patterns in Tashlhiyt. Both systems exhibit a sparse distribution of tones across the utterance and have arguably no word stress. This raises the question as to whether the absence of a lexical determined metrical anchor is correlated with a certain flexibility in tonal placement. Answers to this question remain speculative until more instrumental studies are available. We hope that the used methods and analyses will spark further interest to investigate stress and intonation in other Berber languages. This would be particularly interesting with regard to the interaction of word stress and tonal placement. Other Berber languages such as Zwara Berber, spoken in Libya, have been reported to exhibit word stress. Whether tonal placement exhibits less variability in these varieties is an interesting question. Preliminary results suggest that this is indeed the case (Gussenhoven 2017). Therefore, descriptive and comparative explorations of stress and intonation in other Berber languages could be a very informative departure point from which possible typological generalisations can be made.

As opposed to Ambonese Malay, tonal placement patterns in Tashlhiyt, as presented here (also in Grice, Ridouane & Roettger 2015), exhibit variability that was referred to as discrete variability. Tonal events systematically align with one of two mutually exclusive positions that can be defined in discrete ways, rather than continuously varying between these positions. Thus, the observed variability exhibits a systematic structure. Most interestingly, large amounts of this structured variability can be related to Tashlhiyt's phonotactic patterns.

8.2 Phonotactic restrictions on tonal placement

In Tashlhiyt, many words can be comprised of consonants only. Consonants can be considered poorer carriers of pitch than vowels and even within consonants, some segment types are better suited to convey pitch information than others. In extreme cases, the phonetic opportunity afforded for the execution of pitch movements is exceptionally limited. In spite of these restrictions, communicatively relevant tones in Tashlhiyt show a preference to be located in certain prosodic positions. This creates a functional conflict between privileged prosodic locations and their inherent qualities to carry pitch information. This conflict can be resolved in many different ways. Recall that if the tone bearing word contains

8.2 Phonotactic restrictions on tonal placement

more than one sonorant, the tonal events described in this book associate either to the penult or to the final syllable. If the word does not contain a sonorant, the tones associate either to the vowel of the preceding word or to a schwa within the word. Alternatively, the tones may remain unrealised. With which syllables the tones associate is not only dependent on sentence modality but also on at least three competing factors orthogonal to that: (1) the tones are generally attracted to the right edge, i.e. the tones are more often located on the final syllable than on the penult and they are more often located on schwa than on the preceding word. (2) The tones are attracted to more sonorous elements, i.e. if there are two available sonorants within the word, the tones are preferably located on the more sonorous one. If there is only one sonorant in the word, the tones are almost exclusively located on it, and if there is no sonorant in the word, the tones may be realised on a sonorant of the preceding word. (3) The tone is attracted to heavy syllables, i.e. the tones are more often located on heavy syllables than on light syllables.

These tendencies can all be conceived of as optimising the phonetic prerequisites for the manifestation of pitch. A pitch target or contour has a more salient percept on segments that are higher in intensity and have a richer harmonic structure (Zhang 2004; Barnes et al. 2014). In this sense, tonal events in Tashlhiyt are attracted to positions that are well suited to pitch perception.

With regard to (1), phrase-final elements are often spatio-temporally expanded (among other things, they are longer and louder, see Chapter 2 and 6), not only offering more time for the articulation of a complex pitch movement but also enabling a more salient pitch percept. With regard to (2), a pitch movement on a vowel is easier to perceive than one on a consonant. Even if the consonant is voiced – clearly a prerequisite for pitch – a pitch target is easier to perceive on nasals and liquids than on fricatives and stops. In terms of pitch perception and production, voiced obstruents are weak carriers of the signal. When airflow is inhibited during an articulatory constriction, the leeway for vocal fold modulation is limited. Moreover, voiced obstruents are acoustically manifested by low intensity and a restricted harmonic structure, diminishing the saliency of a pitch percept. Voiceless obstruents are at the extreme end of the scale being the the type of sounds that are least suited for carrying information cued by fundamental frequency. Finally, with regard to (3), a more complex rhyme may also be beneficial for mechanisms of pitch perception. A longer rhyme, i.e. more elements of high intensity and rich harmonic structure, will enable a more salient percept of pitch. This, however, is dependent on the identity of the coda consonant, since not all consonants are well suited to carry pitch.

8 Concluding remarks and future directions

Interestingly, these individual factors not only correlate with pitch perceptibility, they also resonate with cross-linguistic asymmetries.[1] For example, many tone languages restrict contour tones to syllables with rhymes that contain more sonorous elements (Zhang 2001; Gordon 2004). Tashlhiyt is a rare case with regard to sonority determining structures at higher levels of prosodic structure. However, there are some other reports of tone bearing units of intonational tones being defined by sonority. For example, Japanese allows secondary association of edge tones to sonorant moras but not to non-sonorant moras (Pierrehumbert & Beckman 1988). Moreover, there are many languages with weight-sensitive word stress or tone systems (cf. De Lacy 2002; 2007; Gordon 2004; 2006, for overviews), in which syllables with relatively more complex rhymes exhibit more tonal contrasts and are more likely to be the metrically strong syllable of a constituent.

In languages discussed in the above-cited literature, the co-occurrence of a tone with a certain structure appears to be phonologised. In such cases, the quality of a unit for expressing pitch contrasts categorically determines its actual co-occurrence with phonological tones (e.g. a contour tone co-occurs with a certain syllable structure or not). Tashlhiyt, however, does not exhibit such a consistent mapping, but rather allows for several competing possibilities of how the segmental structure affects the realisation of tone.

The most frequently observed option is a temporal shift of the tonal event, i.e. tones move towards segmental material that is better suited to carrying pitch information. This is true for both words with sonorants and words containing no sonorants. In cases with multiple available sonorants, the tone can shift to a position that is segmentally most suitable for the realisation and perception of the pitch movement. In cases with no available sonorants, the tone can even shift to a position that is outside of the tone-bearing word. Similar temporal shifts of tonal events to less restricted material have been observed for Neapolitan Italian (Cangemi & Grice 2016). As opposed to Neapolitan Italian, Tashlhiyt does not exhibit gradual shifts but discrete shifts that can be analysed as changes in the association of the tones.

In addition to temporal shifts, the tonal movement can be undershot. This resembles phenomena referred to as 'truncation', i.e. cases in which a tonal target is not fully reached. In words with available sonorants, truncation mainly applies to the final low tone following the high target. The high target is almost always realised in these cases. Similar observations have been made for other languages

---

[1] It is not implied that there is a causal relationship between the functional motivation of a speech pattern and observed cross-linguistic asymmetries, even though the author considers this hypothesis highly plausible (e.g. Ohala 1993; Blevins 2004, among many others).

8.2 Phonotactic restrictions on tonal placement

such as Catalan, English, German, Russian, Spanish, and Swedish (Erikson & Alstermark 1972; Grabe 1998; Grabe et al. 2000; Prieto & Ortega-Llebaria 2009; Rathcke 2009). Alternatively, Tashlhiyt allows the entire tonal complex to be absent altogether. To our knowledge, the latter case has never been reported on in the literature. From a functional perspective, this is arguably the least desirable pattern. The absence of the tone leaves the listener with no local cue to disambiguate an intonational contrast. All these patterns share a common relationship between segments and tones: the segmental material determines the realisation of tones, or in other words, 'the text drives the tune'.

Alternatively, the text can be adjusted to enable the realisation of the tune. Tashlhiyt allows vowel insertion to bear functionally relevant tonal movements. This is comparable to Italian word-final schwa in loan words, which has been shown to be dependent on the complexity of the tune that needs to be realised (Grice et al. 2015). Similar observations have been made for Moroccan Arabic (Dell & Elmedlaoui 1985) and Tarifiyt Berber (Dell & Tangi 1985), two languages also spoken in Morocco. The mirror image of these phenomena has been reported for Greek and other languages. In Greek, vowels are often deleted in certain prosodic positions. However, this deletion is less likely in prosodically privileged positions, namely those locations that bear complex intonational pitch movements (Kaimaki 2015). Similarly, Heath (1987: 184) described a process in which schwa deletion in word-final syllables is blocked by "list intonation" for Moroccan Colloquial Arabic. Vance (1987: 51) claims that in Japanese high vowel devoicing is blocked "when a final syllable in the devoicing environment must carry a rising intonation." These patterns constitute cases in which the requirement of the tonal realisation causes the segmental structure to adjust or in other words cases in which 'the tune drives the text' (Grice et al. 2015).

All of the discussed patterns can be conceived of as solutions to a functional dilemma: the requirement to realise meaningful pitch movements in privileged prosodic positions and the extent to which segments lend themselves for a clear manifestation of these pitch movements. Most well documented languages such as West Germanic languages usually do not face such extreme conflicts of tune-text-association. The patterns observed for Tashlhiyt, thus, add to our understanding of how conflicting structural preferences can be resolved. Tashlhiyt demonstrates, more clearly than any other language before, that the tune and the text interact in a synergetic way. The text drives the tune and the tune drives the text.

8 Concluding remarks and future directions

8.3 Future directions

Future studies will have to complement the present studies in order to evaluate the proposed analyses and to increase our understanding of prosodic structure and intonation in Tashlhiyt. Fruitful avenues for future research are the investigation of tonal events and phrasing in longer utterances. While the present analysis has discussed the possibility of focus-induced phrasing, the data was restricted to short utterances. Impressionistic observations from semi-spontaneous tasks hint at the possibility of a richer prosodic structure in longer phrases than the patterns described in this book.[2] The question arises as to whether there is robust evidence for prosodic constituents smaller than the intonation phrase and larger than the phonological word. Analyses of corpora of more natural speech may answer remaining questions. Only after gaining a broader understanding of prosodic structure and after considering the full range of tonal events, a complete analysis of intonation in Tashlhiyt can be proposed.

Beyond descriptive and typological purposes, the analysis of Tashlhiyt has clearly demonstrated that presently available formalisms for the description of intonation systems have difficulties in modelling certain types of variability. Both the discrete variability of tonal events and the gradient variability of pitch scaling pose a challenge to the Autosegmental-Metrical model. These types of variability appear to be common in intonational systems and are rather difficult to formalise within the available symbolic representations. The problem appears to be rooted in the traditional assumption that speech can be represented as sequences of discrete symbols using discrete mathematics. Even though practical for description and comparison purposes, more and more evidence suggests that discrete mathematics are insufficient to account for numerous observations even within the segmental domain. For example, processes of assimilation and neutralisation are commonly represented via discrete formalisms resulting in categorical predictions. A segment is assimilated or not; it is neutralised or not. However, these alternations might in fact not always be categorical. Evidence suggests that the assimilation of a segment does not involve a discrete alternation but a continuous modulation of gestural overlap with different degrees of overlap dependent on the context (Browman & Goldstein 1986). Similarly, often-cited neutralisation processes have repeatedly been shown to be incomplete (e.g. Port & O'Dell 1985; Roettger et al. 2014).

---

[2] Some of the recordings involving semi-spontaneous tasks have been made available by Bruggeman & Roettger (2017).

8.3 Future directions

In addition to the continuous nature of categorically formalised phenomena, certain alternations may be categorical but apply only probabilistically depending on several competing factors (cf. /t/ deletion in Chapter 7). Thus, phenomena traditionally formalised as discrete operations or entities are in fact more adequately represented in terms of statistical distribution expressed by continuous mathematics. This comprises both the probability of an event occurring as well as the phonetic variability the event exhibits when it occurs. Developing formalisms that capture these aspects of speech would enable a more detailed comparison of phonological systems, and in turn, more adequate models of human language.

Appendix

A.1 Media Access

The sound files of the examples used in the figures throughout this book can be accessed here: https://doi.org/10.5281/zenodo.815840. The files are saved under transparent names, titled according to their occurrence in respective figures (e.g. "Figure 5.9a").

The data presented in Chapter 5 and 6 were recorded by the author. The data presented in Chapter 4 were recorded by Anna Bruggeman and are used with her permission.

A.2 Participant Information

Table A.1: Speaker information of production experiment discussed in Chapter 4.

Initials	Exp-ID	Gender	Age	Origin
AO	1	M	24	Tata
MO	2	M	34	Tata
AB	3	M	26	Tiznit
L	4	F	24	Tata
S	5	F	22	Tata
E	6	M	26	Tiznit
H	7	F	21	Agadir
S	8	F	21	Tata / Agadir
AC	9	M	28	Tata

Appendix

Table A.2: Speaker information of production experiment discussed in Chapter 5 and 6

Initials	Exp-ID	Gender	Age	Origin
MI	M1	M	21	Agadir
SAS	M2	M	21	Taroudant
BM	M3	M	22	Ait Baha (Anti-Atlas)
AA	F1	F	21	Agadir
IB	F2	F	20	Taroudant
IS	M4	M	23	Tighmi (Anti-Atlas)
BF	F3	F	22	Agadir
FZ	F4	F	24	Agadir
BA	M5	M	27	Agadir
RA	F5	F	19	Anti-Atlas

Table A.3: Speaker information of perception experiment discussed in Chapter 5.

Initials	Exp-ID	Gender	Age	Origin	Note
SB	1	M	23	Ait Baamrane	
OH	2	F	20	Tata	
OZ	3	F	21	Tata	
HDE	4	F	20	Agadir	
LH	5	M	22	Ait Baamrane	
SH	6	M	23	Ait Baamrane	
SaH	7	M	22	Ait Baamrane	excluded
HA	8	F	20	Ait Baamrane	
BJ	9	M	22	Ait Baamrane	

References

Anttila, Arto. 1997. Deriving variation from grammar. In Frans Hinskens, Roeland van Hout & Leo Wetzels (eds.), *Variation, change, and phonological theory*, 35–68. Amsterdam: John Benjamins.

Anttila, Arto. 2012. Modeling phonological variation. In Abigail C. Cohn, Cécile Fougeron & Marie K. Huffman (eds.), 76–91. Oxford University Press.

Applegate, Joseph R. 1958. *An outline of the structure of Shilha*. New York: American Council of Learned Societies.

Applegate, Joseph R. 1971. The Berber languages. In Thomas. A. Sebeok (ed.), *Current trends in linguistics: Linguistics in South West Asia and North Africa*, vol. 6, 586–661. The Hague: Mouton.

Arvaniti, Amalia. 1998. Phrase accents revisited: Comparative evidence from standard and Cypriot Greek. In *Proceedings of the 5th International Conference on Spoken Language Processing*, 2883–2886. Sidney, Australia.

Arvaniti, Amalia. 2001. The intonation of wh-questions in Greek. *Studies in Greek Linguistics* 21. 57–68.

Arvaniti, Amalia. 2011. The representation of intonation. In Marc van Oostendorp, Colin J. Ewen, Elizabeth V. Hume & Keren Rice (eds.), *The Blackwell companion to phonology: Vol. 2. Suprasegmental and prosodic phonology*, vol. 5, 757–780. Malden, MA: John Wiley & Sons.

Arvaniti, Amalia & D. Robert Ladd. 2009. Greek wh-questions and the phonology of intonation. *Phonology* 26(01). 43–74.

Arvaniti, Amalia, D. Robert Ladd & Ineke Mennen. 1998. Stability of tonal alignment: The case of Greek prenuclear accents. *Journal of phonetics* 26(1). 3–25.

Arvaniti, Amalia, D. Robert Ladd & Ineke Mennen. 2000. What is a starred tone? Evidence from Greek. In Michael B. Broe & Janet Pierrehumbert (eds.), *Papers in Laboratory Phonology V: Acquisition and the lexicon*, 119–131. Cambridge: Cambridge University Press.

Arvaniti, Amalia, D. Robert Ladd & Ineke Mennen. 2006. Tonal association and tonal alignment: Evidence from Greek polar questions and contrastive statements. *Language and Speech* 49(4). 421–450.

References

Aspinion, Robert. 1953. *Apprenons le berbère: initation aux dialectes chleuhs*. Rabat: Éditions Félix Moncho.

Atterer, Michaela & D. Robert Ladd. 2004. On the phonetics and phonology of "segmental anchoring" of f0: Evidence from German. *Journal of Phonetics* 32(2). 177–197.

Bannert, Robert & A. Bredvad. 1975. Temporal organisation of Swedish tonal accent: The effect of vowel duration. *Working Papers in Linguistics, Lund University* 10. 1–36.

Barnes, Jonathan, Alejna Brugos, Nanette Veilleux & Stefanie Shattuck-Hufnagel. 2014. Segmental influences on the perception of pitch accent scaling in English. In *Proceedings of 7th Speech Prosody Conference*, 1125–1129. Dublin, UK.

Barr, Dale J., Roger Levy, Christoph Scheepers & Harry J. Tily. 2013. Random effects structure for confirmatory hypothesis testing: Keep it maximal. *Journal of memory and language* 68(3). 255–278.

Bartels, Christine. 1999. *The intonation of English statements and questions: A compositional interpretation*. New York: Routledge.

Basset, André. 1952. *La langue berbère*. Oxford: Oxford University Press.

Bates, Douglas, Martin Mächler, Ben Bolker & Steve Walker. 2015. Fitting linear mixed-effects models using lme4. *Journal of Statistical Software* 67(1). 1–48.

Baumann, Stefan, Christine T. Röhr & Martine Grice. 2015. Prosodische (De-)kodierung des informationsstatus im Deutschen. *Zeitschrift für Sprachwissenschaft* 34(1). 1–42.

Beckman, Mary & Jan Edwards. 1990. Lengthenings and shortenings and the nature of prosodic constituency. In John Kingston & Mary Beckman (eds.), *Papers in Laboratory Phonology I: Between the grammar and physics of speech*, 179–200. Cambridge: Cambridge University Press.

Beckman, Mary & Janet Pierrehumbert. 1986. Intonational structure in Japanese and English. *Phonology* 3(01). 255–309.

Benkirane, Thami. 1998. Intonation in Western Arabic (Morocco). In Daniel Hirst & Albert Di Cristo (eds.), *Intonation systems: A survey of twenty languages*, 345–359. Cambridge: Cambridge University Press.

Bensoukas, Karim. 2001. *Stem forms in the nontemplatic morphology of Berber*. Rabat: Université Mohammed V PhD thesis.

Berdouzi, Mohamed. 2000. *Rénover l'enseignement: De la charte aux actes*. Rabat: Renouveau.

Blevins, Juliette. 2004. *Evolutionary phonology: The emergence of sound patterns*. Cambridge: Cambridge University Press.

Bloomfield, Leonard. 1933. *Language*. New York: Holt.

Boersma, Paul. 1997. How we learn variation, optionality, and probability. In *Proceedings of the Institute of Phonetic Sciences of the University of Amsterdam*, vol. 21, 43–58. Amsterdam.

Boersma, Paul & Bruce Hayes. 2001. Empirical tests of the gradual learning algorithm. *Linguistic inquiry* 32(1). 45–86.

Boersma, Paul & David Weenink. 2015. *Praat: Doing phonetics by computer.* [Computer program]. Version 6.0.05.

Bolinger, Dwight Le Merton. 1951. Intonation: Levels versus configurations. *Word* 7(3). 199–210.

Bolinger, Dwight Le Merton. 1961. *Generality: Gradience and the all-or-none.* The Hague: Mouton & Company.

Bolinger, Dwight Le Merton. 1978. Intonation across languages. In Joseph H. Greenberg (ed.), *Universals of human language*, vol. 2, 471–524. Stanford: Stanford University Press.

Bolinger, Dwight Le Merton. 1989. *Intonation and its uses: Melody in grammar and discourse.* Stanford: Stanford University Press.

Boogert, Nico van den. 1997. *The Berber literary tradition of the Souls: With an edition and translation of "the ocean of tears" by Muhammad Awzal.* Leiden: Nederlands Instituut voor het Nabije Oosten.

Boukhris, Fatima, Abdallah Boumalk, El-Houssaïn El-Moujahid & Hamid Souifi. 2008. *La nouvelle grammaire de l'amazighe.* Rabat: Institut Royal de la Culture Amazighe.

Boukous, Ahmed. 1987. *Phonotactique et domaines prosodiques en berbère (parler tachelhit d'Agadir, Maroc).* Université de Paris VIII, Vincennes è Saint Denis PhD thesis.

Boukous, Ahmed. 2012. *Revitalisation de la langue amazighe: Défis, enjeux et stratégies.* Rabat: Top Press.

Braun, Bettina. 2006. Phonetics and phonology of thematic contrast in German. *Language and Speech* 49(4). 451–493.

Breiman, Leo. 2001. Random forests. *Machine learning* 45(1). 5–32.

Browman, Catherine P. & Louis Goldstein. 1986. Towards an articulatory phonology. *Phonology* 3(01). 219–252.

Browman, Catherine P. & Louis Goldstein. 1990. Gestural specification using dynamically-defined articulatory structures. *Journal of Phonetics* 18. 299–320.

Bruce, Gösta. 1977. *Swedish word accents in sentence perspective.* Lund University PhD thesis.

References

Bruggeman, Anna & Timo B. Roettger. 2017. *CoTaSS: Corpus of Tashlhiyt Semi-spontaneous Speech*. http://cotass.uni-koeln.de/index.php/en/home/. http://cotass.uni-koeln.de/index.php/en/home/.

Bruggeman, Anna, Timo B. Roettger & Martine Grice. 2017. Question word intonation in tashlhiyt berber: is 'high'good enough? *Laboratory Phonology: Journal of the Association for Laboratory Phonology* 8.

Brunelle, Marc. 2017. Stress and phrasal prominence in tone languages: The case of Southern vietnamese. *Journal of the International Phonetic Association*. 1–38.

Brunelle, Marc, Kiều Phuong Ha & Martine Grice. 2012. Intonation in Northern Vietnamese. *Linguistic review* 29(1). 3–36.

Buring, Daniel. 2009. Towards a typology of focus realization. In Malte Zimmermann & Caroline Féry (eds.), *Information structure*, 177–205. Oxford: Oxford University Press.

Byrd, Dani & Elliot Saltzman. 2003. The elastic phrase: Modeling the dynamics of boundary-adjacent lengthening. *Journal of Phonetics* 31(2). 149–180.

Cangemi, Francesco. 2015. *Mausmooth*. Praat script.

Cangemi, Francesco & Martine Grice. 2016. The importance of a distributional approach to categoriality in Autosegmental-Metrical accounts of intonation. *Laboratory Phonology: Journal of the Association for Laboratory Phonology* 7(1). 1–20.

Caspers, Johanneke & Vincent J. van Heuven. 1993. Effects of time pressure on the phonetic realization of Dutch accent-lending pitch rise and fall. *Phonetica* 50(3). 161–171.

Chaker, Salem. 1992. *Une décennie d'études Berbères (1890-1990): Bibliographie critique*. Algiers: Bouchène.

Chaker, Salem. 1996. *Propositions pour la notation usuelle a base latine du Berbère*. Atelier du 24-25 juin 1996, INALCO-CRB. Synthèse des travaux.

Cho, Taehong. 2005. Prosodic strengthening and featural enhancement: Evidence from acoustic and articulatory realizations of /ɑ, i/ in English. *The Journal of the Acoustical Society of America* 117(6). 3867–3878.

Cho, Taehong & Sun-Ah Jun. 2000. Domain-initial strengthening as enhancement of laryngeal features: Aerodynamic evidence from Korean. *UCLA working papers in phonetics* 99. 57–70.

Cho, Taehong & Patricia Keating. 2009. Effects of initial position versus prominence in English. *Journal of Phonetics* 37(4). 466–485.

Cho, Taehong & James M. McQueen. 2005. Prosodic influences on consonant production in Dutch: Effects of prosodic boundaries, phrasal accent and lexical stress. *Journal of Phonetics* 33(2). 121–157.

Choi, Hansook. 2003. Prosody-induced acoustic variation in English stop consonants. In *Proceedings of the 15th International Congress of Phonetic Sciences*, 2661–2664. Barcelona, Spain.

Chomsky, Noam & Morris Halle. 1968. *The sound pattern of English*. New York: Harper & Row.

Clark, Herbert H. 1973. The language-as-fixed-effect fallacy: A critique of language statistics in psychological research. *Journal of verbal learning and verbal behavior* 12(4). 335–359.

Cohen, Antonie & Johan t'Hart. 1968. On the anatomy of intonation. *Lingua* 19(1-2). 177–192.

Cole, Jennifer, Hansook Choi, Heejin Kim & Mark Hasegawa-johnson. 2003. The effect of accent on the acoustic cues to stop voicing in radio news speech. In *Proceedings of the 15th International Congress of Phonetic Sciences*. Barcelona, Spain.

Cole, Jennifer, Heejin Kim, Hansook Choi & Mark Hasegawa-Johnson. 2007. Prosodic effects on acoustic cues to stop voicing and place of articulation: Evidence from radio news speech. *Journal of Phonetics* 35(2). 180–209.

Coleman, John. 1996. Declarative syllabification in Tashlhit Berber. In Jacques Durand & Bernard Laks (eds.), *Current trends in phonology: models and methods*, 175–216. CNRS, Paris X & University of Salford: University of Salford Publications.

Coleman, John. 1999. The nature of vocoids associated with syllabic consonants in Tashlhiyt Berber. In *Proceedings of the 14th International Congress of Phonetic Sciences*, 735–738. San Francisco, California.

Coleman, John. 2001. The phonetics and phonology of Tashlhiyt Berber syllabic consonants. *Transactions of the Philological Society* 99(1). 29–64.

Colin, Georges S. 1937. Les parlers: l'arabe. *Initiation au Maroc*. 208–236.

Cooper, A. 1991. *Glottal gestures and aspiration in English*. Yale University PhD thesis.

Crystal, David. 1969. *Prosodic systems and intonation in English*. Cambridge: Cambridge University Press.

De Lacy, Paul. 2002. The interaction of tone and stress in Optimality Theory. *Phonology* 19(2). 1–32.

De Lacy, Paul. 2007. The interaction of tone, sonority, and prosodic structure. In Paul De Lacy (ed.), *The Cambridge handbook of phonology*, 281–307. Cambridge, MA: MIT Press.

De Saussure, Ferdinand. 1989. *Cours de linguistique générale: édition critique*. Vol. 1. Wiesbaden: Otto Harrassowitz Verlag.

References

Dell, François & Mohamed Elmedlaoui. 1985. Syllabic consonants and syllabification in Imdlawn Tashlhiyt Berber. *Journal of African Languages and Linguistics* 7(2). 105–130.

Dell, François & Mohamed Elmedlaoui. 1988. Syllabic consonants in Berber: Some new evidence. *Journal of African Languages and Linguistics* 10(1). 1–17.

Dell, François & Mohamed Elmedlaoui. 1996. Nonsyllabic transitional vocoids in Imdlawn Tashlhiyt Berber. In Jacques Durand & Bernard Laks (eds.), *Current trends in phonology: models and methods*, 217–244. CNRS, Paris X & University of Salford: University of Salford Publications.

Dell, François & Mohamed Elmedlaoui. 2002. *Syllables in Tashlhiyt Berber and in Moroccan Arabic*. Dordrecht: Kluwer.

Dell, François & Mohamed Elmedlaoui. 2008. *Poetic meter and musical form in Tashlhiyt Berber songs*. Cologne: Rüdiger Köppe Verlag.

Dell, François & Oufae Tangi. 1985. Syllabification and empty nuclei in Ath–Sidhar Rifan Berber. *Journal of African Languages and Linguistics* 13(2). 1–17.

Diercks, Kristin Lena. 2011. *Akustische und artikulatorische Prominenzmarkierung im Tashlhiyt Berber*. University of Cologne MA thesis.

D'Imperio, Mariapaola. 2001. Focus and tonal structure in Neapolitan Italian. *Speech Communication* 33(4). 339–356.

D'Imperio, Mariapaola & David House. 1997. Perception of questions and statements in Neapolitan Italian. In *Proceedings of the 5th European Conference on Speech Communication and Technology*, 251–254.

Edwards, Jan, Mary Beckman & Janet Fletcher. 1991. The articulatory kinematics of final lengthening. *The Journal of the Acoustical Society of America* 89(1). 369–382.

El-Aissati, Abderrahman. 2005. A socio-historical perspective on the Amazigh (Berber) cultural movement in North Africa. *Afrika Focus* 18(1-2). 59–72.

Elmedlaoui, Mohamed. 1995. *Aspects des représentations phonologiques dans certaines langues chamito-sémitiques*. Faculté des lettres et des sciences humaines, Université Mohammed V, Rabat PhD thesis.

Ennaji, Moha. 2005. *Multilingualism, cultural identity, and education in Morocco*. New York: Springer.

Erikson, Y. & Margit Alstermark. 1972. Fundamental frequency correlates of the grave word accent in Swedish: The effect of vowel duration. *Speech Transmission Laboratory, Quarterly Papers and Status Report* 13(2-3). 53–60.

Face, Timothy & Pilar Prieto. 2007. Rising accents in Castilian Spanish: A revision of Sp_ToBI. *Journal of Portuguese Linguistics* 6(1). 117–146.

Féry, Caroline & Frank Kügler. 2008. Pitch accent scaling on given, new and focused constituents in German. *Journal of Phonetics* 36(4). 680–703.

Fougeron, Cécile & Rachid Ridouane. 2008. On the nature of schwa-like vocalic elements within some Berber clusters. In *Proceedings of the 8th International Seminar on Speech Production*, 441–444.

Frota, Sónia. 2002. Tonal association and target alignment in European Portuguese nuclear falls. In Natasha Warner & Carlos Gussenhoven (eds.), *Papers in Laboratory Phonology 7*, vol. 7, 387–418. Berlin, New York: Mouton de Gruyter.

Fry, Dennis B. 1955. Duration and intensity as physical correlates of linguistic stress. *The Journal of the Acoustical Society of America* 27(4). 765–768.

Fry, Dennis B. 1958. Experiments in the perception of stress. *Language and speech* 1(2). 120–152.

Fujimura, Osamu, Marian J. Macchi & Lynn A. Streeter. 1978. Perception of stop consonants with conflicting transitional cues: A cross-linguistic study. *Language and speech* 21(4). 337–346.

Galand, Lionel. 1988. Le berbère. In David Cohen & Jean Perrot (eds.), *Les langues dans le monde ancien et moderne*, vol. 3, 207–242. Paris: Editions du CNRS.

Gårding, Eva. 1983. A generative model of intonation. In Anne Cutler & D. Robert Ladd (eds.), *Prosody: Models and measurements*, 11–25. Berlin: Springer.

Goedemans, Rob & Harry van der Hulst. 2009. StressTyp: A database for word accentual patterns in the world's languages. In Harry van der Hulst (ed.), *The use of databases in cross-linguistics research*, 235–282. Cambridge: Cambridge University Press.

Goedemans, Rob & Ellen van Zanten. 2007. Stress and accent in Indonesian. In Vincent van Heuven & Ellen van Zanten (eds.), *Prosody in Indonesian languages*, 35–62. Utrecht: LOT, Netherlands Graduate School of Linguistics.

Goldinger, Stephen D. 1998. Echoes of echoes? An episodic theory of lexical access. *Psychological review* 105(2). 251–279.

Goldstein, Louis. 2011. Back to the past tense in English. In Rodrigo Gutiérrez-Bravo, Line Mikkelsen & Eric Potsdam (eds.), *Representing language: Essays in honor of Judith Aissen*, 69–88. Santa Cruz, California: University of California, Santa Cruz.

Goldstein, Louis. 2014. *Intrusive vowels and the dynamics of gestural coordination*. Oral presentation at 22nd Manchester Phonology Meeting.

Gordon, Matthew. 2004. Syllable weight. In Bruce Hayes, Robert Kirchner & Donca Steriade (eds.), *Phonetic bases for phonological markedness*, 277–312. Cambridge: Cambridge University Press.

References

Gordon, Matthew. 2006. *Syllable weight: Phonetics, phonology, typology*. New York: Routledge.

Gordon, Matthew. 2014. Disentangling stress and pitch accent: A typology of prominence at different prosodic levels. In Harry van der Hulst (ed.), *Word stress. Theoretical and typological issues*. 8–118. Cambridge: Cambridge University Press.

Gordon, Matthew & Latifa Nafi. 2012. Acoustic correlates of stress and pitch accent in Tashelhiyt Berber. *Journal of Phonetics* 40(5). 70–724.

Gordon, Matthew & Timo B. Roettger. in press. Acoustic correlates of word stress: A cross-linguistic survey. *Linguistic Vanguard*.

Gósy, Mária & Jacques M. B. Terken. 1994. Question marking in Hungarian: Timing and height of pitch peaks. *Journal of Phonetics* 22. 269–281.

Grabe, Esther. 1998. Pitch accent realization in English and German. *Journal of Phonetics* 26(2). 129–143.

Grabe, Esther, Brechtje Post, Francis Nolan & Kimberley Farrar. 2000. Pitch accent realization in four varieties of British English. *Journal of Phonetics* 28(2). 161–185.

Grice, Martine. 1995. *The intonation of interrogation in Palermo Italian; implications for intonation theory*. Tübingen: Niemeyer.

Grice, Martine. 2006. Intonation. In Keith Brown (ed.), *Encyclopedia of Language and Linguistics*, Second, vol. 5, 778–788. Oxford: Elsevier.

Grice, Martine, Amalia Arvaniti & D. Robert Ladd. 2000. On the place of phrase accents in intonational phonology. *Phonology* 17. 143–185.

Grice, Martine, Stefan Baumann & Ralf Benzmülller. 2005. German intonation in Autosegmental-Metrical phonology. In Sun-Ah Jun (ed.), *Prosodic typology: The phonology of intonation and phrasing*, 55–83. Oxford: Oxford University Press.

Grice, Martine, Rachid Ridouane & Timo B. Roettger. 2015. Tonal association in Tashlhiyt Berber: Evidence from polar questions and contrastive statements. *Phonology* 32(2). 241–266.

Grice, Martine, Michelina Savino & Mario Refice. 1997. The intonation of questions in Bari Italian: Do speakers replicate their spontaneous speech when reading. *Phonus* 3. 1–7.

Grice, Martine, Ralf Benzmüller, Michelina Savino & Bistra Andreeva. 1995. The intonation of queries and checks across languages: Data from map task dialogues. In *Proceedings of the 13th International Congress of Phonetic Sciences*, 648–651. Stockholm.

Grice, Martine, Mariapaola D'Imperio, Michelina Savino & Cinzia Avesani. 2005. Towards a strategy for labelling varieties of Italian. In Sun-Ah Jun (ed.), *Prosodic typology: The phonology of intonation and phrasing*, 362–389. Oxford: Oxford University Press.

Grice, Martine, Timo B. Roettger, Rachid Ridouane & Cécile Fougeron. 2011. The association of tones in Tashlhiyt Berber. In *Proceedings of the 17th International Congress of Phonetic Sciences*, 775–778. Hong Kong.

Grice, Martine, Michelina Savino, Alessandro Caffo & Timo B. Roettger. 2015. The tune drives the text – schwa in consonant-final loanwords in Italian. In *Proceedings of 18th International Congress of Phonetic Sciences*. Glasgow, UK.

Grice, Martine, Simon Ritter, Henrik Niemann & Timo B. Roettger. 2017. Integrating the discreteness and continuity of intonational categories. *Journal of Phonetics*.

Grønnum, Nina. 1989. Stress group patterns, sentence accents and sentence interration in Southern Jutland (Sonderborg and Tonder) - with a view to German. *Annual Reports of the Institute of Phonetics, University of Copenhagen* 23. 1–85.

Gussenhoven, Carlos. 2000. The boundary tones are coming. In Michael Broe & Janet Pierrehumbert (eds.), *Papers in Laboratory Phonology V: Acquisition and the lexicon*, 132–151. Cambridge: Cambridge University Press.

Gussenhoven, Carlos. 2002. Phonology of intonation. *Glot International* 6(9/10). 271–284.

Gussenhoven, Carlos. 2004. *The phonology of tone and intonation*. Cambridge: Cambridge University Press.

Gussenhoven, Carlos. 2015. Does phonological prominence exist? *Lingue e linguaggio* 14(1). 7–24.

Gussenhoven, Carlos. 2017. Zwara Tamazight. *Journal of the International Phonetic Association*. 1–17.

Gussenhoven, Carlos & Toni Rietveld. 1992. Intonation contours, prosodic structure and preboundary lengthening. *Journal of Phonetics* 20(3). 283–303.

Gussenhoven, Carlos & Toni Rietveld. 2000. The behavior of H* and L* under variations in pitch range in Dutch rising contours. *Language and Speech* 43(2). 183–203.

Gussenhoven, Carlos & Peter van der Vliet. 1999. The phonology of tone and intonation in the Dutch dialect of Venlo. *Journal of linguistics* 35(01). 99–135.

Guy, Gregory R. 1980. Variation in the group and the individual: The case of final stop deletion. In William Labov (ed.), *Locating language in time and space*, 1–36. New York: Academic Press.

Haan, Judith. 2002. *Speaking of questions*. Utrecht: LOT.

References

Hadding-Koch, Kerstin & Michael Studdert-Kennedy. 1964. An experimental study of some intonation contours. *Phonetica* 11(3-4). 175–185.

Haeseryn, Walter, Kirsten Romijn, Guido Geerts, J. de Rooij & Maarten C. Toorn. 1997. *Algemene Nederlandse spraakkunst*. Groningen: Nijhoff.

Hall, Nancy. 2006. Cross-linguistic patterns of vowel intrusion. *Phonology* 23(03). 387–429.

Halle, Morris & Jean-Roger Vergnaud. 1987. Stress and the cycle. *Linguistic Inquiry* 18(1). 45–84.

Halliday, Michael Alexander Kirkwood. 1967. *Intonation and grammar in British English*. The Hague: Mouton de Gruyter.

Hanssen, Judith, Jörg Peters & Carlos Gussenhoven. 2007. Phrase-final pitch accommodation effects in Dutch. In *Proceedings of the 16th International Congress of Phonetic Sciences*, 1077–1080. Saarbrücken, Germany.

Harms, Robert T. 1976. The segmentalization of Finnish 'nonrules'. In *Texas linguistic forum*, vol. 5, 73–88.

Harrington, Jonathan, Janet Fletcher & Mary Beckman. 2000. Manner and place conflicts in the articulation of accent in Australian English. In Michael Broe & Janet Pierrehumbert (eds.), *Papers in Laboratory Phonology V: Acquisition and the lexicon*, 40–51. Cambridge: Cambridge University Press.

Hawkins, Sarah. 2003. Roles and representations of systematic fine phonetic detail in speech understanding. *Journal of Phonetics* 31(3-4). 373–405.

Hawkins, Sarah. 2012. The lexicon: Not just elusive, but illusory. In Abigail C. Cohn & Cécile Fougeron (eds.), *The Oxford handbook of Laboratory Phonology*, 162–173. Oxford: Oxford University Press.

Haxby, James V., Raja Parasuraman, François Lalonde & Hisham Abboud. 1993. SuperLab: General-purpose macintosh software for human experimental psychology and psychological testing. *Behavior Research Methods, Instruments, & Computers* 25(3). 400–405.

Hayes, Bruce. 1995. *Metrical stress theory*. Chicago: The University of Chicago Press.

Hayes, Bruce & Aditi Lahiri. 1991. Bengali intonational phonology. *Natural Language and Linguistic Theory* 9(1). 47–96.

Heath, Jeffrey. 1987. *Ablaut and ambiguity: Phonology of a Morcoccan Arabic dialect*. New York: SUNY Press.

Hellmuth, Sam, Nabila Louriz, Basma Chlaihani & Rana Almbark. 2015. F0 peak alignment in Moroccan Arabic polar questions. In *Proceedings of the 18th International Congress of Phonetic Sciences*. Glasgow, UK.

Hermes, Anne, Rachid Ridouane, Doris Mücke & Martine Grice. 2011. Gestural coordination in Tashlhiyt syllables. In *Proceedings of the 17th International Congress of Phonetic Sciences*, 859–862. Hong Kong.

Heston, Tyler M. 2014. Prosodic differences between declaratives and polar questions in Fataluku. In *28th Pacific Asia Conference on Language, Information and Computation*, 395–403.

Hirschberg, Julia & Gregory Ward. 1992. The influence of pitch range, duration, amplitude and spectral features on the interpretation of the rise-fall-rise intonation contour in English. *Journal of Phonetics* 20(2). 241–251.

Hirst, Daniel & Albert Di Cristo. 1998. *Intonation systems: A survey of twenty languages*. Cambridge: Cambridge University Press.

Hothorn, Torsten, Frank Bretz & Peter Westfall. 2008. Simultaneous inference in general parametric models. *Biometrical Journal* 50(3). 346–363.

Hothorn, Torsten, Peter Bühlmann, Sandrine Dudoit, Annette Molinaro & Mark J. van Der Laan. 2006. Survival ensembles. *Biostatistics* 7(3). 355–373.

House, David. 2003. Perceiving question intonation: The role of pre-focal pause and delayed focal peak. In *Proceedings of the 15th International Congress of Phonetic Sciences*, 755–758. Barcelona, Spain.

Householder Jr., Fred W. 1956. Unreleased /ptk/ in American English. In Morris Halle, Horace Lunt, Hugh McLean & C. H. van Schooneveld (eds.), *For Roman Jakobson*, 235–244. The Hague: Mouton.

Hyman, Larry. 2011. Does Gokana really have no syllables? Or: What's so great about being universal? *Phonology* 28(01). 55–85.

Hyman, Larry. 2014. Do all languages have word accent? In Harry van der Hulst (ed.), *Word stress. Theoretical and typological issues*, 56–82. Cambridge: Cambridge University Press.

Iivone, Antti. 1998. Intonation in Finnish. In Daniel Hirst & Albert Di Cristo (eds.), *Intonation systems: A survey of twenty languages*, 311–327. Cambridge: Cambridge University Press.

Inkelas, Sharon & William Leben. 1990. Where phonology and phonetics intersect: The case of Hausa intonation. In John Kingston & Mary Beckman (eds.), *Papers in Laboratory Phonology I: Between the grammar and physics of speech*, 17–34. Cambridge: Cambridge University Press.

IPA. 1999. *Handbook of the international phonetic association: A guide to the use of the international phonetic alphabet*. Cambridge: Cambridge University Press.

Jacobs, Joachim. 1991. On the semantics of modal particles. In Werner Abraham (ed.), *Discourse particles: Descriptive and theoretical investigations on the logi-*

References

cal, syntactic and pragmatic properties of discourse particles in German, 141–162. Amsterdam: John Benjamins Publishing.

Jebbour, Abdelkrim. 1996. *Morphologie et contraintes prosodiques en berbère (tachelhit de Tiznit): Analyse linguistique et traitement automatique.* Université Mohammed V, Rabat PhD thesis.

Jebbour, Abdelkrim. 1999. Syllable weight and syllable nuclei in Tachelhit Berber of Tiznit. *Cahiers de Grammaire* 24. 95–116.

Julien, Charles André. 1966. *Histoire de l'Afrique du Nord: Tunisie, Algérie, Maroc.* Lausanne: Payot.

Jun, Sun-Ah. 1993. *The phonetics and phonology of Korean prosody.* The Ohio State University PhD thesis.

Jun, Sun-Ah. 2005. *Prosodic typology: The phonology of intonation and phrasing.* Vol. 1. Oxford: Oxford University Press.

Jun, Sun-Ah & Cécile Fougeron. 2002. Realisations of accentual phrase in French intonation. *Probus* 14(1). 147–172.

Kaimaki, Marianna. 2015. Voiceless Greek vowels. In *Proceedings of the 18th International Congress of Phonetic Sciences.* Glasgow, UK.

Kanerva, Jonni M. 1990. Focusing on phonological phrases in Chicheŵa. In Sharon Inkelas & Draga Zec (eds.), *The phonology-syntax connection*, 145–161. Chicago: University of Chicago Press.

Karlsson, Anastasia. 2014. The intonational phonology of Mongolian. In Sun-Ah Jun (ed.), *Prosodic Typology II*, 187–215. Oxford: Oxford University Press.

Katsika, Argyro, Jelena Krivokapić, Christine Mooshammer, Mark Tiede & Louis Goldstein. 2014. The coordination of boundary tones and its interaction with prominence. *Journal of Phonetics* 44. 62–82.

Keane, Elinor. 2006. Prominence in Tamil. *Journal of the International Phonetic Association* 36(1). 1–20.

Kiparsky, Paul. 1993. *Variable rules.* Handout from Rutgers Optimality Workshop 1.

Kohler, Klaus. 1991. A model of German intonation. *Arbeitsberichte des Instituts für Phonetik der Universität Kiel* 25. 295–360.

Kohler, Klaus. 2006. Timing and communicative functions of pitch contours. *Phonetica* 62(2-4). 88–105.

Kossmann, Maarten. 2009. Loanwords in Tarifiyt, a Berber language of Morocco. In Martin Haspelmath & Uri Tadmor (eds.), *Loanwords in the world's languages. A comparative handbook*, 191–214. Berlin: Mouton de Gruyter.

Kossmann, Maarten & Harry Stroomer. 1997. Berber phonology. In Alan Kaye (ed.), *Phonologies of Asia and Africa*, 461–475. Winona Lake: Eisenbrauns.

Krifka, Manfred. 2008. Basic notions of information structure. *Acta Linguistica Hungarica* 55(3-4). 243–276.

Kroch, Anthony S. 1989. Reflexes of grammar in patterns of language change. *Language variation and change* 1(03). 199–244.

Labov, William. 1969. Contraction, deletion, and inherent variability of the English copula. *Language* 45. 715–762.

Ladd, D. Robert. 1983. Phonological features of intonational peaks. *Language* 59. 721–759.

Ladd, D. Robert. 2008. *Intonational phonology.* Second. Cambridge: Cambridge University Press.

Ladd, D. Robert. 2014. *Simultaneous structure in phonology.* Oxford: Oxford University Press.

Ladd, D. Robert & Rachel Morton. 1997. The perception of intonational emphasis: Continuous or categorical? *Journal of Phonetics* 25(3). 313–342.

Ladefoged, Peter. 1972. *Three areas of experimental phonetics: Stress and respiratory activity, the nature of vowel quality, units in the perception and production of speech.* Oxford: Oxford University Press.

Lahrouchi, Mohamed. 2001. *Aspects morphophonologiques de la dérivation verbale en Berbère (parler Chleuh d'Agadir): Contribution à l'étude de l'architecture des gabarits.* Université Paris VII PhD thesis.

Lambrecht, Knud. 1996. *Information structure and sentence form: Topic, focus, and the mental representations of discourse referents.* Cambridge: Cambridge University press.

Laroui, Abdallah. 2015. *The history of the Maghrib: an interpretive essay.* Princeton, NJ: Princeton University Press.

Lasri, Ahmed. 1991. *Aspects de la phonologie non-linéaire du parler berbère chleuh de Tidli.* Université de la Sorbonne Nouvelle, Paris III PhD thesis.

Laver, John. 1994. *Principles of phonetics.* Cambridge: Cambridge University Press.

Leben, William. 1976. The tones in English intonation. *Linguistic analysis* 2(1). 69–107.

Lehiste, Ilse. 1970. *Suprasegmentals.* Cambridge, MA: MIT Press.

Levin, Juliette. 1987. Between epenthetic and excrescent vowels. In *Proceedings of the 6th West Coast Conference on Formal Linguistics*, vol. 6, 187–202. University of Arizona.

Lewis, M. Paul, Gary F. Simons & Charles D. Fennig (eds.). 2016. *Ethnologue: languages of the world.* 19th edn. Dallas, Texas: SIL International.

References

Liberman, Alvin, Katherine Harris, Howard Hoffman & Belver Griffith. 1957. The discrimination of speech sounds within and across phoneme boundaries. *Journal of Experimental Psychology* 54(5). 358–368.

Liberman, Mark & Janet Pierrehumbert. 1984. Intonational invariance under changes in pitch range and length. In Mark Aronoff & Richard Oerhle (eds.), *Language sound structure*, 157–233. Cambridge, MA: MIT Press.

Liberman, Mark & Alan Prince. 1977. On stress and linguistic rhythm. *Linguistic Inquiry* 8(2). 249–336.

Lickley, Robin J., Astrid Schepman & D. Robert Ladd. 2005. Alignment of "phrase accent" lows in Dutch falling rising questions: Theoretical and methodological implications. *Language and Speech* 48(2). 157–183.

Lieberman, Philip & Sheila E. Blumstein. 1988. *Speech physiology, speech perception, and acoustic phonetics*. Cambridge: Cambridge University Press.

Lisker, Leigh & Arthur Abramson. 1964. A cross-language study of voicing in initial stops: Acoustical measurements. *Word* 20(3). 384–422.

Louali, Naıma & Gilbert Puech. 2000. Etude sur l'implémentation du schwa pour quatre locuteurs Berbères de tachelhit. In *Actes des 23e journées d'études sur la parole*, 25–28.

Lyons, John. 1977. *Semantics*. Cambridge: Cambridge University Press.

Maas, Utz & Stefan Procházka. 2012. Moroccan Arabic in its wider linguistic and social contexts. *STUF - Language Typology and Universals* 65(4). 329–357.

Makarova, Veronika. 2007. The effect of pitch peak alignment on sentence type identification in Russian. *Language and speech* 50(3). 385–422.

Malécot, André. 1958. The role of releases in the identification of released final stops: A series of tape-cutting experiments. *Language* 34(3). 370–380.

Marley, Dawn. 2004. Language attitudes in Morocco following recent changes in language policy. *Language Policy* 3(1). 25–46.

Maskikit-Essed, Raechel & Carlos Gussenhoven. 2016. No stress, no pitch accent, no prosodic focus: The case of Ambonese Malay. *Phonology* 33(2). 353–389.

Mettouchi, Amina & Axel Fleisch. 2010. Topic-focus articulation in Taqbaylit and Tashelhit Berber. In Ines Fiedler & Anne Schwarz (eds.), *The expression of information structure: a documentation of its diversity across Africa*, 193–232. Amsterdam, Philadelphia: John Benjamins.

Meyer, Roland & Ina Mleinek. 2006. How prosody signals force and focus—a study of pitch accents in Russian yes–no questions. *Journal of Pragmatics* 38(10). 1615–1635.

Mountassir, Abdallah El. 2008. Le berbère dans un milieu urbain plurilingue, un difficile équilibre. Exemple de la ville d'Agadir. In Mena Lafkioui & Vermondo

Brugnatelli (eds.), *Berber in contact: linguistic and sociolinguistic perspectives*, vol. 22, 151–163. Cologne: Rüdiger Köppe.

Mücke, Doris & Martine Grice. 2014. The effect of focus marking on supralaryngeal articulation–is it mediated by accentuation? *Journal of Phonetics* 44. 47–61.

Mücke, Doris, Martine Grice, Johannes Becker & Anne Hermes. 2009. Sources of variation in tonal alignment. Evidence from acoustic and kinematic data. *Journal of Phonetics* 37(3). 321–338.

Murphy, Kelly. 2013. *Melodies of Hawai'i: The relationship between Hawai'i Creole English and 'ōlelo Hawai'i prosody*. University of Calgary PhD thesis.

Nespor, Irene & Marina Vogel. 1986. *Prosodic phonology*. Dordrecht: Foris.

Newman, Stanley. 1947. Bella Coola I: Phonology. *International Journal of American Linguistics* 13(3). 129–134.

Niebuhr, Oliver. 2008. Coding of intonational meanings beyond f0: Evidence from utterance-final /t/ aspiration in German. *The Journal of the Acoustical Society of America* 124(2). 1252–1263.

Niebuhr, Oliver. 2009. Intonation segments and segmental intonations. In *Proceedings of the 10th Interspeech Conference*, 2435–2438. Brighton, UK.

Niebuhr, Oliver. 2012. At the edge of intonation: The interplay of utterance-final f0 movements and voiceless fricative sounds. *Phonetica* 69(1–2). 7–27.

Niebuhr, Oliver, Cassandra Lill & Jessica Neuschulz. 2011. At the segment-prosody divide: The interplay of intonation, sibilant pitch and sibilant assimilation. In *Proceedings of the 17th International Congress of Phonetic Sciences*, 1478–1481. Hong Kong.

Niemann, Henrik & Doris Mücke. 2015. Effects of phrasal position and metrical structure on alignment patterns of nuclear pitch accents in German: Acoustics and articulation. In *Proceedings of the 18th International Congress of Phonetic Sciences*. Glasgow, UK.

O'Connor, Joseph Desmond & Gordon Frederick Arnold. 1973. *Intonation of colloquial English: A practical handbook*. London: Longman.

Ohala, John J. 1990. The phonetics and phonology of aspects of assimilation. In John Kingston & Mary Beckman (eds.), *Papers in Laboratory Phonology I: Between the grammar and the physics of speech*, 258–275. Cambridge: Cambridge University Press.

Ohala, John J. 1993. The phonetics of sound change. In Charles Jones (ed.), *Historical linguistics: Problems and perspectives*, 237–278. London: Longman.

Ouakrim, Omar. 1994. Un paramètre acoustique distinguant la gémination de la tension consonantique. *Etudes et documents berbères* 11. 197–203.

References

Ouakrim, Omar. 1995. *Fonética y fonolog'ia del bereber*. Universitat Aut'onoma de Barcelona PhD thesis.

Pierrehumbert, Janet. 1980. *The phonology and phonetics of English intonation*. Bloomington, Indiana: MIT PhD thesis.

Pierrehumbert, Janet. 2012. The dynamic lexicon. In Abigail C. Cohn & Cécile Fougeron (eds.), *The Oxford handbook of Laboratory Phonology*, 173–183. Oxford: Oxford University Press.

Pierrehumbert, Janet & Mary Beckman. 1988. *Japanese tone structure*. Cambridge, MA: MIT Press.

Pierrehumbert, Janet, Mary Beckman & D. Robert Ladd. 2000. Conceptual foundations of phonology as a laboratory science. In Noel Burton-Roberts, Philip Carr & Gerard Docherty (eds.), *Phonological knowledge: Conceptual and empirical issues*, 273–304. Oxford: Oxford University Press.

Pierrehumbert, Janet & Julia Hirschberg. 1990. The meaning of intonational contours in the interpretation of discourse. In Phillip Cohen, Jerry Morgan & Martha Pollack (eds.), *Intentions in communication*, 271–311. Cambridge, MA: MIT Press.

Pierrehumbert, Janet & Shirley A. Steele. 1989. Categories of tonal alignment in English. *Phonetica* 46(4). 181–196.

Pierrehumbert, Janet & David Talkin. 1992. Lenition of /h/ and glottal stop. In Gerard J. Docherty & D. Robert Ladd (eds.), *Papers in Laboratory Phonology II: Gesture, segment, prosody*, 90–117. Cambridge: Cambridge University Press.

Port, Robert & Michael O'Dell. 1985. Neutralization of syllable-final voicing in German. *Journal of Phonetics* 13(4). 455–471.

Prieto, Pilar, Mariapaola D'Imperio & Barbara Gili Fivela. 2005. Pitch accent alignment in Romance: Primary and secondary associations with metrical structure. *Language and Speech* 48(4). 359–396.

Prieto, Pilar & Marta Ortega-Llebaria. 2009. Do complex pitch gestures induce syllable lengthening in Catalan and Spanish. In Marina Vigário, Sonja Frota & Maria J. Freitas (eds.), *Phonetics and phonology: Interactions and interrelations*, 51–70. Amsterdam: John Benjamins.

Prince, Alan & Paul Smolensky. 1993. *Optimality Theory: Constraint interaction in generative grammar*. Tech. rep. 2. Rutgers University Center for Cognitive Science.

R Core Team. 2015. *R: A Language and Environment for Statistical Computing*. R Foundation for Statistical Computing. Vienna, Austria.

Rathcke, Tamara. 2009. *Komparative Phonetik und Phonologie der Intonationssysteme des Deutschen und Russischen*. Vol. 29. München: Herbert Utz Verlag.

Refice, Mario, Michelina Savino & Martine Grice. 1997. A contribution to the estimation of naturalness in the intonation of Italian spontaneous speech. In *Proceedings of the 5th European Conference on Speech Communication and Technology*. Rhodes, Greece.

Remijsen, Bert. 2013. Tonal alignment is contrastive in falling contours in Dinka. *Language* 89(2). 297–327.

Reynolds, William Thomas. 1994. *Variation and phonological theory*. University of Pennsylvania PhD thesis.

Ridouane, Rachid. 2003. *Suites de consonnes en berbère: phonétique et phonologie*. Université de la Sorbonne nouvelle–Paris III PhD thesis.

Ridouane, Rachid. 2007. Gemination in Tashlhiyt Berber: an acoustic and articulatory study. *Journal of the International Phonetic Association* 37(2). 119–142.

Ridouane, Rachid. 2008. Syllables without vowels: Phonetic and phonological evidence from Tashlhiyt Berber. *Phonology* 25(2). 321–359.

Ridouane, Rachid. 2014. Tashlhiyt Berber. *Journal of the International Phonetic Association* 44(2). 207–221.

Ridouane, Rachid & Cécile Fougeron. 2011. Schwa elements in Tashlhiyt word-initial clusters. *Journal of Laboratory Phonology* 2(2). 275–300.

Ridouane, Rachid, Philip Hoole & Susanne Fuchs. 2007. Laryngeal adjustments in the production of voiceless words and sentences in Berber. In *Proceedings of the 16th International Congress of Phonetic Sciences*, 2049–2052. Saarbrücken, Germany.

Rietveld, Toni & Carlos Gussenhoven. 1995. Aligning pitch targets in speech synthesis: Effects of syllable structure. *Journal of Phonetics* 23(4). 375–385.

Ritter, Simon & Martine Grice. 2015. The role of tonal onglides in German nuclear pitch accents. *Language and speech* 58(1). 114–128.

Ritter, Simon & Timo B. Roettger. 2014. Speakers modulate noise-induced pitch according to intonational context. In *Proceedings of 7th International Conference on Speech Prosody*, 890–894. Dublin, UK.

Roettger, Timo B., Anna Bruggeman & Martine Grice. 2015. Word stress in Tashlhiyt: Postlexical prominence in disguise? In *Proceedings of the 18th International Congress of Phonetic Sciences*. Glasgow, UK.

Roettger, Timo B. & Matthew Gordon. in press. Methodological issues in the study of word stress correlates. *Linguistic Vanguard*.

Roettger, Timo B. & Martine Grice. 2015. The role of high pitch in Tashlhiyt Tamazight (Berber): Evidence from production and perception. *Journal of Phonetics* 51(1). 36–49.

References

Roettger, Timo B., Bodo Winter, Sven Grawunder, James Kirby & Martine Grice. 2014. Assessing incomplete neutralization of final devoicing in German. *Journal of Phonetics* 43. 11–25.

Sadiqi, Fatima. 1997. *Grammaire du berbère*. Paris: Editions l'Harmattan.

Sadock, Jerrold & Arnold Zwicky. 1985. Speech act distinctions in syntax. In Timothy Shopen (ed.), *Language typology and syntactic description*, 155–196. Cambridge: Cambridge University Press.

Saltzman, Elliot, Hosung Nam, Jelena Krivokapic & Louis Goldstein. 2008. A task-dynamic toolkit for modeling the effects of prosodic structure on articulation. In *Proceedings of the 4th International Conference on Speech Prosody*, 175–184. Campinas, Brazil.

Sankoff, David, Sali A. Tagliamonte & Eric Smith. 2005. *Goldvarb X: A multivariate analysis application*. http://individual.utoronto.ca/tagliamonte/Goldvarb/GV_index.htm.

Sapir, Edward. 1925. Sound patterns in language. *Language* 1(2). 37–51.

Sasse, Hans-Jürgen. 1984. Case in Cushitic, Semitic and Berber. *Current progress in Afro-Asiatic linguistics* 28. 111–126.

Savino, Michelina. 2012. The intonation of polar questions in Italian: Where is the rise? *Journal of the International Phonetic Association* 42. 23–48.

Savino, Michelina & Martine Grice. 2007. The role of pitch range in realising pragmatic contrasts–the case of two question types in Italian. In *Proceedings of the 15th International Congress of Phonetic Sciences*, 1037–1040. Saarbrücken, Germany.

Savino, Michelina & Martine Grice. 2011. The perception of negative bias in Bari Italian questions. In Sónia Frota, Gorka Elordieta & Pilar Prieto (eds.), *Prosodic categories: Production, perception and comprehension*, 187–206. Berlin: Springer.

Schafer, Amy J., Shari R. Speer, Paul Warren & S. David White. 2000. Intonational disambiguation in sentence production and comprehension. *Journal of Psycholinguistic Research* 29(2). 169–182.

Schepman, Astrid, Robin J. Lickley & D. Robert Ladd. 2006. Effects of vowel length and "right context" on the alignment of Dutch nuclear accents. *Journal of Phonetics* 34(1). 1–28.

Schielzeth, Holger & Wolfgang Forstmeier. 2009. Conclusions beyond support: Overconfident estimates in mixed models. *Behavioral Ecology* 20(2). 416–420.

Schiering, René, Balthasar Bickel & Kristine A. Hildebrandt. 2010. The prosodic word is not universal, but emergent. *Journal of Linguistics* 46(03). 657–709.

Schuyler, Philip D. 1979. Rwais and ahwash: opposing tendencies in Moroccan Berber music and society. *The World of Music* 21(1). 65–80.

Shen, Xiao-nan Susan. 1990. *The prosody of Mandarin Chinese.* Berkeley: University of California Press.

Shlonsky, Ur. In Mohamed Guerssel & Kenneth Hale (eds.), *Studies in Berber syntax*, 1–20. Massachusetts Institute of Technology.

Silverman, Daniel. 2011. Schwa. In Marc van Oostendorp, Colin J. Ewen, Elizabeth V. Hume & Keren Rice (eds.), *The Blackwell companion to phonology*, 628–642. Malden, MA: Wiley-Blackwell.

Snider, Keith L. 1999. *The geometry and features of tone.* Dallas: Summer Institute of Linguistics & the University of Texas at Arlington Publications in Linguistics.

Sosa, Juan Manuel. 1999. *La entonación del español: Su estructura fónica, variabilidad y dialectología.* University of Massachussets PhD thesis.

Steele, Shirley A. 1986. Nuclear accent f0 peak location: Effects of rate, vowel, and number of following syllables. *The Journal of the Acoustical Society of America* 80(S1). S51–S51.

Strobl, Carolin, Anne-Laure Boulesteix, Achim Zeileis & Torsten Hothorn. 2007. Bias in random forest variable importance measures: Illustrations, sources and a solution. *BMC bioinformatics* 8(1). 25.

Strobl, Carolin, Anne-Laure Boulesteix, Thomas Kneib, Thomas Augustin & Achim Zeileis. 2008. Conditional variable importance for random forests. *BMC bioinformatics* 9(1). 307.

Stumme, Hans. 1899. *Handbuch des Schilhischen von Tazerwalt.* Leipzig: J. C. Hinrichs'sche Buchhandlung.

Tagliamonte, Sali A. & R. Harald Baayen. 2012. Models, forests, and trees of York English: Was/were variation as a case study for statistical practice. *Language Variation and Change* 24(02). 135–178.

Trager, George L. & Henry Lee Smith. 1951. *An outline of English structure.* Norman, Oklahoma: Battenberg Press.

Trubetzkoy, Nikolaus. 1939. *Grundzüge der Phonologie.* Prag: Travaux du cercle linguistique de Prague.

Turk, Alice E. & Stefanie Shattuck-Hufnagel. 2007. Multiple targets of phrase-final lengthening in American English words. *Journal of Phonetics* 35(4). 445–472.

t´Hart, Johan & Antonie Cohen. 1973. Intonation by rule: A perceptual quest. *Journal of Phonetics* 1. 309–327.

t´Hart, Johan & René Collier. 1975. Integrating different levels of intonation analysis. *Journal of Phonetics* 3(4). 235–255.

References

Vance, Timothy J. 1987. *An introduction to Japanese phonology*. New York: SUNY Press.

Varga, László. 2002. *Intonation and stress: Evidence from Hungarian*. Berlin: Springer.

Vayra, Mario & Carol A. Fowler. 1992. Declination of supralaryngeal gestures in Italian. *Phonetica* 49(1). 48–60.

Wang, William S. Y. 1959. Transition and release as perceptual cues for final plosives. *Journal of Speech, Language, and Hearing Research* 2(1). 66–73.

Ward, Gregory & Julia Hirschberg. 1985. Implicating uncertainty: The pragmatics of fall-rise intonation. *Language* 61(4). 747–776.

Warner, Natasha, Allard Jongman, Anne Cutler & Doris Mücke. 2001. The phonological status of Dutch epenthetic schwa. *Phonology* 18(03). 387–420.

Whalen, Douglas H. & Yi Xu. 1992. Information for Mandarin tones in the amplitude contour and in brief segments. *Phonetica* 49(1). 25–47.

Williams, Briony. 1999. The phonetic manifestation of stress in Welsh. In Grzegorz Dogil & Briony Williams (eds.), *Word prosodic systems in the languages of Europe*, 311–344. Berlin; New York: Mouton de Gruyter.

Winter, Bodo. 2011. Pseudoreplication in phonetic research. In *Proceedings of the 17th International Congress of Phonetic Sciences*, 2137–2140. Hong Kong.

Xu, Yi. 2005. Speech melody as articulatorily implemented communicative functions. *Speech communication* 46(3). 220–251.

Yip, Moira. 1989. Contour tones. *Phonology* 6(01). 149–174.

Zhang, Jie. 2001. *The effects of duration and sonority on contour tone distribution—typological survey and formal analysis*. University of California, Los Angeles PhD thesis.

Zhang, Jie. 2004. The role of contrast-specific and language-specific phonetics in contour tone distribution. In Bruce Hayes, Robert Martin Kirchner & Donca Steriade (eds.), *Phonetically based phonology*, 157–190. Cambridge: Cambridge University Press.

Zouhir, Abderrahman. 2013. Language situation and conflict in Morocco. In *43rd Annual Conference on African Linguistics*. Somerville, MA: Cascadilla Proceedings Project.

Name index

Abramson, Arthur, 5
Alstermark, Margit, 20, 157
Anttila, Arto, 147, 148
Applegate, Joseph R., 31, 36, 45
Arnold, Gordon Frederick, 13
Arvaniti, Amalia, 14, 17, 18, 27, 28, 45, 66, 133–135, 138
Aspinion, Robert, 36
Atterer, Michaela, 18

Baayen, R. Harald, 110
Bannert, Robert, 20
Barnes, Jonathan, 155
Barr, Dale J., 51
Bartels, Christine, 62
Basset, André, 31, 39
Bates, Douglas, 51, 76, 92
Baumann, Stefan, 10, 66, 140, 145, 146, 148
Beckman, Mary, 7, 10, 11, 16, 24, 25, 47, 67, 120, 121, 134, 138, 142, 148, 156
Benkirane, Thami, 65, 66, 148
Bensoukas, Karim, 36
Benzmülller, Ralf, 10, 66, 140, 145
Berdouzi, Mohamed, 34
Bickel, Balthasar, 10, 43
Blevins, Juliette, 156
Bloomfield, Leonard, 6
Blumstein, Sheila E., 55
Boersma, Paul, 50, 75, 90, 147

Bolinger, Dwight Le Merton, 13, 66, 145, 150
Boogert, Nico van den, 36
Boukhris, Fatima, 41
Boukous, Ahmed, 36, 118, 124
Braun, Bettina, 66
Bredvad, A., 20
Breiman, Leo, 110
Bretz, Frank, 76
Browman, Catherine P., 128, 147, 158
Bruce, Gösta, 20
Bruggeman, Anna, 48, 63, 119, 138, 139, 158
Brunelle, Marc, 59, 65
Buring, Daniel, 66
Byrd, Dani, 122, 123

Cangemi, Francesco, 21, 75, 146, 156
Caspers, Johanneke, 21
Chaker, Salem, 31, 36
Cho, Taehong, 12, 47, 67, 120, 121
Choi, Hansook, 12
Chomsky, Noam, 7
Clark, Herbert H., 48
Cohen, Antonie, 15, 16
Cole, Jennifer, 12, 47
Coleman, John, 38, 101, 102, 104, 105, 142
Colin, Georges S., 32
Collier, René, 15, 16
Cooper, A, 12
Crystal, David, 13

Name index

D'Imperio, Mariapaola, 15, 18, 21, 68, 138
De Lacy, Paul, 156
De Saussure, Ferdinand, 6
Dell, François, 36–39, 41, 43, 45, 80, 101, 102, 104, 105, 125–128, 135, 137, 140–142, 157
Di Cristo, Albert, 13, 65
Diercks, Kristin Lena, 121, 122, 135

Edwards, Jan, 47, 120
El-Aissati, Abderrahman, 33, 34
Elmedlaoui, Mohamed, 36–39, 41, 43, 45, 80, 101, 102, 104, 105, 125–128, 135, 137, 140–142, 157
Ennaji, Moha, 34
Erikson, Y., 20, 157

Face, Timothy, 18, 138
Fennig, Charles D., 31, 32
Fleisch, Axel, 40, 41, 140
Fletcher, Janet, 47, 67, 120, 121
Forstmeier, Wolfgang, 51
Fougeron, Cécile, 36, 101, 106, 107, 126, 153
Fowler, Carol A., 55
Frota, Sónia, 22
Fry, Dennis B., 44
Fuchs, Susanne, 122
Fujimura, Osamu, 107
Féry, Caroline, 146

Galand, Lionel, 31, 36
Gili Fivela, Barbara, 21, 138
Goedemans, Rob, 43, 59
Goldinger, Stephen D., 7
Goldstein, Louis, 123, 128, 147, 158

Gordon, Matthew, 36, 44–48, 50, 58–60, 112, 117, 121, 123, 125, 135, 156
Gósy, Mária, 65, 66, 68
Grabe, Esther, 20, 23, 26, 157
Grice, Martine, 9, 10, 19, 21, 22, 26–28, 45, 47, 48, 63, 65–68, 72, 84–89, 96, 98, 117, 119, 121, 133–135, 137–146, 148, 154, 156, 157
Grønnum, Nina, 23
Gussenhoven, Carlos, 6, 10, 11, 15, 18, 23, 26, 47, 59, 136, 150, 153, 154
Guy, Gregory R., 147
Gårding, Eva, 65

Haan, Judith, 65
Hadding-Koch, Kerstin, 65
Haeseryn, Walter, 62
Hall, Nancy, 101, 104, 125
Halle, Morris, 7, 43
Halliday, Michael Alexander Kirkwood, 13
Hanssen, Judith, 23
Harms, Robert T., 125
Harrington, Jonathan, 47, 67, 120, 121
Hawkins, Sarah, 7
Haxby, James V., 91
Hayes, Bruce, 43, 65–67, 136, 146–148
Heath, Jeffrey, 126, 157
Hellmuth, Sam, 135
Hermes, Anne, 36, 121
Heston, Tyler M., 22
Heuven, Vincent J. van, 21
Hildebrandt, Kristine A., 10, 43
Hirschberg, Julia, 14, 16, 66

Name index

Hirst, Daniel, 13, 65
Hoole, Philip, 122
Hothorn, Torsten, 76, 110
House, David, 15, 18, 21, 65, 68
Householder Jr., Fred W., 107
Hulst, Harry van der, 43
Hyman, Larry, 10, 43, 58

Iivone, Antti, 65
Inkelas, Sharon, 65, 149

Jacobs, Joachim, 62
Jebbour, Abdelkrim, 36, 104
Julien, Charles André, 33
Jun, Sun-Ah, 12, 66, 67, 153

Kaimaki, Marianna, 157
Kanerva, Jonni M., 67
Karlsson, Anastasia, 153
Katsika, Argyro, 47
Keane, Elinor, 59
Keating, Patricia, 120, 121
Kiparsky, Paul, 147
Kohler, Klaus, 13, 146
Kossmann, Maarten, 1, 31
Krifka, Manfred, 63
Kroch, Anthony S., 147
Kügler, Frank, 146

Labov, William, 147
Ladd, D. Robert, 7, 9, 12, 14, 16–18,
    20, 21, 23, 27, 28, 45, 64–66,
    133–135, 138, 145, 148–150
Ladefoged, Peter, 55
Lahiri, Aditi, 65–67, 136, 146, 148
Lahrouchi, Mohamed, 36
Lambrecht, Knud, 63
Laroui, Abdallah, 33
Lasri, Ahmed, 36

Laver, John, 72
Leben, William, 12, 65, 149
Lehiste, Ilse, 53
Levin, Juliette, 125
Lewis, M. Paul, 31, 32
Liberman, Alvin, 6
Liberman, Mark, 12, 66
Lickley, Robin J., 20, 21
Lieberman, Philip, 55
Lill, Cassandra, 24
Lisker, Leigh, 5
Louali, Naıma, 107, 108
Lyons, John, 62

Maas, Utz, 35
Macchi, Marian J., 107
Makarova, Veronika, 65, 66, 68
Malécot, André, 107
Marley, Dawn, 34, 35
Maskikit-Essed, Raechel, 59, 153
McQueen, James M., 120
Mennen, Ineke, 17, 18, 134, 138
Mettouchi, Amina, 40, 41, 140
Meyer, Roland, 66
Mleinek, Ina, 66
Morton, Rachel, 150
Mountassir, Abdallah El, 35
Mücke, Doris, 18, 19, 21, 80, 121, 146
Murphy, Kelly, 65

Nafi, Latifa, 36, 45–47, 50, 58, 112, 117,
    121, 123, 125, 135
Nespor, Irene, 12
Neuschulz, Jessica, 24
Newman, Stanley, 58
Niebuhr, Oliver, 24
Niemann, Henrik, 80

O'Connor, Joseph Desmond, 13

185

Name index

O'Dell, Michael, 158
Ohala, John J., 107, 156
Ortega-Llebaria, Marta, 20–22, 157
Ouakrim, Omar, 36

Peters, Jörg, 23
Phuong Ha, Kiều, 65
Pierrehumbert, Janet, 7, 9–12, 15, 16, 18, 24, 25, 66, 67, 134, 138, 142, 148, 150, 156
Port, Robert, 158
Prieto, Pilar, 18, 20–22, 138, 157
Prince, Alan, 12, 147
Procházka, Stefan, 35
Puech, Gilbert, 107, 108

Rathcke, Tamara, 20, 157
Refice, Mario, 22
Remijsen, Bert, 138
Reynolds, William Thomas, 148
Ridouane, Rachid, 36–38, 43, 47, 84–89, 96, 98, 101, 103–108, 117, 119, 121–123, 126, 135, 140–144, 154
Rietveld, Toni, 15, 47, 150
Ritter, Simon, 24, 146
Roettger, Timo B., 24, 44, 47, 48, 59, 60, 63, 72, 84–89, 96, 98, 117, 119, 121, 135, 138–144, 154, 158
Röhr, Christine T., 146, 148

Sadiqi, Fatima, 40, 41, 46, 140
Sadock, Jerrold, 62
Saltzman, Elliot, 122, 123
Sankoff, David, 147
Sapir, Edward, 6
Sasse, Hans-Jürgen, 39
Savino, Michelina, 21, 22, 65, 66, 68, 133

Schafer, Amy J., 146
Schepman, Astrid, 20, 21
Schielzeth, Holger, 51
Schiering, René, 10, 43
Schuyler, Philip D, 103
Shattuck-Hufnagel, Stefanie, 12, 120
Shen, Xiao-nan Susan, 65
Shlonsky, Ur, 41
Silverman, Daniel, 125
Simons, Gary F., 31, 32
Smith, Eric, 147
Smith, Henry Lee, 16
Smolensky, Paul, 147
Snider, Keith L., 149
Sosa, Juan Manuel, 148, 149
Steele, Shirley A., 15, 18, 21
Streeter, Lynn A., 107
Strobl, Carolin, 110
Stroomer, Harry, 1
Studdert-Kennedy, Michael, 65
Stumme, Hans, 36, 46

Tagliamonte, Sali A., 110, 147
Talkin, David, 12
Tangi, Oufae, 125, 127, 157
Terken, Jacques M. B., 65, 66, 68
Trager, George L., 16
Trubetzkoy, Nikolaus, 6, 16
Turk, Alice E., 12, 120
t'Hart, Johan, 15, 16

Vance, Timothy J., 157
Varga, László, 66, 133
Vayra, Mario, 55
Vergnaud, Jean-Roger, 43
Vliet, Peter van der, 26
Vogel, Marina, 12

Wang, William S. Y., 107

Name index

Ward, Gregory, 14, 16
Warner, Natasha, 125
Weenink, David, 50, 75, 90
Westfall, Peter, 76
Whalen, Douglas H., 23
Williams, Briony, 44
Winter, Bodo, 48

Xu, Yi, 13, 23

Yip, Moira, 149

Zanten, Ellen van, 59
Zhang, Jie, 155, 156
Zouhir, Abderrahman, 33
Zwicky, Arnold, 62

Language index

Arabic, 34
Arabic (Moroccan), 35, 65, 66, 126, 127, 133, 135, 148, 157

Bengali, 65–67, 133, 136, 138, 146, 148
Berber (Tamazight), 31
Berber (Tarifiyt), 31, 125, 127, 157
Berber (Zwara), 154
Bulgarian, 66

Cantonese, 149
Catalan, 21, 157
Chicheŵa, 67

Dutch, 15, 20, 120, 150
Dutch (Venlo), 26

English, 5, 7, 10–12, 14, 17, 18, 43–45, 62, 65, 67, 96, 120, 145, 147, 149, 157
English (AE), 65
English (BE), 20

Fataluku, 22
Finnish, 65
French, 34, 36, 120, 153

German, 11, 17, 20, 23, 67, 96, 120, 140, 145, 148, 157
Gokana, 43
Greek, 18, 27, 66, 133, 134, 157
Greek (Cypriot), 134, 136

Hausa, 65, 149

Hawaiian, 65
Hungarian, 27, 65, 66, 68, 134, 136

Indonesian, 59
Italian, 45, 66, 67, 120, 133, 134
Italian (Bari), 22, 65, 68
Italian (Neapolitan), 15, 21, 68, 156
Italian (Palermo), 26, 27, 134

Japanese, 11, 24, 26, 67, 137, 156, 157

Korean, 67, 153

Limbu, 43

Malay (Ambonese), 59, 154
Mandarin, 24, 65, 149
Mongolian, 153

Nuxalk, 58

Portuguese, 22

Romanian, 27, 134
Russian, 65–68, 157

Spanish, 21, 149, 157
Swedish, 20, 65, 68, 146, 157

Tamil, 59

Vietnamese, 43, 59, 65

Subject index

boundary, 8

compression, 19, 20, 22

declination, 55, 56, 58, 59

echo question, 49, 51, 62, 63, 66, 68, 78–80, 84, 95, 149, 150

edge tone, 8, 12, 16–18, 24, 26, 27, 66, 134–137, 139, 140, 143, 144, 150, 151

falsetto, 72, 78

focus, 17, 21, 26, 27, 47, 49, 61–64, 67, 68, 70, 71, 85, 95, 136, 139, 140, 146

gestural coordination, 102, 106–108, 120, 122–125, 158

incomplete neutralisation, 158
information status, 146

just noticeable difference, 53, 58

microprosody, 56, 58, 59

Optimality Theory, 148

paralinguistic, 9, 148, 150
phrase accent, 27, 134, 135
pitch accent, 8, 16–19, 22, 26, 27, 45, 47, 66–68, 134–136, 140, 146

pitch scaling, 4, 24, 65–67, 72, 75, 76, 78, 79, 84, 89, 91, 93–95, 137, 138, 140, 145, 148–151

secondary association, 24, 26, 27, 134–136, 143, 144, 151, 156
segmental pitch, 24
syllable weight, 4, 50, 86, 89, 96, 103, 104, 155, 156

tonal alignment, 4, 16–21, 26, 67, 68, 75, 80–84, 89, 91, 93–95, 97, 134, 135, 137–140, 143, 147, 154
tonal association, 16–18, 26, 134–138, 143, 144, 148, 151
tonal crowding, 19, 20, 146
tonal shift, 19, 21, 22, 100, 157
tone bearing unit, 8, 16, 17, 19, 24, 26, 89, 134–138, 141–144, 151, 155
truncation, 19, 20, 22, 24, 26, 27, 70, 157

vowel insertion, 19, 22, 101, 102, 118–120, 123–127, 129

word stress, 2, 3, 44–49, 59, 121, 135, 154

yes-no question, 21, 22, 26, 27, 49, 62, 63, 66, 68, 78–80, 84, 85, 95, 136, 137, 149, 150

www.ingramcontent.com/pod-product-compliance
Lightning Source LLC
Chambersburg PA
CBHW080603170426
43196CB00017B/2885